CHANGING GAMES, CHANGING STRATEGIES

MANCHESTER
UNIVERSITY PRESS

New Approaches to
Conflict Analysis

Series editor: Peter Lawler, Senior Lecturer in
International Relations, Department of Government,
University of Manchester

Until recently, the study of conflict and conflict resolution
remained comparatively immune to broad developments in
social and political theory. When the changing nature and
locus of large-scale conflict in the post-Cold War era is also
taken into account, the case for a reconsideration of the
fundamentals of conflict analysis and conflict resolution
becomes all the more stark.

New Approaches to Conflict Analysis will promote the development of new theoretical insights and their application to
concrete cases of large-scale conflict, broadly defined. The
series does not intend to ignore established approaches to
conflict analysis and conflict resolution, but contribute to
the reconstruction of the field through a dialogue between
orthodoxy and its contemporary critics. Equally, the series
will reflect the contemporary porosity of intellectual border-
lines rather than simply perpetuate rigid boundaries around
the study of conflict and peace. *New Approaches to Conflict
Analysis* seeks to uphold the normative commitment of the
field's founders yet also recognise that the moral impulse to
research is properly part of its subject matter. To these
ends, the series will be comprised of the highest quality
work of scholars drawn from throughout the international
academic community, and from a wide range of disciplines
within the social sciences.

FORTHCOMING

Deiniol Jones
*Mediation in international affairs:
culture and authority*

Helena Lindholm Schulz
*Reconstruction of Palestinian nationalism:
between revolution and statehood*

Changing games, changing strategies

Critical investigations in security

K. M. FIERKE

Manchester University Press

MANCHESTER AND NEW YORK

distributed exclusively in the USA by St. Martin's Press

Published by Manchester University Press
Oxford Road, Manchester M13 9NR, UK
and Room 400, 175 Fifth Avenue, New York, NY 10010, USA

Distributed exclusively in the USA by
St. Martin's Press, Inc. 175 Fifth Avenue, New York, NY 10010, USA

Distributed exclusively in Canada by
UBC Press, University of British Columbia, 6344 Memorial Road,
Vancouver, BC, Canada V6T 1Z2

British Library Cataloguing-in-Publication Data
A catalogue record for this book is available from the British Library

Library of Congress Cataloging-in-Publication Data applied for

ISBN 0 7190 5475 3 *hardback*

First published 1998

05 04 03 02 01 00 99 98   10 9 8 7 6 5 4 3 2 1

Typeset in Photina
by Koinonia, Manchester
Printed in Great Britain
by Bookcraft Bath (Midsomer Norton) Ltd

For Eleanore and Marland

CONTENTS

ABBREVIATIONS

ABM	anti-ballistic missile
CDPSP	*Current Digest of the Post-Soviet Press*
CDSP	*Current Digest of the Soviet Press*
COMECOM	Council for Mutual Economic Assistance
CP	*Current Policy*
CPD	Committee on the Present Danger
CSCE	Conference on Security and Cooperation in Europe
DSB	*Department of State Bulletin*
END	European Nuclear Disarmament
FRG	Federal Republic of Germany
IKV	Interkerkelijk Vredesberaad (Interchurch Peace Council)
INF	intermediate-range nuclear forces
ISG	Instituut voor Sociale Geschiedenis (Institute for Social History)
KOR	Komitet Obrony Robotnikow (Workers' Defence Committee)
LFEE	*Labour Focus on Eastern Europe*
LRTNF	long-range theatre nuclear forces
MAD	mutually assured destruction
NACC	North Atlantic Cooperation Council
NATO	North Atlantic Treaty Organisation
NR	*NATO Review*
OSCE	Organisation for Security and Cooperation in Europe (formerly the CSCE)
PPB	*Palach Press Bulletin*
SALT	Strategic Arms Limitation Treaty
SDI	Strategic Defence Initiative
UN	United Nations
VSD	*Vital Speeches of the Day*
WEU	Western European Union

PREFACE AND ACKNOWLEDGEMENTS

This book has two goals. One is to explore the later Wittgenstein's concepts of rule-following, language games and grammars, and their relevance for the analysis of international change. The second is to apply these methodologically to the historical context of changing East–West security relations over the last two decades, from the Helsinki Final Act to the signing of the North Atlantic Treaty Organisation (NATO)–Russia Founding Act in May 1997.

The analysis is explicitly descriptive. I do not claim to provide an explanation of the end of the Cold War or changing East–West security relations in its aftermath. Nothing in the conclusions denies the role of a failing Soviet economy or Reagan's intention to leave communism on the 'ashheap of history', but the guiding question is a very public one about the *political* circumstances under which it became possible to introduce major changes in both East and West. The end of the Cold War is usually associated with the dramatic events of 1989 or 1991. In the argument of this book, these events were the culmination of a much longer process. I have attempted to 'map' the contours of this change. The description does raise a counter-factual question about whether the Cold War would have ended in the absence of the processes described here. The question is intriguing and important, but must be left for another time, since the two central tasks of this book are so large in and of themselves.

The beginnings and endings of the story have changed over time. The study began in the late 1980s, before the Cold War was 'over', as an analysis of Dutch foreign policy texts covering the five years from 1983–88. I had no idea of what I was looking for and, at the time, no familiarity with Wittgenstein or his notion of a grammar. The archive expanded over time, to include a larger time span and a growing cast of characters. Some of the insights from the 'test case' were confirmed in the course of the larger analysis, but others emerged along the way. The study evolved against the background of a rapidly changing world.

The analysis from which this book was derived relied on a large archive of primary documents, including over 650 texts, from the Soviet Union, NATO, speeches given by Ronald Reagan, the Committee on the Present Danger in the United States, Western peace movements and Eastern European human rights initiatives. Given space limitations, it has only been possible to refer directly to a small number of these documents in order to illustrate, on the basis of a sample, the empirical basis of the narrative.

Despite this extensive archive, some have asked why I did not include a more diverse array of sources or actors or metaphors, and whether the story would have changed if I had. I cannot make definitive claims in this respect, but I can provide some food for thought. Generally, I argue that this is a 'better' description of these changes but not the 'best' possible. In an ideal world, the researcher could explore every angle of a situation; in reality, limits are necessarily imposed. First, more actors could always be included. There was a rationale for choosing those represented here. The point of departure was the public documents of states and particularly the Cold War alliances. As non-state actors emerged as a major source of concern for states, separate archives of their documents were created. The analysis does not include all possible players, but it does, I believe, represent the major angles of conflict in the East–West dimension of the late Cold War, both between states in the two blocs and between state and non-state actors.[1]

Second, as Chilton (1996) has demonstrated, the meaning of the Cold War was constituted in a much more diverse array of metaphors than explored here. Metaphor in itself is not the central concern of this study; rather, metaphor is a point of departure for identifying grammars of change. Four different grammars are explored in what follows. In so far as the different layers of the description overlap and correspond, I expect that the inclusion of further grammars would not present a qualitatively different 'map' of the changes but would only 'thicken' the description.

Finally, in an attempt to be systematic, I have tried, whenever possible, to rely on the same source, for instance, *NATO Review*, the *Current Digest of the Soviet Press* and the *Current Digest of the Post-Soviet Press*. Some have asked whether the analysis would look different if I had relied on other sources, such as internal documents from state leaders or a more diverse array of publications. I chose these sources in the hope of tapping that diversity without losing the systematicity. *NATO Review* includes the perspective of the range of countries within NATO. *The Current Digest* is a compilation of the Soviet press. In choosing these public texts I was not in search of 'facts' or 'motives'. My concern was the boundaries within which truth claims were justified and transformed, and the shared language and assumptions within which actors were entangled or from which they were liberated. I might note that, in my experience, the very same categories

---

1 I have, for instance, been asked why an analysis of the role of 'epistemic communities' or 'specialist networks' has not been included. Others (for instance, Herman in Katzenstein, 1996; Adler, 1992; Checkel, 1993) have looked at this issue, particularly in relation to Soviet policymakers. While there is some overlap between these knowledge elites and social movements, I have focused on the latter since my central concern is how these changes became politically possible in a larger domestic and international context.

were also present in confidential documents and other sources, although this issue requires further exploration.

The form of analysis is unconventional at best; subsequently, its significance is sometimes difficult to grasp. International relations scholarship has tended to be confined either to explaining causality, in a world independent of human meaning, or to understanding the motives or subjective experience of individuals (Hollis and Smith, 1991). By contrast, the point of departure for this study is that we – including the theorist or analyst – are always already embedded in a social and political world that constructs the boundaries of what can be said and done. Policymakers or other actors are not determined in their actions; nor is the world infinitely malleable. Change is possible but, in the world of international politics, the process is explicitly *political* and *social*.

The inspiration for this project grew out of my professional experience prior to academia during which I had the good fortune to observe a portion of the history described in these pages, first as a staff member in the national office of the US Nuclear Weapons Freeze Campaign and later as an editor of a small international publication based in the Netherlands.

During my academic development I have received the generous support of three different universities in three different countries. I would like to thank in particular the Centre for European Studies and the Political Science Department, University of Minnesota; the Amsterdam School for Social Science Research, University of Amsterdam; and Nuffield College, Oxford University, for providing financial and intellectual support as well as a stimulating work environment during different stages of my research.

Throughout this long journey, I have grown enormously from the intellectual support and friendship of a large number of people. Several of them have played an indispensable role in the development of this book. The order of thanks is based on a chronological placement over the last fifteen years. I would like to thank Sandra Ball for guiding me through the political intricacies of Western European peace movements and their dialogue with counterparts in the East; David Sylvan, my University of Minnesota adviser, for teaching me to look at language, and therefore the world, through different eyes, for the skills to apply these insights and for his incisive comments over many years; Hans Righart, my University of Amsterdam adviser, for his support and guidance as I steered my way through the joys and frustrations of researching and writing the dissertation, for his ongoing insightful critique of my work and for challenging me to go beyond my training as a political scientist to think more historically; Hans Sonneveld for his patience and flexibility in negotiating the relationship between two universities in two different countries; Wim Bartels for granting me access to the archives of the Dutch Interchurch Peace Council; Bert

Bomert for his steadfast companionship and for his meticulous editing of the dissertation; Nicholas Onuf and Peter Lawler for their insightful comments on many versions of the text and for helping me to negotiate the publishing world; Nicholas Wheeler, whose probing questions and comments during the process of rewriting the book version helped me to see more clearly the significance of what I was trying to say and how to communicate it to others more effectively; Richard Ned Lebow and Hayward Alker for providing helpful comments and identifying weak spots in the book version; Maja Zehfuss for her incisive comments and careful editing of the (almost) final text; Nicola Viinikka for her enthusiasm for the manuscript and flexibility during the publishing process, as well as the staff, copy-editor and referees for Manchester University Press for their helpful assistance in preparing the final text.

In addition to the indispensable role of these individuals, there have been many others along the way whose comments and support have challenged and inspired me, including, but not confined to, Ron Aminzade, Andreas Behnke, Thomas Biersteker, David Blaney, Ken Booth, Lars-Erik Cederman, Simon Dalby, Tibor Dessewffy, Mary Dietz, Stephen Dudink, Tim Dunne, Raymond Duvall, Scott Erb, Rosemary Foot, Andrew Hurrell, Yuen Fong Khong, Keith Krause, Marianne Marchand, Jennifer Milliken, Kim Munholland, Iver Neumann, Michael Nicholson, Martin Sampson, Byron Schafer, Ben Schennink, Michael Shapiro, Siep Stuurman, J. Ann Tickner, R. B. J. Walker, Jutta Weldes, Lawrence Whitehead and Michael Williams. Finally, I would like to thank my family for their support and encouragement along the way.

K. M. F.

INTRODUCTION

Investigations usually begin with a puzzle. The goal is often to identify the cause of some outcome or to identify the motive or rationale behind a particular behaviour. There are cases, however, where a different and prior concern dominates. Consider the following puzzle presented in a British detective series, titled *Jonathan Creek*. A man was found dead in a deeply fortified fallout shelter that he had built himself. The man was holding a gun in his hand and the only entrance to the room was locked from the inside. Naming this outcome to be a suicide or a potential murder depended on an answer to two questions: first, was it possible for someone to enter this space from outside, and second, was it possible for this elderly man, whose hands were crippled by arthritis, to bolt a heavy door and then not only to hold a gun but to pull the trigger. The motive of a potential killer, as opposed to the victim's own motive for suicide, was necessarily secondary to the question of what was possible under these circumstances. It is not that the motive was unimportant; but rather that a question about motive could not be asked until the context had been established. It could not conceivably be a context of murder if there was no possible way to exit the room and leave the door bolted from inside. It could not conceivably be a context of suicide if the victim was incapable of holding a gun. Before a 'why' question could be asked, the context had to be established, which required knowing how either act was possible under the circumstances.

A similar problem hangs over our investigation. There is no shortage of explanations of the end of the Cold War or of the changing relationship between the former antagonists in its aftermath. Far less attention has been paid to the criteria for establishing the context and how a range of acts and outcomes which had been viewed as unrealistic and highly improbable became possible.

Charles Kegley (1994), troubled by a similar concern, outlined procedures for undertaking an autopsy of the Cold War. The autopsy was necessary because existing explanations for the death of the superpower conflict had aroused the author's suspicions. The first problem was the wide range of explanations for the phenomenon, most of which relied on the assumptions of particular theories that had been called into question by the death itself.[1]

---

1 See Grunberg and Risse-Kappen in Allan and Goldman (1992). This was particularly true of realism. Since that time a range of realist explanations has emerged. See, for instance, Dolan (1990), Glynn (1992), Perle (in Kegley and Schwab, 1991), Schweizer (1994), Wells (in Hogan, 1992) and Wohlforth (1994–95).

1

The various explanations also represented a particular political position, either Left or Right. Kegley argues that a more complex analysis, attentive to multiple causes rather than singular, is needed. His initial question regards the object of analysis, that is, whether the death to be explained is that of the Cold War itself or of the Soviet Union. This is a question about context. How do we establish the contours of the 'body' to be examined, which is prior to determining a cause?

Establishing the context

While identifying an important problem, Kegley's procedures for an autopsy are insufficient. He does not draw on the assumptions of a particular theory, for instance, realist or liberal. He does, however, establish the meaning and boundaries of the context prior to the analysis. He names the changes to be a death. The need for an autopsy implies that the death may not have been natural. There is an examiner who stands outside the body, taking it apart, seeking clues to the causes of death. Kegley begins by questioning whether the cadaver is the Cold War or the Soviet Union, but he at least implies, along with others, that it is the latter. He uses the end of the Cold War interchangeably with 'a hegemon's withdrawal from global competition', 'the reversal of seventy years of Soviet practice' and 'the need to trace the causes of the Soviet Union's withdrawal from the Cold War competition'.

Kegley asks a question about how the Soviet Union died. His analysis is superior to those he criticises; he is open to the possibility of multiple causes. However, like the others, the investigator establishes the context prior to the analysis. He suggests first naming the object of explanation, delineating the units of analysis and then proceeding with the autopsy. One begins with the scientist's categories and then moves to the observation of reality. This process of articulating the question and naming the object of explanation establishes the parameters of the context prior to the analysis itself. The procedures do not go far enough in addressing the problem Kegley identifies because they are not qualitatively different from those he criticises.

The first section of this book makes an argument for a particular method for establishing the context of the end of the Cold War. The method builds on the work of the later Wittgenstein.[2] Aside from some of the theoretical work by Onuf (1989), Kratochwil (1989), and Hollis and Smith (1991),[3] Wittgenstein's work remains largely unexplored within international

---

2 This application of Wittgenstein's ideas is indebted to a number of primary sources on Wittgenstein (1958, 1969, 1979), as well as a range of secondary sources, including Finch (1995), Gier (1981), Johnston (1991), Phillips (1977) and Pitkin (1972).

3 Two more recent contributions to the literature on Wittgenstein and international relations theory are Holt (1997) and Pin-Fat (1997a).

relations. His thought is a useful point of departure for an analysis of this kind for several reasons. First, Wittgenstein argued the need to move away from the formulation of abstract theoretical languages and the search for essences to 'look and see' how language is put to use in everyday practice. In this case, rather than beginning with the analyst's hypothesis, the central task is to uncover the meanings that the subjects of study brought to their interactions. While the positivist model assumes language to be a set of labels which can be compared with the world, Wittgenstein demonstrates that language is constitutive of the world. We cannot get behind our language to compare it with that which it describes.

Second, Wittgenstein's approach to rules belonging to multiple games is useful for making sense of a context of dramatic change. With the end of the Cold War we have been confronted with a number of particular and surprising outcomes, not least of which was the end of the Cold War itself. Many of the existing theoretical and methodological tools of international relations are more suited to the analysis of continuity than change. Practices of fixing the meaning of terms in order to compare them with a reality which, it is assumed, is characterised by repetition and recurrence, are not very useful for analysing a process of change which culminates in a unique outcome.[4] In sum, Wittgenstein's concept of a *language game* is a useful tool for describing a process of change based on the shared categories by which the social world is constituted.

In Part I, I lay out the basis for the analysis in five chapters. In Chapter One I explore Wittgenstein's notion of *rule-following*, and in particular the implications of this approach for how we understand the relationship between word and world. This intersubjective approach to rules is contrasted with other orientations in the discipline, including approaches to laws, rationality and interpretation.

In Chapter Two I discuss a particular type of language game, expressed in *metaphor*. Linguists have long argued that everyday speech is dependent on metaphor for attributing meaning and making sense of the world. This is all the more true at the international level where we cannot isolate and directly observe the subjects of analysis and where the actors are often abstract collective entities such as states and alliances. Cultural forms of life

---

4 Nicholson (1996: 118) indirectly points to the problem. He argues that a concept of social rules – as opposed to laws – need not detract from the positivist enterprise during a stable period: 'If the rules are stable, the generalisations about behaviour are stable; if not, then not ... By instability, I mean changes in the rules of such frequency that we cannot predict behaviour in the sorts of contexts we wish to.' The implication of his claim is that positivist methods are far more suited to the analysis of stable periods than contexts of change. Scholars, such as Gilpin (1981), have generalised about processes of international change. In these studies, war is usually a central mechanism of the change. With the end of the Cold War, by contrast, many were surprised by the absence of interstate conflict.

are drawn on 'as a matter of course' to metaphorically attribute meaning and boundaries to life at the international level.

In Chapter Three, I argue that this understanding of metaphor can be put to use in the systematic analysis of a process of change. Metaphors do not only refer to isolated objects. The use of a dominant metaphor to conceptualise international relations constitutes a *grammar* of possibilities for the transformation of the named object. The central point is that the structure of change is not to be identified in a reality independent of human meaning, but rather in the shared language games and grammars by which international identities and practices are constituted.

Chapter Four goes a step further to argue that these shared grammars provide a unique point of departure for *describing* a change, such as the end of the Cold War. Given the complexity of international life, criteria are needed for making choices about which details to privilege. By looking at the weakness of various existing approaches, I rethink the criteria for a 'better' description of a process of change. A better description describes a 'reality', but this reality is explicitly social; the focus is on the *actions* of a *range* of players, actions which are dependent on rules for their meaning. The analysis identifies the parameters of a dominant game and moves, over time, by which it was transformed.

Chapter Five illustrates this approach to description by presenting an overview of the unfolding of the end of the Cold War over a sixteen year period, from 1975 to 1991, based on a shared grammar of structure. This narrative does not describe every detail of the situation. Like all narratives, it preferences some aspects over others. The criteria for privileging are based on the shared categories of different players who situate their acts within a particular type of game. The purpose of the description is to highlight shifts in the game and in the position and acts of players over time.

How possible?

In Jonathan Creek's puzzle, establishing the context was necessary in order to determine how the death of the victim was possible. In our investigation, the goal is to trace a change towards a particular outcome that was not predicted by theories that assumed more of the same.[5] The Cold War superpowers were locked in a pattern of action and reaction. The space for thinking about possible options was limited by the confines of their shared space. International relations theories in the realist tradition articulated the reasonable boundaries of action for great powers. Great powers were concerned primarily with their own survival. Great powers would act to

5 Everts in Allan and Goldman (1992).

maintain their empires. It was more rational for great powers to arm than to disarm. Stability and preservation of the balance of power were to be prized above all else. In this context, defensive systems would contribute to instability in so far as they encouraged a first strike capability. Alliances would disband in the absence of an enemy.

That these were boundaries, enclosing the two superpowers, is only reinforced by the sense of surprise accompanying a range of moves since the mid-1980s.[6] When Reagan introduced the Strategic Defence Initiative (SDI), against the background of a taboo against defensive systems going back more than a decade, the response was one of surprise. At Reykjavik, when Reagan and Gorbachev agreed in principle to a nuclear-free world, some were shocked and some celebrated, but no one anticipated this particular outcome. Disarmament became possible for the first time during the Cold War. When the Iron Curtain and the Berlin Wall were dismantled, followed by the Velvet Revolutions in Eastern Europe, social scientists were surprised that the Soviet Union did not step in to maintain its empire. When later the Soviet Union gave up its identity and East Germany merged with the Federal Republic of Germany (FRG), the world was once again caught by surprise. When NATO survived the end of the Cold War, in the absence of an enemy, realists were confounded.

The second question of this book is how alternatives to the realist game of the Cold War became possible. If we accept realist assumptions that states were constrained by their context of interaction, how did the two superpowers move beyond those constraints to introduce possibilities that had previously been considered unrealistic? With this question as the point of departure, not only the disarmament initiatives of the Soviet Union but Reagan's proposal of SDI become the subject of enquiry; not only the collapse of the Eastern bloc or the Soviet Union but the survival of NATO in their absence must be drawn into the investigation.

If states were constrained in their actions, within the context of the Cold War, the analysis needs to be broadened to account for the potential influence of other types of actor. Realists have tended to isolate states as the most relevant actors at the international level. An answer to the question of how the Cold War came to an end requires looking at the relationship between different *types* of actor. A more flexible approach capable of capturing the multiplicity of identities and games is needed.

While traditional positivist scholarship in international relations has asked 'why necessary?' questions, that is, why one variable necessarily caused another, post-positivists or post-structuralists have asked how certain acts

6 A number of scholars have analysed the failure to predict the end of the Cold War. See, for instance, Gaddis (1992–93), Lebow and Risse-Kappen (1995), and Allan and Goldman (1992).

become possible.[7] Roxanne Doty (1993), for instance, asked how intervention in the Philippines became possible and David Campbell (1993) asked how intervention in the Gulf became possible. The critical intent of these analyses is to expose the role of realist language and argument in constituting a realist agenda and marginalising alternative voices. Generally, these studies make a claim that alternatives are possible, that spaces *should* be created for alternative voices to speak, but they do not provide much insight into *how* alternatives to the realist discourse become possible in actual contexts. As a result, they also emphasise a particular dominant game rather than the trans-ition from a 'realist' game to alternatives originally thought to be unrealistic. A central theme of post-structural analysis is how dominant state discourses and practice are reproduced. By contrast, I concentrate on how antagonistic self–other relationships are broken down, analysing the relationship between multiple identities embedded in multiple interfacing games.

Given the emphasis on how dominant discourses, as opposed to alter-natives, prevail, post-structuralists, like realists, have been preoccupied with state-level practice. The analysis in this book examines the relationship between the practices of state and non-state actors in both East and West, which has implications for how we understand the role of language at the international level. Realists have traditionally articulated a concern that there is a distinction between the words of state actors and their material interests or practices. Yet state leaders try publicly to justify their acts for a reason. As some realists have recognised, these justifications constitute the power to act (Donnelly in Nardin and Mapel, 1994: 94; Kissinger, 1977: 200).

E. H. Carr (1964: 2) starts his classic work, *The Twenty Years' Crisis* with a claim that the birth of International Relations as a science was given impetus by the conviction, after World War I, that international politics could no longer be left to statesmen in light of changes in warfare which made it the business of populations. One point of his argument is the complexity yet the centrality of public opinion in shaping what state leaders do. Carr suggests the role of theories and ideas in convincing populations or other states of the desirability of a certain state of affairs. He warns of the consequences of too great a gap between theories and ideas about morality and what the 'ordinary man' is thinking (Carr, 1964: 146–9). Public opinion, in addition to economic and military capabilities, is an important category of power in his analysis, which is a point that has been largely lost on later realists.

A central theme of this book is the relationship between a *language of manoeuvre* by states, that is, the strategic use of language, and the *entanglement* of states in their own public justifications. Michael MccGwire (1991: 11),

---

7 For a discussion of the distinction between 'why' and 'how' questions, see Doty (1993), Little (1991) and Wendt (1987).

an analyst of Soviet strategy, notes that there is often a confusion between the multiple factors that lead to a decision and the rationalisation that is used to justify the decision, 'which then takes on a life of its own'. Whatever the original factors giving rise to a decision or strategy, it has to be justified in a political environment, at which point it takes on a life that may be different to that originally intended. Because states must justify their actions, they may also be held accountable for them if the gap between the rationalisation and the practice becomes too wide.

The purpose of Part II is to unpack the dynamics of the challenge to state practice during the latter part of the Cold War, by analysing the role of critical movements in both East and West. There is an extensive literature on the role of social movements in these changes, a literature that has been largely marginalised (Reus-Smit, 1992). The analysis presented in this book is unique in a number of ways. First, many studies of social movements adopt more traditional positivist methods or the assumptions of liberal or neo-liberal theory.[8] By contrast, I develop an alternative methodology, specific to the task of analysing a process of change. Second, few studies have looked at the relationship *between* movements in East and West.[9] They instead tend to focus on either the Western European peace movements or the Eastern European dissidents.

Each chapter in Part II thickens the description of changing games of East–West security by adding new layers that approach the context from a different angle, exploring the identities occupying the Cold War structure and their relationships to one another. I argue that a change on the part of the superpowers towards options originally considered to be unrealistic has to be understood in a context of changing games.

Realists have argued that there is only one game in a condition of anarchy, and this game limits the room for manoeuvre by states. In Chapter Six, I explore the contours of an alternative emancipatory game and the clash of the two in the early 1980s. Emancipatory movements, which positioned themselves outside the dominant rules of the Cold War, came to the conclusion that states were trapped in a zero-sum logic, which defined possibilities in terms of individual or state survival. One step in transforming the game was to *denaturalise* the 'objective' basis of the dominant rules in order to convince public opinion that multiple games were possible. Against

---

8 See Cortright (1993), Goldman in Allan and Goldman (1992) and Risse-Kappen (1991).

9 The foremost exception is the work of Kaldor which explored the détente from below process. See Kaldor (1991) and Kaldor, Holden and Falk (1989); these are collections of essays by a range of authors. See also Dalby (1990). Cortright (1993) and a number of pieces in Lebow and Risse-Kappen (1995) emphasise the role of Western peace activists. Koslowski and Kratochwil (in Lebow and Risse-Kappen, 1995) examine changes in the Eastern bloc, as does Waller (1993).

the background of 'permanent' alliances, social movements engaged in emancipatory acts which altered the meaning of security and insecurity across the Cold War divide.

Chapter Seven begins with the realist assumption that the words of state leaders may disguise other interests, but then asks a question about what happens if the disguise is exposed. In the early 1980s a 'battle' for public opinion emerged between states and independent movements in each bloc over the meanings at the foundation of each bloc. Processes of *immanent critique* by independent movements in both East and West – processes that exposed the contradiction between state words and practice – created *spaces of opportunity* for both Reagan and Gorbachev to move towards alternative policies.

Chapter Eight situates the rationality of changing moves by the two superpowers in a context of changing games. Traditional international relations theory has privileged questions of rationality or processes 'inside the mind' of individuals. *Changing Games, Changing Strategies* shifts attention to the *rules of the game* which are necessarily prior to the rationality of any particular move. Reagan and Gorbachev shifted from a negotiating game between 'adversaries' to a game of dialogue between 'friends', a new game within which their identities and practices changed. Their actions were not determined, however. It is possible that other leaders would have continued to follow the rules of the realist game. Lebow and Stein (in Lebow and Risse-Kappen, 1995: 9) highlight the relationship between Gorbachev's context and his policy changes. The context made the changes possible, but did not determine the character of the change. In their argument:

> someone other than Gorbachev could have come to power with very different conceptions of internal reform and foreign policy. Grigory Romanov or Yegor Ligachev, other contenders for power in 1985, would probably have pursued a kinder and gentler version of Brezhnevism, as had Konstantin Chernenko and Yuri Andropov. East–West relations might have improved, but the two blocs probably would have retained their essential character and antagonism.

The actions of Gorbachev and Reagan were not determined; they were made possible, however, by the intersubjective constitution of an alternative in a broader context. As more and more people began to engage in this new game, the wall dividing Western and Eastern Europe was dismantled and Cold War institutions in the Eastern bloc began to collapse.

This introduction began with a claim that diagnosis is potentially distorted by premature efforts to name a context to be either a murder or a suicide. Once Jonathan Creek established the context, he found it was both. The killer had entered the room with the victim, bolted the door, committed the murder and placed the gun in the victim's hand. He then proceeded to reconstruct a wall in the room, take a suicidal dose of pills and crawl behind his artificial wall, sealing the last brick, so that only the most astute investigator could identify an alteration in the room. The simple picture was one of a murder or a suicide; the more complex picture situated both within a broader field of possibilities. Similarly, in the case of the end of the Cold War, we get a more coherent and complex understanding of the relationship between Reagan's SDI, Gorbachev's domestic and international proposals, and the eventual collapse of the wall separating East and West, by looking at the larger context within which these actions became possible.

Implications?

Scholars in the post-Cold War world have been perplexed by the changing nature of security.[10] Questions have been raised about the referent object of security, that is, whether states or individuals, as well as questions about what constitutes a security threat. A theme running throughout this book is the contrast between two distinct constructions of what it means to be secure in relation to others. The first defines security as something acquired by a *referent object vis-à-vis* another. Security is defined in contrast to an enemy other. The focus is on the constitution of distinct and isolated identities engaged in a zero-sum game. The second defines security as a *process* of dialogue and cooperation in partnership with others.[11] The two are embedded in distinct language games that came into conflict as the Cold War was ending. The end of the Cold War was constituted in the tension between these two games of security; this tension continues to define the possibilities for security in the post-Cold War world.

This description of the end of the Cold War is the point of departure for an alternative understanding of post-Cold War changes in strategy by both NATO and Russia. Both are caught in the tension between two language games of security. The rules of these games are followed strategically, in different ways, by each side. But both have also become entangled in these rules, which limit the space for manoeuvre and constrain their response to one another. NATO expansion has now become 'inevitable'; from a realist perspective, Russia had no choice but to accept this development. Others have argued that expansion is an error of historical importance and may lead to a new division of Europe (Brown, 1995; Mandelbaum, 1996; MccGwire, 1998). I provide a more nuanced view of a continuing process that could result in a different outcome.

10 For a review of recent debates on the meaning of security, see Krause and Williams (1996).

11 This type of positive-sum game, emphasising dialogue and cooperation, has been explored by feminist theorists. See, for instance, Tickner (in DerDerian, 1995), Sylvester (1994) and Jabri (1996).

Chapter Nine raises a question about the conventional wisdom that the end of the Cold War was a case of the West 'winning'. When situated in a larger context, NATO's victory over the Soviet Union takes on a different meaning. The alliance *constructed* its victory, at a very late date, by strategically adopting the language games of its opponents in the public opinion battles of the 1980s. In so far as we accept the victory explanation as 'true', it affects a closure on our thinking about the lessons to be drawn from the past and the future implications. The end of the Cold War becomes a static picture of a war that was won. When we 'look and see' the contestation between language games, spaces are opened for rethinking the past, the present and the future.

In Chapter Ten, I argue that NATO tried to lay down the rules of a new post-Cold War game of security, but became increasingly entangled in its own rules as its survival became linked to eastward expansion. Despite the claim to victory, with the end of the Cold War many were questioning why NATO, as an organisation created primarily to counter the Soviet threat, should continue. In order to survive, NATO had to adapt and change. While initially reluctant to expand militarily, the eventual 'inevitability' of expansion was driven by NATO's concerns about survival.

Chapter Eleven raises a question about Russia's agreement to the NATO–Russia Founding Act in May 1997, after years of arguing that expansion would re-create the Cold War conflict. The Russian response can be seen less as a concession or a recognition of defeat, than a move to change the game in a way that would potentially realise its long-term interest in a pan-European security structure. By remaining firm in its opposition to expansion, while calling for a special relationship to NATO, it put the alliance in a position where it would have to live up to its stated intent of dialogue in 'true partnership' or be exposed as the agent in creating a new division of Europe.

In the final chapter I explore the implications of this analysis for how we think about the relationship between language and power. This 'thick' description (Geertz, 1973) represents more than a mapping of conflicting language games. It also represents an exploration of the relationship between two different types of power, as they relate to strategy. The one is a tradition of coercive power; the other form of power has historically been employed by the weak, or by those who play with a losing hand. In the last section of the chapter I discuss the implications both for security policy and for the way the relationship between theory and practice is conceptualised.

A critical investigation?

In the post-Cold War world, international relations theorists have been in search of a research agenda that addresses some of the problems of the positivist model but is not purely critical. Ole Waever (in Smith, Booth and Zalewski, 1996) argued that the international society tradition is one meeting place between two extremes of international relations theorising. What distinguishes the British School from the American realists is the emphasis on the *sociality* of the international system and on rules of the game. The language game argument provides a link for thinking about the analysis of rules of the game in practice.

While the international society literature has tended to focus on macro rules of the international system, such as sovereignty, international law and rules of war, the analysis of this book looks at the everyday rules by which practices are given meaning. The language game argument provides a bridge between two genres of international relations theory that have occupied the extremes of Waever's spectrum of the field of international relations in the 1990s. At one end, at a boundary of boredom, he places the game theorists; at the other, at a boundary of negativity, he places the post-structuralists.

Given the abstract nature of the theory, game theorists have had a hard time with empirical analysis (Schelling, 1980: v–vi; Bennett, 1995: 25–6). The following analysis moves closer to the actors, identifying the structure of a change in the political context itself. It traces the contest and transition between multiple games.

Constructivists, more to the centre of Waever's spectrum, have theorised about the intersubjective nature of changing games (Wendt, 1992; Barnett, forthcoming).[12] They have emphasised that identities and interests are constituted through the interactions of players. While *Changing Games, Changing Strategies* is compatible with much of the work in this genre,[13] it pushes further on two points. First, constructivists have tended to maintain a separation between material factors and ideas, arguing the causal force of the latter (Katzenstein, 1996; Adler, 1997). Second, the role of language, and its relation to practice, has not been adequately explored.[14] By contrast, I argue that material possibility is linguistically constituted. At the international level, strategic action can no more be detached from language than the meaning of the objects with which chess is played, or the

---

12 For a more humanistic methodological approach to games, see Alker (1996).
13 Dunne (1995) has argued that the international society tradition is compatible with a constructivist approach to international relations.
14 Notable exceptions include Weldes (forthcoming), Weldes and Saco (1996) and Milliken and Sylvan (1996).

rationality of moves within this game, can be detached from a language of chess.

Post-structuralists have analysed how the actions of states become possible, arguing that spaces should be opened for marginalised voices to speak. This analysis includes those marginalised voices and argues that they were fundamental to constituting the possibility of an alternative to the realist games of the Cold War.

Game theorists have remained largely at the level of abstract theory. Post-structuralists, equally abstract in many cases, have emphasised the importance of discourse and language. By constructing an alternative methodology of language games, this book occupies a middle space between the two. It is compatible with the international society literature's emphasis on historically specific rules of the game, but provides the methodological tools to analyse these in actual contexts of change.

But what makes this investigation critical? In addition to Wittgenstein, the critical theory of the Frankfurt School has shaped this analysis. While Wittgenstein provided a critique of logical positivism, critical theory emerged from a challenge to the overwhelming dominance of instrumental rationality in modern culture. One of the central concerns of Adorno and Horkheimer, representatives of the early Frankfurt School, was that positivism had contributed to the dehumanisation of society and the objectification of individuals. The project of critical theory was to recover the capacity to be fully human.

A marriage of the two overcomes the criticism that post-Wittgensteinian scholarship has not adequately addressed issues of power and repression, history and social change (Thompson, 1981; George and Campbell, 1990). A marriage of the two also addresses some of the weaknesses in the philosophy of Habermas, the most prominent member of the Frankfurt School.

Habermas was influenced by Wittgenstein's argument about the social nature of language and communication. From Wittgenstein he took the idea that human subjects are always already united with one another through language (Honneth, 1995: 86). This led to his critique of Marx. If human society is distinguished by its dependence on linguistic understanding, then societal reproduction cannot be reduced to the single dimension of labour, as Marx proposed. Collective processes of securing a material existence are dependent from the beginning on the maintenance of communicative agreement.

Habermas, influenced by Wittgenstein, recognised the intersubjective nature of human action. He has, however, been criticised on two points which, I would argue, are contrary to the spirit of his Wittgensteinian move. The first criticism relates to his reliance on abstract and universal criteria of rationality (Hoy and McCarthy, 1994). Wittgenstein countered the claim that the world could be abstractly represented in theory; instead it is necessary to 'look and see' what language game is being played. The second criticism regards Habermas's distinction between communicative and strategic action (Smith, 1997: 114–20). While the former is dialogical, in search of agreement, the latter is monological, seeking to impose. From a Wittgensteinian perspective, all communication, both communicative and strategic, is intersubjective and dependent on shared rules for its meaning.

The following study explores the role of several concepts from critical theory, such as denaturalisation, emancipation, immanent critique and dialogue, as put to use by critical actors in this context of change. Critique, from the perspective of the Frankfurt School, was a tool for identifying contradictions within the social world and therefore the potential for change within it. Part II explores the attempt of these critical actors to identify and expose the contradictions of the Cold War. In Part III, I, as analyst, take these earlier efforts as a point of departure for identifying the contradictions of post-Cold War security relations between NATO and its former enemies.

The inclusion of critical voices goes against the grain of the traditional realist emphasis on states. But the analysis is not primarily critical because it includes a range of practices that have in the past been ignored. There is not necessarily anything critical about the mere description of a change, even if it includes dissident voices. This volume is first and foremost critical because it makes us look again, in a fresh way, at that which we assume about the world because it has become overly familiar. In this way, new spaces are opened for thinking about the meaning of the past and the present and, therefore, how we construct the future.

PART I

The social construction of games

1

Rules

The rule can only seem to me to produce all its consequences in advance if I draw them as a matter of course. As much as it is a matter of course for me to call this colour 'blue'. (Wittgenstein, 1958: para. 238)

REALISTS ARGUE THAT rules at the international level are of minimal significance because states do not always follow them. Existing rules of international law, for instance, do not constrain states when it is not in their self-interest to comply. Emphasis is placed on the choice of whether or not to follow a rule. One might argue, in response, that the possibility of cheating or breaking a rule is dependent on its prior existence and, in fact, states do in most cases follow the rules. The more crucial problem, however, is the exclusive focus on a regulative notion of rules. Rules are norms that constrain or do not constrain, such as the rule that 'one should not cheat' in playing a game. Rules do not only regulate though; they also constitute identity and action.[1] The purpose of this chapter is to explore an alternative approach to rules that does not deny the regulative dimension, but shifts attention to the constitutive nature of rules that we follow 'as a matter of course'. Wittgenstein's metaphor of the language game is a useful point of departure for exploring this distinction.

The term 'language game' is often used in a disparaging way to suggest that a person is playing with words or manoeuvring with language rather than being sincere. This use of the concept is consistent with the prevailing view of language within the field of international relations. Language is considered to be largely irrelevant. Leaders are assumed to be more motivated by their self-interest in power or material constraints than the words of others. To the extent that language is considered, it is most often assumed to be mere windowdressing, a disguise for other interests or propaganda.

One of the central issues I explore in this book is the relationship between a 'language of manoeuvre', that is, using language strategically,

---

1 There has been an ongoing debate about the extent to which these two forms of rule can be separated; see Onuf (1989) and Kratochwil (1989). The emphasis on the regulative function is at least implied by the language of norms used in another genre of constructivist literature; see Katzenstein (1996).

versus the constraints imposed on actors by their 'entanglement' in a shared language. Wittgenstein's concept is useful for starting to think about this relationship. On the one hand, the metaphor of the game implies the possibility of strategic action and manoeuvre with language. On the other hand, the game metaphor also imposes boundaries on the room for manoeuvre. One makes moves strategically within the boundaries of a specific game from a particular position within that game and, in doing so, one employs the rules. Normally, one follows these rules 'as a matter of course'. One cannot play chess without moving knights or bishops according to the rules which dictate what can be done with these pieces. One does not play chess with houses and hotels; or monopoly with bishops and pawns; or poker with a baseball. The meaning of the objects with which a game is played, and the moves that can be made with them, are constituted by the rules. As long as we are engaged in playing this game, we do not choose whether to follow these rules; we do so blindly (Wittgenstein, 1958: para. 219).

In what follows I contrast the assumptions of this approach to games with three strands of international relations theory. First, a rule is distinguished from the positivist notion of a law. Second, the rational action of game theory is contrasted with a notion of rationality dependent on the 'rules of the game'. Third, the difference between a rule and an interpretation is explored.

Rules and laws

In using the term 'language game' Wittgenstein makes the point that using language is like making moves in a game. It is on the basis of shared rules that we know 'how to go on' in particular contexts (Wittgenstein, 1958: paras 179, 186, 198, 566, 167). The positivist model denies the importance of language, yet implicitly assumes a position regarding the relationship between word and world. Words are labels that we apply to discrete objects in an objective world. The notion of hypothesis testing relies on the assumption that the scientist can compare his or her statements with reality to see whether they correspond.

In his later work, Wittgenstein (1958: paras 357, 401) was very clear about the impossibility of getting behind our words to compare them with that which they describe. Rather than understanding words as labels, he approaches language use as a form of action in itself, which cannot be isolated in the description of discrete objects; agents, actions and objects are given meaning within the context of game, that is, a set of practices based on rules within which they are constituted in relation to one another (Wittgenstein, 1958: paras 1, 7, 23, 65, 66).

A chess analogy is useful for elaborating the significance of this approach.

Imagine a chess board with all of its pieces. Based on the 'words as labels' approach, we are immediately confronted with the question of whether to attach the label 'piece of wood' or 'piece of plastic', whatever the case might be, to the various pieces or, by contrast, the labels 'knight', 'bishop', 'pawn', and so on. Once we concede that one of the latter is the most concise label, we are forced to recognise the dependence of these identities on the larger game of chess. The identity of a piece of wood as a knight and what one does with it cannot be detached from the rules of the game of chess (Wittgenstein, 1958: para. 31). A piece of wood, when situated in another language game, might be a club to hit someone with or a component of a potential bonfire.[2]

Likewise, we could not begin to observe two players moving objects around on a board and say anything meaningful or strategic about these moves or the process by which the game unfolds without knowledge of the rules. Any move within a game of chess is an expression of following or breaking these rules, which prescribe the boundaries of what can reasonably be said about it or done within it. It would be meaningless, as well as nonsensical, to begin invoking the rules of monopoly to describe the interactions between players of chess.

A central point of this chess analogy is to begin to think about patterns belonging to social relations in a way that can be distinguished from the regularities and patterns presupposed by the notion of a causal law.[3] The search for causal laws is considered to be important because of a desire to establish the existence of recurring features of international relations. The source of regularity in this case is assumed to be independent of human meaning. To explain something is to identify that which necessarily caused it. This relationship, at least in reference to a covering law model, is necessary because of a recurring pattern under which it can be subsumed. A law either exists or it does not. The purpose of falsification is to make an effort to demonstrate that it probably does by looking at the most difficult case in which it might not.

By contrast rules are explicitly social and the patterning or regularities we associate with them are dependent on people following them over and

---

2 Language cannot be divorced from practices involving material objects. Both a baseball bat and a pawn from a game of chess might be made of wood, but it is nonsensical to think that because of this common property the two could be used in the same way. Just try hitting a baseball with a pawn! It is not that the material reality of wood is missing in this case, but rather how the material object is invested with *meaning* which then informs practice in relation to it. The 'woodness' of both objects fades in importance against the background of games within which each has a very distinct meaning and use.

3 In this approach to rules, actions are constituted within the contours of a particular game; they are not caused, as argued within the dominant literature on social constructivism within international relations. For a discussion of cause as it relates to the constructivist literature, see Adler (1997: 329).

over again. The game of chess would change significantly if we stopped following the rule that knights move two spaces forward and one sideways or vice versa. A rule cannot be applied just once; it is like a custom that is continuously reproduced through our practice (Wittgenstein, 1958: para. 199). Rules do not determine behaviour in the way that causal laws are said to. We follow rules in acting but it is perfectly possible to break a rule or begin following a different set of rules (Wittgenstein, 1958: para. 201). Failing to follow a rule in no way falsifies it. However, in a situation governed by a consistently applied set of rules, if everyone for some reason stopped following them and took up another game, one might say that one set of rules had replaced another. For instance, a person travelling from one country to another, such as the United States to Britain, replaces the rule that a piece of paper has a dollar value with a different rule that it has a pound value.[4] While laws are the basis for identifying causal relationships in an objective reality, rules constitute the *meaning* of practices within specific games.

The question is, why choose an approach that assumes the existence of one or the other, that is, causal laws or rules? The standard argument is that causal laws are superior because they allow us to explain why one variable necessarily caused another by identifying this relationship with a recurring pattern. The goal is to construct theories of international relations of equal status to theories of the natural sciences. The problem is how we ever identify any two events across time as the same, which is a necessary step in order to make the claim that a pattern has recurred. On the basis of the positivist model, this involves an act by the scientist of naming two contexts as similar. Explanation, in this case, begins with the categories of the scientist which he or she sets out to compare with the world.

The analysis of this book shifts attention to acts of naming by the subjects of study. As a result, it is not explanatory in the way that a positivist model claims to be explanatory. Following rules does not involve the determinacy associated with causal law. However, by providing a descriptive account of a particular world, including the meaning of acts in relation to objects and in relation to the acts of others, we do explain what happened. We explain the unfolding of a context in much the same way that the observer of a chess match explains to an audience the relationship between different moves and the eventual outcome of the game. As the

4 Searle (1995: 41) refers to social constructions, such as money, which we tend to treat as objective, as 'institutional or social facts'. We are surrounded by 'objective' institutions and practices of this kind. But this does not detract from a recognition that a piece of paper with a government stamp on it has a much different value and social use than the piece of paper in my printer. In each of these cases, we know the meaning of these symbols or objects, and therefore how to act, on the basis of a rule.

analogy suggests, the unfolding of one game is not a guide to how future matches will unfold. This approach makes it possible to explain the 'particularity' of an outcome by situating it within the rules of a game. It is useful for the cases examined in this book in so far as each explores a *change* in policy or strategy from what had originally been defined as 'realistic'.

The specificity of an outcome can be understood by reference to a system of rules. Rules are social in nature and, therefore, inseparable from human meaning. If one says she would like to play a game of chess but does not know the rules, and the other responds by saying 'sorry, they are a secret', it is not possible to go on. Rules constitute not only the identity of the pieces with which the game is played but the meaning of any particular move, which can be repeated by anyone who engages in play (Wittgenstein, 1958: para. 54). Moving a knight two spaces one way and a single space another is meaningful because it relies on a rule by which innumerable players – and even a computer – move a knight 'in this way' in each game of chess that is played. The pattern is evident in what is done, that is, an act, repeated over and over again by players of chess who will never know one another but know what it means to play this game. No two games of chess will follow precisely the same course, however. In fact, the future chess champion may recognise, in the range of possible moves from any one position on the board, the wisdom of avoiding certain past mistakes. The only sense in which one can meaningfully introduce the possibility of encouraging or discouraging a particular outcome is in recognising particular 'strategies' that grandmasters have employed, strategies which encompass more than a single move. Achieving precisely the same outcome would require that both players repeat precisely the moves of a particular chess match.

The point is that each chess match unfolds in a distinct way rather than recurring in exactly the same way, as the logic of recurring cause and effect would seem to suggest. Yet the game of chess is constituted by rules which make it possible for particular acts to be repeated by players who will never know or see one another.

Rules and rationality

Rules provide an alternative way to think about patterns at the international level. A shift to an emphasis on rules also makes us think differently about rationality. Game theories have emphasised the rationality of individual moves but say very little about the 'rules of the game'. The question is whether strategic rationality can ever be detached from the context of a specific game. The analyst wants to know what Kasparov is thinking prior to a move in order to predict what he will do. The prediction is not only dependent on what Kasparov rationally decides, but on the range of possible moves and strategies available to him from a position within an ongoing game. Deep Blue was able to beat the grandmaster because it was programmed to sort through a much larger range of possible strategies than the grandmaster himself. It is not that the computer was ultimately more *rational* than Kasparov; rather, the computer was able to access a wider range of possibilities for putting the rules to use because it had been programmed to do so at a very rapid speed.[5] The point is that one cannot begin to sort through the range of possible moves, and therefore choose the most rational one, in the absence of what is possible within a particular game. Knowing what is possible from any one position is dependent on knowledge of the rules. These rules are learned via language. It would make no sense to say that Kasparov reasons about his next move by drawing on a language other than the one by which he knows the rules of chess.

The question, of course, is whether international relations resembles a game of chess or a single game at all. Kasparov's defeat by Deep Blue provides an insight into how the two may be different. One commentator in this context asked why it is that programmers have succeeded in teaching computers to play chess or to do maths, yet have been less successful in teaching a computer natural language (Naughton, 1997: 7). While all three depend on rules, there is a difference between the rules of chess or maths, on the one hand, and those of natural language, on the other. The first two represent single games dependent on a context of rules, within which one knows 'how to go on' from point A to point B. These rules are fixed in a way that the rules of language are not.

The use of language and other forms of action in everyday life, as well as at the international level, are no less interwoven with material practice and no less dependent on rules than moving a knight *in this way* is bound up with the rules of chess. However, any two games played in a social or political context are not incommensurable in the way that playing any two games, for example chess and monopoly, are.[6] The use of language, employing the rules, knowing how to go on, is as dependent on a context as a game of chess or maths, but the possibilities for changing games within a single context are much greater.

This requires elaboration. One can say that chess and monopoly are incommensurable. They represent two internally coherent sets of rules which cannot be employed simultaneously in the same space. One cannot play chess and monopoly at the same time, in the same space, at least in

5 A rational choice analyst might argue that Deep Blue had more complete information, but the point, ignored in the rational choice literature, is the dependence of this information on the range of ways that the rules of a specific game can be put to use.
6 For an in-depth analysis of the incommensurability argument in relation to theories of international relations, see Wight (1996).

any rational sense, *without* devising a new set of rules by which one could move the pieces of monopoly on a chess board or vice versa with *purpose*, that is, to some end (Wittgenstein, 1958: 564–6). This is less true of language games in the political world. President Reagan, for instance, after the introduction of SDI in the early 1980s, engaged simultaneously in two distinct language games about the meaning of deterrence. On the one hand, he increasingly argued that deterrence was a prison that had to be escaped. The logic or purpose of this argument was that it was necessary and possible to move away from reliance on nuclear weapons. In this case, he was providing a justification for SDI as an alternative. At the same time, he engaged in a conflicting game about the need to maintain deterrence until SDI was realised. This was in conflict with the first argument in so far as the latter had traditionally been – and was still within NATO – guided by a logic that the prison of deterrence was inescapable. To play both at once constructed a conflicting logic by which the inescapable was escapable. The logic of playing both games simultaneously has to be situated in a larger context of *contestation* in which Western populations and elites were divided over the desirability and potential consequences of nuclear deterrence. This problem is explored in more depth in Chapter Seven.

Another type of situation involving multiple changing games might involve two players following different but interfacing rules. For instance, in the context of Bosnia, NATO made a threat to compel the Serbs to stop their aggressive acts towards the safe havens. This threat was explicitly presented as a 'Gulf War' game, and relied on the assumption that the threat of overwhelming force would persuade a rational aggressor to stop its aggressive behaviour. However, given the context and the identities involved, the Serbs had an alternative move available to them which transformed the game. Just as Saddam Hussein, in the context of the Gulf War, took Westerners hostage in order to deter NATO from realising its threat, the Serbs took peacekeepers hostage and used this as leverage in bargaining for a promise that the bombing would stop.[7] From the perspective of the original Western game of compellence, this move may not have initially been imagined or it may have been categorised as 'irrational'. However, within a game involving players possessing *different types* of power, that is, with one having the potential to do massive damage from the air and the other to do massive damage to humans on the ground, the move on the part of the Serbs may be considered rational in so far as it involved following the rule of a different but interfacing game. This move transformed the

---

7 The Russian press identified the reliance of the Serbs on the prior example of Hussein. See *Current Digest of the Post-Soviet Press (CDSP)*, 67:21 (1995), p. 6.

context of choice for the West.[8] They were then confronted with a 'terrorist' game within which they could either make concessions to get the peace-keepers back, which they did, or to refuse to make concessions, which is normally understood to be more 'correct' in this type of game.

The latter example clarifies two points. First, the Serb act was situated in a terrorist game, which constituted the meaning of material practices such as taking hostages. Stated differently, taking 'hostages' – as opposed to 'prisoners', for instance – is an act that is dependent on a larger framework of meaning belonging to terrorism. Second, in a context of change the key issue is less the incommensurability of games at the international level than how new possibilities are created as multiple games intersect. Serb action cannot be understood merely in terms of cooperation or defection within a compellence game. They transformed the game and therefore the meaning of action within it. The goal here is to explore an approach that will allow us not only to identify the structure of individual games or matches, but the 'processes' by which one game is transformed into another.

Game theory relies on a high degree of abstraction. The scientist con-structs the structure of the game, the payoffs and incentives, and therefore the rationality of any particular move. In this study, the task is to identify the structure of change within the language games of the actors. How is this done? Wittgenstein (1958: para. 66) instructs us to 'look and see' what language games are being played in a given place and time. This raises one further question: if in fact any number of games can be played simul-taneously, are we not simply confronted with a multiplicity of contending interpretations and subsequently a complete lack of order or coherence at the international level?

Rule and interpretation

Wittgenstein argued against two prevailing assumptions about language. The first, explored earlier, was the tendency to understand language as a set of labels that we apply to discrete objects in the world. The second was the tendency to view language as a product of the mental processes of individuals. The latter often implies that meaning is first and foremost a

---

8 The alternative move by the Serbs was dependent on the fact that the 'West' was already playing with two strategies simultaneously which positioned the peace-keepers as potential hostages. On the one hand, the original game of peacekeeping relied on an impartiality rule. While the bombing strategy was meant to maintain this impartiality by making the peacekeepers, rather than the Bosnian population, the target of protection, it also constructed the peacekeepers as potential targets of retaliation, since the threat was directed specifically at the Serbs and was therefore open to an interpretation of partiality or taking sides with the Muslims. See Fierke (1996).

matter of subjective interpretation. A distinction between the two can be made.

An 'interpretivist' might argue that the interpretation of a natural phenomenon, such as an earthquake, depends on a discursive field which does not simply describe an event, but interprets it, for instance, as a 'natural phenomenon' or the 'wrath of God' (Laclau and Mouffe, 1985: 108; Campbell, 1993: 8). However, given a distinction between interpretation and rule, the relationship might be stated differently. Persons situated in different cultural or historical contexts may be inclined to interpret an earthquake differently, as a 'natural phenomenon' or as the 'wrath of God'. However, within any one of these contexts, individuals possess a rule for identifying an earthquake as one type of phenomenon rather than another. It would be unusual at best in Western culture, unless one is a member of a particular type of religious sect, to interpret an earthquake as an 'act of God', while in another time and place this would have been the rule for attributing meaning to it.

The distinction is even more important in relation to a socially constructed phenomenon. Consider the distinction between a totem pole and a ballistic missile. Based on the interpretivist argument, two people looking at a projectile-like object may see different things. The one may see a totem pole and the other a ballistic missile. Yet the possibility of differing interpretations, in this case, is only meaningful if, for instance, Martians were to come to Earth and knew nothing of the culture they confronted, or if representatives of two totally separate cultures were to come into contact, much like Columbus meeting the 'Indians' in the New World for the first time. The single object being observed would, however, already have a meaning in the culture from which it originated. The object would have been *constructed* to be either a totem pole or a ballistic missile. The central issue is the *practices* that relate to totem poles or ballistic missiles; that is, not what is seen, but how one understands the rules for interacting with one type of object as opposed to another. One would no more dance around a ballistic missile than one would attempt to launch a totem pole.

· Wittgenstein (1958: para. 201) makes the distinction between a rule and an interpretation as follows:

> This was our paradox: no course of action could be determined by a rule, because every course of action can be made out to accord with the rule. The answer was: if everything can be made out to accord with the rule, then it can also be made out to conflict with it. And so there would be neither accord nor conflict here. It can be seen that there is a misunderstanding here from the mere fact that in the course of our argument we give one interpretation after another; as if each one contented us at least for a moment, until we thought of yet another standing behind it. What this shews is that there is a

24

way of grasping a rule which is *not* an *interpretation*, but which is exhibited in what we call 'obeying the rule' and 'going against it' in actual cases.

Hence there is an inclination to say: every action according to the rule is an interpretation. But we ought to restrict the term 'interpretation' to the substitution of one expression of the rule for another.

Interpretation is about the possibility that objects or situations can be viewed through multiple lenses and that perspectives may vary from person to person. Yet there are any number of phenomena within a given culture that are not subject to interpretation, that are meaningful because of the stable rules attached to them in that context. One does not interpret a stop sign, but rather follows the rule that one stops when confronted with this symbol. One does not interpret the word 'men' when placed on a door in a public building; its meaning belongs to a stable context. One does not interpret the meaning of a piece of paper with a value and a government water stamp attached to it.

Two different kinds of question become meaningful if one shifts attention to a concept of rule-following. First, how are practices relating to a particular object, such as a ballistic missile, constrained by the rules of a particular game? Second, what are the limits and possibilities for reconstituting the meaning of an object, and subsequent action towards it, within an alternative game? The meaning and use of a ballistic missile is quite different within a game dictated by the logic that nuclear deterrence is inescapable than within one in which nuclear deterrence is a guillotine which needs to be destroyed. These questions are crucial to an exploration of how alternatives to the dominant Cold War game became possible.

The point is not that there are only rules and no interpretations. I am instead making an argument about the need to specify the difference, in order to distinguish cases of following a rule from acts of interpretation. The main criterion for distinguishing the two is the degree of stability attached to a meaning. Rules are followed 'as a matter of course' in a context where there is an agreement about the meaning of words, practices and objectives. As Wittgenstein (1958: para. 241) says '"So you are saying that human agreement decides what is true and what is false?" – It is what human beings *say* that is true and false; and they agree in the *language* they use. That is not agreement in opinions but in form of life.'

For language use, and therefore communication, to be possible, there must be an agreement about meaning. Within any one culture there is agreement about the value attached to money, how one puts money to use and certain institutional practices attached to money, for example cashing a cheque. There is agreement about the nature of certain identities and what they do – for instance, babysitter, parent, teacher, student – and their relationship to others within a context. These rules may *seem* to belong to an objective order. Interpretation comes into play when meanings are contested. Critical theorists emphasise interpretation over rules because they have been primarily engaged in acts of 'denaturalising' that which has come to be understood to be objective. The purpose is to destabilise meanings that have become fixed and to make the point that multiple interpretations are possible.

The former argument was that much of our social world is not open to interpretation, at least not all of the time. A second argument is that interpretations necessarily rely on rules that are meaningful because of past use. One familiar context of conflicting interpretations is in the greeting rituals of acquaintances across cultures. In this context, a Texan might give a bear hug, a Belgian three kisses on each side of the cheek and an Englishman a handshake. Each relies on a distinct set of rules for how one greets acquaintances within a culture; when participants of these three games collide, the result can be comic at best and embarrassing at worst.

The problem of interpretation arises from a lack of agreement or clarity about the nature of a context. If meaning is dependent on a context, then knowing 'how to go on' requires an ability to identify or 'name' a context as one type rather than another. In everyday life this isn't normally an issue. We unproblematically recognise the difference between the context of a greengrocer and the context of a supermarket and how each shapes the range of speech acts and practices specific to it. One might argue that in the context of the Cold War, moves by the superpowers had become so familiar after decades of playing that they more often involved the employment of a rule rather than interpretation, to such an extent that the actions of states seemed law-like. As the Cold War crumbled, and with it old practices, the difficulty of situating ourselves within a game, and therefore of knowing how to go on, became more apparent, most particularly in the former Yugoslavia where the naming of this context was, from the beginning, very controversial. While generally referred to as a war, the issue of *which* war it most closely resembled – World War I or II, Vietnam, the Gulf War – was significant in establishing the parameters of how to go on in this context, not to mention the identities of the different players involved.

As with the multicultural greeting, each distinct interpretation of the conflict drew on rules, in this case drawn from a past context of war.[9] These rules constituted the identities of the players and the boundaries of reasonable action, that is, what was considered a rational move as opposed to a mistake. In the World War II interpretation, the actions of the Serbs shared a family resemblance with those of Hitler; they were trying to capture territory in the name of an ethnically pure state and to ethnically

---

9 For a more detailed analysis of this case, see Fierke (1996).

cleanse territory of a particular category of people: the Muslims. This naming constituted clear categories of an aggressor (Bosnian Serbs), victim (Bosnian Muslims) and potential liberator (the West, NATO). Within this game, inaction on the part of the West was a form of appeasement that would have predictable consequences. This interpretation emphasised avoiding a mistake from the past, which in this case was Chamberlain's appeasement of Hitler at Munich. The most rational form of action would be intervention, involving a range of primarily military actions, including fighting on the ground, as distinguished from talking, which would result in appeasement. Talking and fighting are in an oppositional relationship in this game.

By contrast, an interpretation of Bosnia as like World War I constituted a different set of identities and practices, based on a different rule from the past. The central fear was that the Bosnian conflict would spiral out of control, drawing in the major powers. Sarajevo, the site where World War I broke out, was on the faultline of historical great power conflict. Peacekeeping, as a strategy, was an attempt to avoid the mistake of World War I, by preventing an escalation of tensions while attempting to respond to the humanitarian disaster. Great power conflict was to be avoided by involving the major contemporary powers directly in decisionmaking over the conflict in a peaceful way within the Security Council. Within this game, no one local party was associated with guilt. All contributed to the construction of the conflict. United Nations (UN) troops were neutral, meaning that they would not engage in armed conflict with any one party. All of the major powers and conflicting parties in Bosnia were actors in this game. An eruption of the conflict beyond the parameters of Bosnia was to be avoided at all costs. In contrast to an intervention game, negotiations were clearly privileged over military engagement.

This contrast between interpretations of Bosnia illustrates several points. First, it is not possible simply to observe reality unproblematically, to understand its meaning in the absence of language, any more than we know or can learn the meaning of various chess pieces or the rules by which they are used in the absence of language. Language is woven into the range of acts constituting a game and language is the means by which we are socialised into, or learn the rules of how to proceed in, any context. In each case, a rule from the past establishes the parameters for reasoning about what should or should not be done. An interpretation drawing on the World War II rule became an argument for intervention; an interpretation based on the mistake of World War I became an argument for peacekeeping and negotiation. Similarly, an interpretation referring to the mistake of Vietnam became an argument for avoiding entanglement; and an interpretation building on the success of the Gulf became an argument for massive

27

bombardment from the air.

Second, the naming of a context is an act in itself which establishes a set of distinctions and the boundaries of action (Hinds and Windt, 1991: 9).[10] In many cases, the naming of a context is settled and rules are followed as a 'matter of course'. But some contexts may be characterised by a contest over the correct name or meaning of what is seen. The different interpretations were not purely individual; they were meaningful because of rules drawn from the past or a history of past use. The contestation, in this case, took place in the public realm. This process of public reasoning contributed to the construction of one interpretation or another as dominant. Once dominant, an interpretation became the rule. Avoiding the mistake of World War I was initially established as the rule, which constituted a range of practices relating to peacekeeping and negotiations.

Third, the possibilities for naming the context were not infinite and the choice was only relative in a positional sense. The meaning of the conflict was relative to geographical position and history. The events in Bosnia and the prospect of involvement pulled different kinds of emotional chords for Europeans and Americans. The boundaries of debate in the United States and Western Europe were quite different, and in part this difference was due to historical experience. In the United States, games invoking Vietnam and the Gulf War were dominant, while World Wars I and II framed the debate in Europe. Peacekeeping and negotiations (avoiding the mistake of World War I) dominated as the most reasonable and realistic response throughout the conflict until the Americans stepped in to play a guiding role with the realisation of NATO's Gulf War strategy in August 1995. Other alternatives, less defining of the experience of these two continents, such as references to Bosnia as another 'Lebanon' or the potential for creating a 'Palestinian problem', did not capture attention in the same way as these other historical experiences.

Interpretations are not the property of individuals; they are dependent on rules for their meaning. Yet not all interpretations will be equally meaningful. For an interpretation to become the rule, it must be meaningful not simply to isolated individuals but to a broader public, both because of past experience and because of a family resemblance between the past and the present. Each of the interpretations of Bosnia represented a packaging of the conflict in meaningful terms. Each was meaningful because Bosnia *did*

---

10 This reference to naming must be distinguished from the correspondence view of language. Naming in this case is not a label unproblematically applied to discrete objects. The point is that there is no one-to-one correspondence; we are always making distinctions, focusing attention on some details to the exclusion of others. Names are not labels; rather, things only have a name within a language game. See Wittgenstein (1958: paras 47, 49).

share a family resemblance with these different historical contexts in quite different ways, with the possible exception of the Gulf War.[11] Each of the scenarios focused attention on different details of this very complex situation.

Conclusion

The purpose of this chapter has been to explore a Wittgensteinian notion of rule-following by making a number of distinctions. The first distinction between a rule and a law makes it possible to think differently about patterns at the international level. While a law is assumed to be discovered in an objective reality, independent of human meaning, rules are explicitly social and reproduced through practice. Rules, and the practices they inform, are bound up with our language. While laws are said to be based on recurring patterns of cause and effect, rules make it possible to trace the unfolding of a game towards a distinct outcome.

The second distinction, between a Wittgensteinian notion of a game and game theory, makes us think differently about rationality. While game theory emphasises the rationality of individual moves, largely ignoring the 'rules of the game', the language game argument situates rationality within the context of specific games. Games relying on language are different to other types of game, however. Language games are not by definition incommensurable. Because the rationality of a game such as chess is internal to a particular structure, it is problematic to play two games simultaneously or to trace the reasons for, or process of, change from one game to another. This is less the case with language games. Particularly in a context of contestation, actors may play two conflicting games simultaneously. It is also possible for actors to take steps that will transform the game. While the rationality of decisions in game theory relies on a high degree of abstraction, we have to go directly to an empirical context to identify the structure of a changing game.

The third distinction is between an interpretation and a rule. The possibility of multiple games raises a concern that there are in fact no patterns at the international level, at least in a context of dramatic change; only a multiplicity of interpretations. But a distinction can be made. On the one hand, not everything is open to interpretation. Many practices are structured by relatively stable rules that seem to belong to an objective order but are in fact socially constructed. On the other hand, even in a

---

11 Many desired to reproduce the successful strategy of the Gulf War, while recognising that the terrain and political circumstances were very different. After NATO began its bombing campaign, a resemblance began to emerge as Bosnian Serbs, who wanted the bombing to stop, took UN peacekeepers hostage and used them as a human shield, much as Saddam Hussein took Western citizens hostage and used them as a human shield.

context of contesting interpretations, these interpretations will depend on rules for their meaning; as one interpretation becomes dominant, it becomes the rule, that is, it informs the practices of actors and, therefore, the construction of a particular reality.

The following three chapters will take these distinctions a step further to explore how language games can be analysed in practice.

2

Metaphor

The more narrowly we examine actual language, the sharper becomes the conflict between it and our requirement (For the crystalline purity of logic was, of course, not a result of investigation: it was a requirement.) ... We have got on to slippery ice where there is no friction and so in a certain sense the conditions are ideal, but also, just because of that, we are unable to walk. We want to walk: we need friction. Back to the rough ground! (Wittgenstein, 1958: para. 107)

WORDS HAVE MEANING within the context of a language game. Rules are the basis for knowing 'how to go on' in making certain moves. A totem pole or a ballistic missile are knowable neither on the basis of a label representing a discrete object in reality nor as pure interpretation. Each can be situated in culturally specific games by which the distinct practices associated with them are given meaning. In the case of Bosnia, the implications of situating the conflict in one language game or another were significant: the World War I scenario provided a framework for reasoning that intervention should be avoided at all costs, and the World War II scenario that intervention was necessary.

The Bosnia examples represent language games of a particular kind. They rely on analogy. Bosnia is like World War I, World War II, the Gulf War, Vietnam. There exists an extensive literature on the role of analogies in international relations (Jervis, 1976; Khong, 1992). The analogy is possible because of a family resemblance between some feature of the present and the past. I have used the term 'language game' instead of analogy, however. Rather than a comparison of two pictures, as suggested by the analogy, a language game is more dynamic, insofar as it establishes a playing field populated by certain types of identity which can manoeuvre in a variety of ways. In addition, the analogies to Bosnia were not always directly stated as analogies. In many cases they were identifiable as language games because of a network of categories that constituted the family resemblance. For instance, a network of concepts, such as ethnic cleansing, victim and aggressor, appeasement and intervention, constitutes a language game that relies on a family resemblance to the context of

31

World War II for its meaning, even when the analogy is not directly stated.

The analogy provides a way to make sense of a context by identifying a family resemblance with the past. In so doing, each selectively focuses on certain details, placing them within a coherent framework. Another type of language game is expressed in metaphor. Lakoff and Johnson (1980: 153) state that 'the primary function of metaphor is to provide a partial understanding of one kind of experience in terms of another kind of experience'. They argue that most of our everyday language is metaphoric. For instance, in Western culture our concept of an argument relies on a metaphor of war. Just as the categories of various analogies were embedded in our language for conceptualising Bosnia, the metaphor of war is embedded in our language of argument:

> ARGUMENT IS WAR[1]
> Your claims are *indefensible.*
> He *attacked every weak point* in my argument.
> His criticisms were *right on target.*
> He *demolished* his argument.
> I have never *won* an argument with him.
> You disagree? Okay, *shoot!*
> If you use that *strategy*, he'll *wipe you out.*
> He *shot down* all my arguments.

We are not necessarily conscious, each time we engage in an argument, that there is a metaphoric connection between acts involved in argu-mentation and acts of war. The similarity between the two is built into our language for argumentation and this similarity is *structural*. In Western culture, argumentation and warfare share a range of structural features by which they are recognisable as coherent, yet distinct, language games. There is a family resemblance between the range of acts, the types of move, that can be made in a context of argumentation or war, even though the meaning of these moves is quite different in each case; the objects of war are vastly different from the words employed in argumentation. However, the metaphoric value of the latter is not merely at the level of language. The metaphor is rather constitutive. It structures our understanding of what it means to conduct an argument, as well as 'how one goes on' or performs in this type of context.

If our concept of an argument were structured by a different metaphor, for instance, love, the types of act characteristic of a context of argument would change dramatically. A metaphoric connection between argument and love seems almost nonsensical, unless one understands love in terms of a battle between the sexes, which returns full circle to the notion that

---

1 Lakoff and Johnson (1980: 4).

'argument is war'. The way we carry out an argument is grounded in the knowledge and experience of physical combat. We conceive of arguments and execute them according to the 'argument is war' metaphor because the metaphor is built into the conceptual system of our culture.

At the international level, one could argue that metaphor is even more essential for attributing meaning and therefore knowing 'how to go on' than in everyday life. Metaphor involves understanding one kind of experience in terms of another. When Waltz (1979) theorises the state as 'economic man' or a 'firm' and the international system as a 'marketplace', he metaphorically conceptualises relations between states in terms of relations in a capitalist economy. When deterrence is theorised as a 'prisoner's dilemma', the decisionmaking processes of states are metaphorically conceptualised in terms of the calculations of prisoners held in a police station. When the arms race is presented as a 'game of chicken', states are metaphorically engaged in a game played by teenage boys in 1950s America. The metaphor is possible and meaningful because of a structural similarity between two types of context. Given the unwieldy nature of international relations as a phenomenon potentially including the entire globe and abstract collective actors called states, metaphor is an essential means for bringing the structure of processes at this level down to a place where they are understandable for decisionmakers, students of international relations or the everyday newspaper reader.

Not only international relations theorists, but political actors use metaphor to communicate the meaning of a context. In the following two examples the 'argument is war' metaphor structures understanding of a particular kind of experience at the international level. In 1983, after NATO decided to proceed with deployment of cruise and Pershing II missiles, the ongoing 'battle' for public opinion relied on the entailments of an 'argument is war' metaphor. One author in the *NATO Review* presented interactions with the peace movement as follows:

> The alliance has lived through one of the *toughest, most sustained* and *most nearly successful attacks* in its history. The *struggle* with public opinion is not over, even if this particular *battle* may have *reached its climax*. Anti-NATO *forces* will be able to *use the territory* they *have won* as a platform for the *next onslaught* if we do not apply ourselves much more consciously to the communication of security policy. [...] In order to *survive*, [the alliance] must make itself relevant to the post-war generations ... The need for a public opinion *strategy* is therefore quite as urgent as for a military one.[2]

The struggle for public opinion is a battle. This was not merely the opinion of a single individual, but rather structured the dominant meaning of this

2 G. Vaerno, 'A Public Opinion Strategy', *NATO Review* (*NR*), 31: 3/4 (1983).

context, on the part of NATO. Another example in the same year enlarged the battle to include the Soviet Union:

> We are witnessing a crisis of political elites that is both the cause and the result of the crumbling framework within which political *battles were fought* for most of the post-war period. ... It is the commitment to keep differences over security challenges within manageable bounds which is in the process of disappearing. [...] It may be true that the first *round of the war* for peace will probably *be won* by those who think the balance of terror is less terrifying than an imbalance of terror ... It is a fashionable notion today that the West is currently *engaged with the Soviet Union in a Battle* for the Soul of Europe. A *battle* is clearly *being waged* and the public is even, in one sense, an *object of that battle.* East and West are *battling* over the basic principles to govern their relationship, while Western political elites are *battling* each other over the guidelines for Western policy towards the East.[3]

Understanding takes place in terms of domains of experience or contexts rather than isolated concepts. The metaphor does not refer to an isolated object, but has a range of entailments. The battle is made up of 'rounds of war' and requires a 'strategy'. Acts of battle include 'successful attacks' and 'onslaughts'. The battle has an object: public opinion. It has different stages: 'reaching a climax', 'winning territory'. The battle is 'over' something: the basic principles to govern the relationship between East and West and the guidelines for Western policy towards the East. Use of the 'war' metaphor also implies the stakes of the contest. War is not a situation of compromise. Rather, wars are won or lost. The stakes are therefore high.

The metaphor is not an *objective* label referring to the inherent properties of the context. The battle between NATO and the peace movements for public opinion was not a battle fought with conventional or nuclear weapons. The sense of being embattled in that context came from the experience of being in a situation that was structurally similar to a war, even though the struggle for public opinion was nonviolent and took place in the media and halls of parliament. The peace movement was experienced as an adversary which was attacking and which NATO needed to defend itself against. The NATO response required a strategy. Together the different acts are part of a whole that is coherent. The use of the metaphor does not refer to inherent properties of the context – that is, objective properties, independent of human meaning – but rather interactive ones. The metaphor grows out of a type of interaction which relates to human experience.

The choice of metaphor is also not *subjective*. Dominant metaphors do not spring from the heads of individuals; they are cultural in origin. Categories are chosen and have meaning within a culture. This suggests that

---

3 G. Flynn, 'Public Opinion and Atlantic Defence', *NR*, 31: 5 (1983).

the meaning of a single metaphor can vary from culture to culture. Chilton and Ilyin's (1993) analysis of the European house metaphor illustrates how the attachment of different meanings to the same phenomenon can result in different entailments. The meaning Gorbachev attached to the European Common House metaphor was different from the interpretation of his use by Western leaders. The confusion related in part to the different meaning of 'house' and '*dom*', the Russian word, in East and West. '*Dom*' referred to a large complex of apartments with several entrances. When Gorbachev used the term 'European Common House', he was suggesting a European security structure enclosing East and West that maintained the distinctiveness of the different political systems contained within. For Western leaders, a 'house' is more likely to be a single family dwelling with a single entrance. They therefore interpreted Gorbachev's proposal in terms of a Soviet desire to enclose Western Europe within the Soviet system. Given this interpretation, the Common House was not an acceptable policy for the West.

Structures of security

Chilton (1996) argues that the structural metaphor relates to a particular conceptualisation of security. Structures have clear insides and outsides, distinguishing the secured within from the threat outside. In this sense, there is a complementarity between the dominant use of the 'container' metaphor to conceptualise security during the Cold War and the 'structural' metaphors used by Gorbachev and, later, NATO. The West's containment strategy drew a line across Europe and the central goal was to keep the Soviet Union out.

Chilton's analysis leaves the impression that the structural metaphor replaced the container metaphor as the Cold War was ending. In contrast, I would argue that the container and structural metaphors overlapped and together constituted the meaning of security in the Cold War. The entailments of the structural metaphor were constitutive of both Western and Soviet categories of the Cold War at the height of détente and through the 1980s. The structure had particular components, such as foundations, cornerstones and frameworks. Note the role of structural entailments in a text by the Belgian Minister of National Defence, Paul van den Boeynants, in 1976:[4]

> For over twenty-five years, the Atlantic Alliance has provided *an irreplaceable framework* for our collective security ... The credibility of the United States' nuclear guarantee, which *is the corner-stone* of the Atlantic Alliance, depends on the credibility of each element of the triad (emphasis added).

4 P. van den Boeynants, 'European Security in 1976', *NR*, 24: 3 (1976).

The idea that NATO *rests on the foundation* of deterrence was central to the alliance's self-definition during the Cold War. As stated by Joseph Luns, the Secretary General of NATO, in the mid 1970s:[5]

> The deterrent capacity of the Alliance is the *foundation* for the security of every member. Were we to allow its credibility to be *undermined* we would be guilty of provocation of the most serious kind.
>
> We have to be willing to devote sufficient resources *to maintain* the credibility of the deterrent shield.
>
> The Atlantic Alliance ... gives Europe its security and *stability* and [...] there is little prospect of a common European defence policy in the near future. This is indeed true. Not that this fact in any way diminishes Europe's defence role, or the need to strengthen the European contribution to collective defence within the Alliance *framework*.

The alliance is a container of a particular kind. It is a structure with a framework, a cornerstone and foundations. The structure provides stability and rests on the foundations of deterrence. The central act towards this foundation is one of maintenance and making sure that it is not undermined.

Metaphors of structure are also laced through Cold War texts of the Soviet Union. The Soviet Union also had foundations, cornerstones and frameworks; it also engaged in acts of maintenance, but the objects of maintenance were different, relating not to deterrence but to socialist production and alliances within the Soviet Union and with its allies in Eastern Europe. Related metaphors appeared repeatedly in the pages of the Soviet press, for instance:

> The strength of our state lies in the fact that its economic *foundation* is socialist production relations, which have evolved on the basis of ... public ownership.[6]

> All the activity of all the Communist Parties *rests on* adherence to Marxism-Leninism, which *is the basis* for their international unity.[7]

> The social *foundation* of the USSR is the indestructible alliance of workers, peasants and intelligentsia.[8]

> One of the *cornerstones* of our fraternal relations is the Treaty of Friendship, Cooperation and Mutual Aid.[9]

> The solidarity of Communists has been and remains a powerful factor in *maintaining* ... the great achievements of the forces of peace, democracy and socialism.[10]

5 J. M. A. H. Luns, 'The Present State of East–West Relations', *NR*, 24: 2 (1976).
6 'Why the Role of the State is Growing', *Current Digest of the Soviet Press (CDSP)*, 27: 39 (1975).
7 'Communist Pluralism vs. the Single Truth', *CDSP*, 29: 6 (1977).
8 'The New USSR Constitution', *CDSP*, 29: 41 (1977).
9 'Brezhnev Visits Czechoslovakia', *CDSP*, 30: 22 (1978).
10 'Prague Meeting Calls for Communist Unity', *CDSP*, 29: 17 (1977).

The container and the contained occupied two structures standing side by side. The one rested on the foundations of socialism and the other on the foundations of deterrence. The central act in relation to both structures was one of maintenance.

Family resemblances

The structural metaphors during the Cold War were less explicit than the Common House or the architecture, both of which denote a particular kind of building. But the nature of these structures was expressed in another overlapping metaphor, which says something about the character of the occupants, that is, that they were families. The following is one of the more blatant articulations of the US–Europe relationship as a *marriage*:

> The United States and Europe are *an old couple*. Almost *forty years of marriage* is a long time at the end of the twentieth century! The *knot was tied* at the end of the 1940s *in a storm of passion* ... The U.S.–European relationship has never really fully developed; it has never acquired the calm resignation of those *couples* who understand that, while *their love is imperfect*, wisdom and happiness in some ways involves a readiness to live with the faults and shortcomings of the other party [...] The U.S. European *couple cannot be divorced*. For the United States, such a divorce would mean surrendering the role of superpower; for Europe, it would mean re-examination of everything which it has been since 1945. But can this *couple devise a relationship which, while no longer exclusive,* would remain privileged?[11]

The metaphors 'alliance is marriage' and 'security is a structure', are not specific to the Cold War but relate to a longer tradition of conceptualising security in terms of structures whose boundaries distinguish the intimate relations inside from those which threaten from outside. What now finds expression in metaphor can be traced back to historical forms of life which continue to be meaningful for understanding the more abstract relationship between states. The impenetrable walls of the fortress or castle existed to protect the more intimate relations inside from those outside which threatened to penetrate these barriers. When deterrence, during the Cold War, was referred to as a foundation of Western security, the structural metaphor conveyed a similar meaning that the nuclear threat worked to keep the Eastern enemy out of the nuclear fortress occupied by the transatlantic family.

Marriage and courtship are forms of human life which in an earlier period were practices constituting diplomacy. Alliances were sealed through

---

11 P. Moreau-Defarges, 'Anti-American Feeling in Europe: Between Fear of War and Obsession with Abandonment', *NR*, 35: 2 (1987).

marriage contracts between members of royal families by which control was gained over territory and military potential increased (DerDerian, 1987: 77–8). Conceptualisations of the classical European balance of power rely on related language games. Take, for instance, the following discussion of the working of that system:

> With more than two states, the politics of power turn on the diplomacy by which alliances are made, maintained, and disrupted. Flexibility of alignment means that the country one is *wooing* may *prefer another suitor* and that one's present alliance partner may defect. A state's strategy *must please a potential or satisfy a present partner* ... Similarly, with a number of approximately equal states, strategy is at least partly made for the sake of *attracting and holding allies. Suitors alter their appearance* and adapt their behaviour *to increase their eligibility* ... Ever since the Napoleonic wars many had believed that the 'Republic' and the 'Cossack' could never *become engaged*, let alone *contract a marriage*. The *wooing* of France and Russia, with each adapting somewhat to the other, was nevertheless *consummated* in the alliance of 1894 and duly *produced* the Triple Entente as *its progeny* ... (Waltz, 1979: 165–6).

The language of courtship structures an understanding of the classical European balance of power; language games relating to intimacy also constitute alliance relations within the Cold War. By comparing the two, both the common origin and the distinction in the rules structuring the two eras become evident.

While security within the Cold War is heir to an earlier culture of international relations, it shares only a family resemblance, since the two were structured by two different sets of rules which are quite opposite. The classical European balance of power worked largely to prevent a major power from securing the space of a smaller state in anything more than a temporary sense. The language of the classical balance of power was one of 'courtship' and 'wooing', not permanent alliance. It was only with the Cold War that this game of courtship was replaced by one of 'commitment' and 'marriage' and with it the securing of spaces larger than particular states on what seemed to be a permanent basis.

Both the difference and the commonality of the two eras are expressed in a metaphor of relationship. This is significant on two levels. First, the distinctions illustrate the relationship between contextual games and particular cultural forms. NATO's nuclear family is structurally similar to cultural representations of the nuclear family in the West in the post-World War II context. Language games from one level of human experience are projected metaphorically to the realm of interstate relations.

Second, these language games construct particular spatial distinctions, which emphasise certain aspects of identity while obscuring others. The heterogeneous national landscape of Europe, or its numerous divisions into separate states, faded against the background of a spatial division between two blocs, East and West. Western and Eastern Europe were homogenised, constructed as members of a family, sharing a single set of values. This particular distinction between families relied on a much different division of space than the 'courtship' games of an earlier period within which separate European states 'wooed' or 'attempted to remain attractive' in a context of ever-changing affairs. Language games construct a field of action involving specific possibilities.

The point, which will be developed throughout this book, is that the meaning of the Cold War was constituted and given structure by a variety of overlapping metaphors. These metaphors were shared by both East and West, although expressed in different forms. The latter claim will become clearer in later chapters. The task here is to fill out this picture of the Cold War as comprising structures containing families.

Communicating with criminal neighbours

The families had a particular relationship to one another, that is, each viewed the 'other' as a criminal. In the speeches of President Reagan in the early 1980s, the Soviet Union was portrayed as a criminal that was imprisoning its own people and holding Western Europe hostage:

> [The Soviets] can resort to *lying or stealing or cheating or even murder* if it furthers their cause.[12]

> We never needed walls or mine fields or barbed wire *to keep our people in*.[13]

> Soviet systems targeted upon Europe were meant to break the link, to isolate Europe, to threaten it from a Russian sanctuary which Europe could not in turn put at risk, and so hold Europe a nuclear *hostage*.[14]

The Soviet Union also accused the United States of a whole range of crimes, not to mention holding Western Europe hostage:

> The main objective was for the US to become able to dictate its will to other countries, *blackmail* them with *impunity*.[15]

> As events in Poland have shown, U.S. special services have made extensive use of methods of economic *sabotage*.[16]

12 R. Reagan, interview with W. Cronkite, CBS News, 3 March 1981, *Department of State Bulletin (DSB)* (April 1981).
13 R. Reagan, 'State of the Union 1982, January 26, 1982', *Vital Speeches of the Day (VSD)*, 48: 9 (1982).
14 R. Bert, 'NATO and Nuclear Deterrence', *DSB* (November 1981).
15 'A Pessimistic Look at U.S. Foreign Policy', *CDSP*, 34: 28 (1982).
16 D. Ustinov, 'Military Leaders Assail "Hostile" US Policy', *CDSP*, 34: 19 (1982).

Inspirers of [Western policy towards Poland] are letting loose streams of *slander*.[17]

[NATO countries] went to Madrid to *poison* the international atmosphere.[18]

Washington ... is making Western Europe a *hostage* of its aggressive policy.[19]

Like the structure and marriage metaphors, there is a tradition in political writing of comparing rulers to criminals (Hurwitz in DerDerian and Shapiro, 1989). Chomsky (1986: 1) cites the example of St Augustine's anecdote of the pirate who, asked by Alexander the Great how he dared molest the sea, replied, 'How dare you molest the world? Because I do it with a little ship only, I am called a thief. You, doing it with a great navy, are called an emperor'.

The self–other constructions of the Cold War relied on the metaphor of the criminal neighbour. The two criminal superpowers communicated with one another in a particular way, that is, they negotiated. An act of negotiation by states is less a case of metaphor than 'metonymy'. To use metaphor is to conceptualise one thing in terms of another: 'argument is war', 'alliance is marriage', 'love is a journey'. Metonymy, by contrast, allows us to conceptualise one thing by its relation to something else. Metonymy pervades most discussions of states. A statement such as 'The Soviet Union threatened to boycott the next round of SALT [Strategic Arms Limitation Treaty] talks' or 'The United States committed itself to the defence of Europe' makes acts by representatives of these collective entities equivalent to acts by the entities themselves. States, as abstract concepts, cannot threaten or make a commitment. These are acts carried out on behalf of the state by individual representatives. Nonetheless, our language constitutes the imagined community (Anderson, 1991) of the state or alliance as an individual that can act in these ways.

The two criminal others, the United States and the Soviet Union, engaged in negotiations, which, as I shall argue in Chapter Eight, can be distinguished from other forms of communication. Negotiations took place in a context of bargaining. Each side proposed solutions that were rejected by the other. Each side also made claims about the distinction between the words and deeds of the other. Examples of these moves are as follows:

UNITED STATES
If we had not begun to modernise, the Soviet negotiators would know we had nothing to *bargain* with except talk. They would know that we were *bluffing* without a good hand because they know what cards we hold just as we know what is in their hand.[20]

17 'Gromyko Review Soviet Foreign Policy', *CDSP*, 35: 25 (1983).
18 L. Brezhnev, 'Brezhnev Announces a Missile Freeze', *CDSP*, 34: 11 (1982).
19 'More Details on Missile Cut Proposal', *CDSP*, 34: 6 (1982).
20 R. Reagan, 'Arms Control: MX Missile', *VSD*, 49: 5 (1982).

I've just sent another message to the Soviet leadership. It's a simple, straightforward yet historic message. The United States *proposes* the mutual reduction of conventional, intermediate-range nuclear and strategic force.[21]

The United States, with the full support of its allies, has been *negotiating* in Geneva for more than a year to persuade the Soviet Union that it is a far better course for both of us to agree to eliminate totally this entire category of weapons ... So far the Soviet Union has *resisted this proposal* and has *failed to come up with a serious alternative.*[22]

Cooperation and understanding are built *on deeds, not words.*[23]

SOVIET UNION

The *proposals* that [the Soviet Union] *placed on the negotiating table* with the US last year ... express a readiness to discuss and resolve the question of limiting and reducing medium-range nuclear arms in Europe.[24]

The United States *not only has refused* to eliminate the obstacles created by the deployment of the new American missiles in Western Europe, it is continuing to deploy them.[25]

It is hard not to be bitter when one thinks of how much time was wasted during the year-and-a-half-long *obstruction of the Soviet proposals.*[26]

If sometimes peace loving rhetoric is heard from Washington it is impossible [...] to detect behind it even the slightest sign of readiness to *back up these words with deeds.*[27]

The two criminals engaged in similar acts of proposing and rejecting, accusing the other of a distinction between their words and deeds, while claiming the sincerity of their own words and intentions.

Conclusion

The Cold War was structured by a number of metaphors by which we begin to see the contours of a multi-layered language game which constitutes a range of specific practices. Practitioners were not necessarily any more conscious of the metaphoric nature of their language games than anyone engaged in argument recognises that the coherence and structure of the context is provided by the metaphor 'argument is war'.

21 R. Reagan, 'United States Foreign Affairs Policy: Arms Reduction', *VSD*, 48: 4 (1981).
22 R. Reagan, 'Nuclear Weapons: An Interim Agreement', *VSD*, 49: 13 (1983).
23 R. Reagan, 'U.S.–Soviet Relations: A Policy of Credible Deterrence', *VSD*, 50: 8 (1984).
24 'NATO's Tough Stance on Nuclear Arms Hit', *CDSP*, 33: 19 (1981).
25 'Chernenko Sees Hope for Better US Ties', *CDSP*, 36: 42 (1984).
26 'Moscow Weighs US Arms Control Stand', *CDSP*, 34: 22 (1982).
27 'Chernenko: No Real Changes in US Policy', *CDSP*, 36: 14 (1984).

A security analyst making the statement that NATO *maintained* the nuclear deterrent or the US *reaffirmed its commitment* to NATO would probably say he or she was making an empirical statement about interests or observing what these actors were doing. Two elements of language are, however, expressed in these examples. *Maintaining* deterrence or *making a commitment* were practices of NATO and to invoke these practices is, on one level, *descriptive*. But the language also represented action of another sort. Stating these words publicly, over and over again, was *constitutive* of the deterrent in so far as the credibility of the threat was dependent on a sense of cohesion between the European partners and the US, as well as a shared understanding that maintaining the deterrent was necessary and therefore desirable.

Maintaining deterrence or making a commitment are acts, but they are not isolated. Their meaning is *thickened* when placed in the contours of a particular kind of game. Even though the role of metaphor is often denied in traditional international relations scholarship (Chilton, 1996), it is constitutive of action at this level. We only attribute action by constituting an actor. Given the practice of referring to states as if they were individuals, it should not be surprising that state practice would draw meaning from human life forms and specific cultural patterns.

When an act of commitment is situated within a context of marriage, the metaphoric quality of the language games becomes more obvious than it probably was to the actors themselves. The description of these acts is thickened by embedding them in layers of meaning and recovering the cultural forms to which they relate.

In reflecting on the distinction between Wittgenstein's early and later work, Finch (1995: 160) contrasts two methods: analytic and rearrangement. The difference is between attaining generality and synoptic understanding through a method of abstract reduction as opposed to obtaining it through a method of conceptual clarification. In relation to the latter, he introduces a concept of metaphoric connection, which he sees as a new method of 'rearrangement of what everybody already knows' (Finch, 1995: 159). Precisely because the everyday language of international relations is so familiar, we have become blinded to its significance. Showing the interrelationship between different overlapping metaphors of the Cold War is a first step in presenting this method. This does not by any means represent a comprehensive overview of the metaphors that structured the Cold War (see Chilton, 1996).

Dominant metaphors can provide a point of departure for identifying patterns and situating the actions of particular players. This cursory analysis of structuring metaphors used by states provides a picture of the Cold War as a metaphoric 'neighbourhood' composed of structures containing families of differing values, who viewed their neighbours as criminals, with whom they engaged in acts of bargaining. This metaphoric picture is the starting point for constructing a description or narrative of the end of the Cold War.

Given the range of metaphors populating any one text, one might raise a question about the criteria for choosing one metaphor over another. By my criteria, a dominant organising metaphor was one that recurred in the public documents of all of the actors included in the larger analysis of this book, that is, both state and non-state, both East and West. These metaphors did not find expression in precisely the same way in each case, however. While the organising metaphor provides a connection between texts, the different entailments (that is, acts, attributes) are the means to identify a change over time. In the next chapter, I explore the notion of a 'grammar' related to these metaphors.

3

Grammars

We feel as if we had to *penetrate* phenomena: our investigation, however, is directed not towards phenomena, but, as one might say, towards the *'possibilities'* of phenomena. We remind ourselves, that is to say, of the *kind of statement* that we make about phenomena ... Our investigation is therefore a grammatical one ... this may be called an 'analysis' of our forms of expression, for the process is sometimes like one of taking a thing apart. (Wittgenstein, 1958: paras 90–1)

METAPHORS PROVIDE BOUNDARIES and meaning to the otherwise unwieldy and abstract experience of international relations. The various metaphors of the Cold War made the identities and objects populating East–West relations understandable in terms of more familiar experiences. The use of a particular metaphor represents a form of naming. The international system is not physically a structure with walls, but in naming it metaphorically to be an object of this kind, we establish a framework for interacting with it as if it were a structure. Alliances are not literally marriages between individuals, but a form of relationship between states. However, the construction of this identity, the meaning attached to it and the types of act undertaken within an alliance (commitment, sharing, etc.) are dependent on a structural similarity to marriage, by which the identity acquires coherence.

Metaphors do not represent isolated objects. The meaning and the significance of the structural similarity are constituted in a language game. Up to this point I have discussed the language game as being similar to a game of chess, that is, as a context of rules. Wittgenstein's use of the concept is not clearly defined. This is consistent with his position that the meaning of words cannot be fixed in place; rather, we have to 'look and see' what language game is being played in a particular context. Just as it is not possible to come up with a single definition of a game, there is no one thing which we can point to as the essence of a language game:

> Consider for example the proceedings that we call 'games'. I mean board-games, card-games, ball-games, Olympic games, and so on. What is common to them all? – Don't say: 'There *must* be something common, or they would

44

not be called "games"' – but *look and see* whether there is anything common to all. – For if you look at them you will not see something that is common to *all*, but similarities, relationships, and whole series of them at that. To repeat: don't think, but look! – Look for example at board-games, with their multifarious relationships. ... In ball games there is winning and losing; but when a child throws his ball at the wall and catches it again, this feature has disappeared ... And we can go through the many, many other groups of games in the same way; can see how similarities crop up and disappear.

And the result of this examination is: we see a complicated network of similarities overlapping and criss-crossing; sometimes overall similarities, sometimes similarities of detail.

I can think of no better expression to characterise these similarities than 'family resemblances'; for the various resemblances between members of a family: build, features, colour of eyes, gait, temperament, etc. etc. overlap and criss-cross in the same way. (Wittgenstein, 1958: paras 66–7)

The definition of a game cannot be formulated *a priori*. We have to 'look and see' what language game is being played in a context. By what criteria do we distinguish one game from another? The game of chess is easily distinguished from monopoly. Each comes packaged in a nice box with a name on the front. The packaging of language games at the international level isn't quite so apparent. Any one text or speech includes hundreds or thousands of words. Metaphor is one place to begin. Metaphors of marriage constitute alliance relationships. The metaphor itself is not always so explicitly expressed, however; it may be present in a range of alliance practices, including acts such as the *commitment* between the alliance partners, the *sharing of burdens, the promise to protect and defend*, and the *hierarchical* constitution of a relationship based on *shared values*. These acts are repeated frequently in the texts of NATO even when the marriage metaphor is not explicitly stated.

The 'marriage' game of the Cold War also shares a family resemblance with the 'courtship' game of the classical European balance of power. Both relate to some form of intimate relationship, but the structure of the relationship is different in each case. The one involved a stable partnership and unchanging alliances; the other depended on 'remaining attractive' in order to be able to change alliances. Gorbachev's Common House shared a family resemblance with NATO's architecture, in so far as both were games involving structures. In this case, the two forms of structure would have occupied different spatial locations (East and West versus West-centred), were based on different models (the Conference on Security and Cooperation in Europe (CSCE) versus interlocking institutions with NATO as the central pillar), and denoted different degrees of intimacy (homes are more intimate than architectures). In this case, the two language games arose in competition with one another.

45

The contestation between language games that share a family resemblance is a central theme of Part II of this book. Here I want to explore the idea that games sharing a family resemblance are related by a 'grammar'.[1] Wittgenstein (1958: para. 373) claimed that 'grammar tells us what kind of object anything is'. A grammatical investigation is, therefore, one that looks to the possibilities of phenomena. We know different regions of language or an object through an investigation of their grammar. For instance, international relations, science or theology can be thought of as grammars. It is on the basis of a grammar that any practitioner within one of these fields knows 'how to go on' in constructing an argument or acting in the world. The practitioner or theorist of international relations is dependent on a grammar that includes concepts such as sovereignty, balance of power and just war. The Christian theologian or priest relies on a grammar, including concepts such as God, Christ, communion and bible.

A grammar can also be thought of more specifically in relation to objects. For instance, we have a grammar for buildings or chairs or nuclear missiles by which we know what kinds of object these are and 'how to go on' in dealing with them. A central point of Wittgenstein's argument is that the 'essence' of any object or language region is not to be found in a reality independent of human meaning; rather, the essence is constituted through our forms of expression or through our grammar.

As with the language game, it is not possible to establish a clear boundary around a grammar, given the fluidity of meaning and language. Grammars are not bounded. They may overlap. For instance, one can 'clean' a chair as well as a room; one can 'sit' on a bed as well as a chair. Sovereignty is a concept that can belong to any number of grammars, from international relations to religion. There are numerous ways of categorising, distinguishing and focusing attention in relation to any one object. As a result, a grammatical investigation requires that we 'look and see' how boundaries are established in practice by the subjects of analysis, that is, what are the objects populating their world and what are the possibilities of these objects, given their grammar for them.

Through a grammar we identify the range of possibilities belonging to a phenomenon. The language game, by contrast, is more or less synonymous with a 'way of operating with language in action' (Pitkin, 1972: 147). While a grammar provides a point of departure for analysing a larger process of change, the language game is more specific and contextual; it refers to

---

1 For alternative approaches to the notion of a 'grammar' in international relations, see Milliken (1994), Polany *et al.* (1993).

specific moves with language.[2] A grammar of nuclear missiles might include the range of acts and attributes that expresses the essence of this object, from developing to deploying, to negotiating with, to disarming. By contrast, threatening is a specific language game that can involve nuclear missiles. The act of threatening is a language game that represents a 'whole, consisting of language and the actions into which it is woven' (Wittgenstein, 1958: para. 7).

Alternatively, a grammar of intimate relations might include the range of possibilities belonging to this language region, from courtship to marriage, to divorce, to emancipation. This grammar can be distinguished from specific language games such as making a commitment or protesting one's dependence within a relationship.

Moral discourse is also a region of language which is expressed in a grammar that includes a range of possibilities defining good and bad, or right behaviour in contrast to wrong or criminal behaviour. This larger grammar can be distinguished from specific language games, such as placing blame or confessing one's guilt.

Each example of a language game relies on the larger grammar of an object or language region to make moves within a specific context. The context of threatening with nuclear missiles is different from one of disarming, although both belong to a grammar of nuclear missiles. The context of making a commitment is different from that of protesting one's dependence, although both possibilities belong to a grammar of intimate relations. The context of placing blame is different from one of confessing guilt, although both belong to a grammar of moral discourse. There are no 'objective' criteria for making distinctions; the distinctions belong to our language as used in a context.

The dominant organising metaphors of the Cold War identified in Chapter Two are not only contextually specific language games, encompassing a range of moves, but also relate to a larger grammar of possibilities. Think about a range of possibilities belonging, for instance, to a grammar of structure (see table below).

All of these categories can be identified as belonging to a grammar of structure, by which we know the possibilities of this object. 'Structure' was a particular naming of the international system, shared by scholars and practitioners alike from the mid-1970s into the 1980s. Not everyone attached precisely the same meaning to this structure, but the recurrence of these categories in text after text and across the texts of different actors

---

2 Wittgenstein says: 'Here the term "language *game*" is meant to bring into prominence the fact that *speaking* a language is part of an activity or form of life.' This passage (Wittgenstein, 1958: para. 23) is followed by a list of examples illustrating the multiplicity of language games.

Types	Attributes
house	foundations
prison	walls
church	ceiling
apartment complex	framework

Acts	Alterations
maintaining	deterioration
restoring	erosion
dismantling	collapse

suggests that during this period there existed a shared understanding about the nature of the international system. It is perhaps not incidental that a range of structural theories of international relations were published at about this time.[3]

It is not that foreign policy actors or theorists sat down and consciously chose a metaphor that would best represent the international system. Rather, these categories preceded any consciously formulated opinion, or were constitutive of it. The categories were drawn on 'as a matter of course'.[4] While Western actors during the first part of the Cold War engaged in 'building' an international structure,[5] by the second half their central concern was one of 'maintenance'. The essence of the Cold War was expressed in this grammar.

This grammar included a range of possible acts. If one looks at the texts of actors in different positions, one sees them engaged in specific moves, much like the knight or the bishop in a game of chess move in prescribed but different ways. For instance, as suggested in the Chapter Two, in the mid-1970s, state actors in both East and West were engaged in actions of maintaining their respective structures. By the early 1980s, the United

3 The emphasis on the state within a stable structure was widespread among historians and international relations scholars during this period (see Waltz, 1979; Gaddis, 1985–86; Deporte, 1986; Bowker and Brown, 1993). The structural theory of *The Capitalist World Economy* by Wallerstein (1979) emerged at about the same time as Waltz's (1979) structural theory of international relations. Realists emphasised the stability and enduring features of this structure. Cox (in Bowker and Brown, 1993) also notes that radicals were convinced that the new Cold War would remain in being for a long time.

4 Wittgenstein (1958: paras 217, 238).

5 See, for instance, 'NSC 68: The Strategic Reassessment of 1950', in Etzold and Gaddis (1978).

States was also engaged in acts of restoration and rebuilding, as is evident from the speeches of President Reagan:

> By *restoring* America's military credibility ... we have strengthened our country's position as a force for peace and progress in the world.[6]

> Unless [the US] demonstrates the will to rebuild our strength and *restore* the military balance and rebuilds its strength, the Soviets ... have little incentive to negotiate.[7]

> We said we would *restore* our ability to protect our freedom on land, sea and air.[8]

Maintaining and restoring are acts that are complementary. Restoring may be part of maintaining. Relationships of complementarity as well as opposition were also to be found. While states were more likely to be engaged in acts of maintenance and restoration, critical movements in both blocs were more likely to be breaking down the structure of the Cold War. The latter are in a relationship of opposition to acts of maintenance:

> [The new peace movements, East and West] are setting themselves an astonish-ing objective: to *break down* ... in the next ten years, the Cold War itself.[9]

> [The campaign for European Nuclear Disarmament's (END's) objective] is to begin to *break down* the unnatural barriers which divide our continent, and to prepare the way for the ending of the bloc system.[10]

> An intra-German dynamic could be the lever which so changes the consensus in both German states that their hostile images of each other *break down* and disarmament becomes possible.[11]

At the same time, state leaders had a tendency to view the other side, as well as critical movements within their own blocs, as engaged in acts of undermining or eroding the current order. The difference is between the meaning movements attributed to their own actions and that attributed by states to the same acts:

> WEST
> This attitude [of a long-term divergence of interest between Western Europe and the US] can only *undermine* Atlantic cohesion and foster anti-Americanism.[12]

---

6 R. Reagan, 'State of the Union 1982', *VSD* (15 February 1982).
7 R. Reagan, 'Arms Control: MX Missile', *VSD* (15 December 1982).
8 R. Reagan, 'Remarks on Accepting the GOP Nomination, 23 August 1984', in Reagan (1989).
9 E. P. Thompson, 'The Normalisation of Europe', *Praxis International*, 3: 1 (1983).
10 M. Beresford, 'An Open Letter to the Soviet Peace Committee', *New Statesman* (21 January 1983).
11 R. Bahro, 'The Peace Movement, the Cold War and Germany', *Labour Focus on Eastern Europe (LFEE)*, 6: 1–2 (1983).
12 G. Vaerno, 'A Public Opinion Strategy', *NR*, 31: 3/4 (1983).

A critical variable is precisely the existence of those willing to organise themselves outside existing political structures ... threatening to *erode* support from at least some traditional party institutions.[13]

Psychological war, which has been waged by the Soviet Union against the West [...] is aimed at *undermining* the West's will to preserve its way of life.[14]

EAST

It is clear that the deployment in Western Europe of nuclear systems ... in no way squares with the US's commitment to refrain from actions *undermining* the SALT II Treaty.[15]

It is time that Washington, Bonn and the other NATO capitals renounce a policy that leads to the *undermining* of the foundations of peace.[16]

Psychological warfare centres in the West are helping the counterrevolutionary forces in Poland to stir up anti-social sentiments, destabilise the situation and *undermine* the Socialist system.[17]

The criteria for delineating the boundaries of a grammar of structure belong to our language. That actors in different positions attributed meaning to their own acts and those of others on the basis of the *same* grammar suggests the extent to which they were 'entangled' in the language of a context and constrained by its boundaries.[18]

In Part III I look more closely at the relationship between this entanglement and a 'language of manoeuvre' used by state leaders to realise their own interests. The point here is that the naming of a structure established a range of possible acts in relation to it. Social movements which were trying to transform the structure relied on this same grammar to communicate the meaning of their acts. They were dependent on the rules of the game established by states. The precise meaning of the structure and the objectives in relation to it differed for each type of actor. States were maintaining a part of the structure, that is, deterrence in the West and socialism in the East. Social movements named the Cold War itself to be a structure which had to be broken down and dismantled.

A grammar of moves

Earlier in the chapter I made a distinction between a language game and grammar, stating that the one was a contextually specific structure of

13 G. Flynn, 'Public Opinion and Atlantic Defence', *NR*, 31: 5 (1983).
14 W. Hofmann, 'Is NATO's Defence Policy Facing a Crisis?', *NR*, 32: 4 (1984).
15 'US Said to Break Arms-Control Pledges', *CDSP*, 36: 4 (1984).
16 'Tass Assails NATO's Militarisic Course', *CDSP*, 36: 22 (1984).
17 'Poland: "Antisocialists" in Solidarity Scored', *CDSP*, 33: 17 (1981).
18 Wittgenstein (1958: para. 125).

action, and the other an expression of the range of *possibilities* belonging to an object or language area. This distinction will be analysed in more depth in Part II when I look at the dynamics underlying the change. For purposes of simplification and description, at this point I would like to present the grammar as a tool for analysing the unfolding of a context over time, by analogy to the unfolding of a single match of a game, in order to identify the coherence of the change.

The structuring role of a grammar shares some similarities with the notion of a game tree. Actors may have any number of options, but the range of options will change as the interaction evolves. With the game tree, outcomes are analysed in terms of utility functions assigned by the analyst. In the descriptive analysis of grammars, the central task is to trace the relationship between the moves made by different actors as a game unfolds. The range of possible moves and one's objective in making one move or another cannot be separated from one's position within a context of rules. In the context of a structure, the range of possible moves might be as follows:

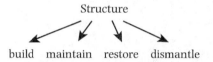

Structure

build   maintain   restore   dismantle

An actor's choice of options may depend on two factors. First, it will depend on the state of the object. A decision to build or maintain, for instance, belongs to two different states; one builds a structure that is not yet complete, while one maintains a structure that is already in existence. Acts exist in *temporal* relation to a context. In the early days of the Cold War, NATO was engaged in building a structure; in the late 1970s and 1980s it was primarily concerned with its maintenance.

Second, a choice will be dependent on one's *role* within a context. Much as a queen moves according to different rules than a pawn, states are likely to engage in different acts than social movements. States, as the central players in the Cold War, were more likely to want to maintain the structure, so long as it served their interests. Social movements, as actors who oppose an existing order, are more likely to engage in acts of dismantling. The relationship between players is less determined by uncertainty over the moves of the other or a strategic rationale for defection or cooperation; rather, each follows a rule specific to their position within a particular type of context. However, just as a queen can move in a variety of ways, it is not inconceivable that states may find themselves in a position within an unfolding game where their interests may be better served by a change in action, for instance, moving from acts of maintenance or

51

restoration to acts of dismantling or breaking down. The narrative in Chapter Five demonstrates the relationship between acts by the social movements to dismantle the structure of the Cold War and moves, later in the game, by the two superpowers which contributed to the eventual collapse of the structure.

The analysis of the grammar of a context makes it possible to identify the correlation, or lack of correlation, between particular acts and an outcome. There is a negative correlation between acts of maintenance, restoration or building and the collapse of a structure. There is a positive correlation between acts of dismantling, breakdown and undermining – or passive states such as deterioration or erosion – and the eventual collapse of a structure. These correlations do not belong to a reality independent of human meaning; they are possibilities expressed in our grammar for a particular object or region of language. The narrative in Chapter Five provides an overview of moves by a range of players over a sixteen year period. Before proceeding to that narrative, Chapter Four will explore in more depth what it means to construct a description based on the criteria of a dominant grammar.

Conclusion

A grammar can be distinguished from a language game. Language games provide the rules of contextually specific acts. Grammars express possibilities belonging to an object or language region. The identification of a grammar shared by a range of players, occupying different roles, can provide a basis for tracing the unfolding of a context over time. Like the notion of a game tree, a grammar can be used to identify how the boundaries of movement are transformed at different points in a game. In contrast to the game tree, where outcomes are determined on the basis of utility functions assigned by the analyst, the structure of the game is to be identified in the practices of the actors themselves.

4

Description

The concept of 'seeing' makes a tangled impression. Well, it is tangled. – I look at the landscape, my gaze ranges over it, I see all sorts of distinct and indistinct movement; *this* impresses itself sharply on me, *that* is quite hazy. After all, how completely ragged what we see can appear! And now look at all that can be meant by 'description of what is seen' ... It is the same when one tries to define the concept of a material object in terms of 'what is really seen'. – What we have rather to do is to *accept* the everyday language game, and to note *false* accounts of the matter as false. (Wittgenstein, 1958: 200).

METAPHORS WERE DRAWN on to name different aspects of the international system. Metaphors of structure, partnership and crime made the experience of the Cold War meaningful in terms of more familiar everyday experiences. These metaphors relate to a grammar of possibilities. This approach to grammar provides a unique point of departure for describing a process of change such as the end of the Cold War.

To describe a change is to construct a narrative of what happened. Yet the world is a complex place. At the international level, the number of events, actors, places and times to choose from is overwhelming. Criteria are needed for selecting from the detail, for focusing attention on certain aspects to the exclusion of others. The need to select has contributed to a privileging of theory over description in international relations. In contrast to narrative, which details the unfolding of a story over time, international relations theory has been conceived of in terms of 'pictures'. Kenneth Waltz (1979: 8), in his classic *Theory of International Politics*, described theory as follows:

> A theory is a picture, mentally formed, of a bounded realm or domain of activity [...] The question, as ever with theories, is not whether the isolation of a realm is reality, but whether it is useful. And the usefulness is judged by the explanatory and predictive powers of the theory that may be fashioned.

A picture holds a particular reality in place.[1] Its usefulness is judged by its

---

1 For an analysis of theories of international relations as 'pictures' that 'hold us captive', see Pin-Fat (1997b).

explanatory and predictive powers. Yet the dominant theories of international relations were called into question by the events giving rise to the end of the Cold War, at least initially. There was a general failure to predict these changes. John Lewis Gaddis (1992–93: 53) made the point that 'prediction' has been a central objective of the major theoretical approaches to international relations during the Cold War, and none of these approaches 'came anywhere close to anticipating how the Cold War would end'. The failure has been ignored by some; the importance of prediction *vis-à-vis* explanation is minimised by others.[2] Nonetheless, prediction is commonly understood to be inseparable from explanation. Brian Fay (1975: 122), for instance, states that 'In light of the structural identity of explanation in science and prediction it may be said [...] *that an explanation is not complete unless it could have functioned as a prediction.*' Both are possible by reference to a covering law which establishes the regularity and recurrence of causal correlations.

The widespread acknowledgement of a failure to predict the most significant international change of this century should at least give us pause to look again at this context, to examine the detail more closely. While theory specifies regularities and recurrences, the goal in this case is to account for a unique outcome, that is, the collapse of the Cold War. As an introduction to this alternative, I shall explore three existing approaches to description, which relate to the distinct ends of explanation, understanding and interpretation. I argue that a fourth approach provides the criteria for a 'better' description of a context of change.

Explaining

Theory seeks to explain, and therefore describe, particular cases as a part of testing. To test a law, one moves from the formulation of a hypothesis, based on the categories of a theory, to a comparison of this hypothesis with reality. The end of the Cold War provides fertile ground for exploring the problem with this way of proceeding. Charles W. Kegley (1994) presented a range of explanations of the end of the Cold War. The following is a shortened version of those he presents.

1 The West's preparations for war forced the USSR into submission.
2 Nuclear deterrence drove the Soviet leaders to abandon any hope they might have harboured about prevailing militarily over the West.
3 The West's extensive alliance network was instrumental in hastening the Soviet Union's submission.
4 Soviet militarism destroyed the Soviet economy.

---

2 Nicholson (1996: 122), for instance, argues that prediction is a particularly severe criterion for satisfactory explanation.

5 Gorbachev's cooperative initiatives towards the United States came when the current and potential costs of competition were weighing heavily on a struggling Soviet economy.

6 The metamorphosis of the US–Soviet relationship was the result of recognition by the Soviet Union and the United States that cooperation was necessary if they were both to address their economic problems.

7 Eastern European demonstrators were inspired by the ideological appeal of liberal democracy.

8 Communism lost the Cold War, not Russia, due to internal democratic reforms.

9 Gorbachev, as an individual, initiated changes that transformed the world.

10 The flawed character of the Soviet Union made it vulnerable to chance events.

11 The fall of communism started outside the Soviet Union, in the Eastern bloc, and necessitated changes within.

12 The Soviet Union was discredited by publication of its human rights record and distortions in its moral and ethical principles.

13 Domestic dissatisfaction convinced Soviet leaders to agree to arms control measures that required more cuts on the part of the Soviets than the United States.

14 Pressure from grassroots peace movements contributed to ending the Cold War.

15 Communism collapsed because of the rise of nationalism in the former republics.

The explanations, with the exception of the first three, are drawn from a table entitled 'Rival Images of the Causes of Communism's Collapse' within an article entitled 'How Did the Cold War Die?'. The first three are characteristic of 'right-wing realists' in the United States, and represent a category of explanation that is compatible with the dominant realist picture of these changes. The rest represent a 'plethora of additional plausible explanations for the Cold War's death' (Kegley, 1994: 21). Given the range of different answers, it is interesting to think about the more specific question that each explanation implies. Look what happens if a particular question, based on the subject and object of attention, is superimposed:

1 *Why did the Soviet Union change?*
   The West's preparations for war forced the USSR into submission.

2 *Why did the Soviet Union change?*
   Nuclear deterrence drove the Soviet leaders to abandon any hope they might have harboured about prevailing militarily over the West.

3 *Why did the Soviet Union change?*
   The West's extensive alliance network was instrumental in hastening the Soviet Union's submission.

4 *Why did the Soviet economy collapse?*
Soviet militarism destroyed the Soviet economy.

5 *Why did the Soviets begin to cooperate with the West?*
Gorbachev's cooperative initiatives towards the United States came when the current and potential costs of competition were weighing heavily on a struggling Soviet economy.

6 *Why did the United States and Soviet Union begin to cooperate?*
The metamorphosis of the US–Soviet relationship was the result of recognition by the Soviet Union and the United States that cooperation was necessary if they were both to address their economic problems.

7 *Why did Eastern Europeans take to the streets?*
Eastern European demonstrators were inspired by the ideological appeal of liberal democracy.

8 *Who lost the Cold War?*
Communism lost the Cold War, not Russia, due to internal democratic reforms.

9 *Why did the Cold War come to an end?*
Gorbachev, as an individual, initiated changes that transformed the world.

10 *Why did the Soviet Union collapse?*
The flawed character of the Soviet Union made it vulnerable to chance events.

11 *Why did the Soviet Union change?*
The fall of communism started outside the Soviet Union, in the Eastern bloc, and necessitated changes within.

12 *Why did the Soviet Union collapse?*
The Soviet Union was discredited by publication of its human rights record and distortions in its moral and ethical principles.

13 *Why did the Soviet Union change its arms control position?*
Domestic dissatisfaction convinced Soviet leaders to agree to arms control measures that required more cuts on the part of the Soviets than the United States.

14 *Why did the Cold War end?*
Pressure from grassroots peace movements contributed to ending the Cold War.

15 *Why did communism collapse?*
Communism collapsed because of the rise of nationalism in the former republics.

One of Kegley's central concerns is whether to name the object of autopsy to be the death of the Cold War or the death of the Soviet Union; nonetheless, there is a high degree of agreement – although not a consensus – that the object of explanation is in fact a change on the part of the Soviet Union. To the extent that the United States or the West is involved, it is – in most cases – less as part of the change than as causal force, outside, influencing the behaviour of the other superpower.

Despite the underlying agreement, each explanation implies a different story; some focus on military factors, some on economic, some on issues of legitimacy, some on interactions between the superpowers, and others on the internal relationship between the Soviet Union and its subject populations. The diversity of potential explanations/descriptions raises a critical concern about the criteria by which one chooses from the vast array of movements, from the complexity of the international system, to construct one story about these changes rather than another.

Kegley suggests first naming the object of explanation, delineating the units of analysis and then proceeding with the autopsy. One begins with the scientist's categories and then moves to the observation of reality. Yet this process of articulating the question and of naming the object of explanation is the beginning point for a *particular* description of events. This 'way of proceeding' sets the stage for emphasising certain details and ignoring or excluding others.

To complicate matters further, despite the similarity of the question in most cases, the range of answers illustrates the extent to which the same question can have different meanings (Garfinkel, 1981). Consider the following two explanations from above, filled out with a bit more descriptive detail. Both answer the question 'Why did the Soviet Union change?'. The first is an explanation from the Right that the West's preparations for war forced the Soviet Union into submission:

> By engaging Moscow in a prohibitively expensive arms race, and by staging, in 1984, a fake 'disinformation' test of the SDI system to fool the Soviets, the United States forced the Soviet Union into a competition which exhausted their economic capacity and compelled them to jettison their objective of increasing their influence throughout the globe. (Kegley, 1994: 13)

The second relates to a loss of credibility due to human rights violations:

> It was the moral reassessment of the seventy-odd years of this socialist experiment that shook the nation, not Ronald Reagan's Star Wars. It was the flood of publications of the Soviet Union's human rights record and the tremendous distortions of moral and ethical principles that discredited the system, especially when introduced into the everyday lives of its individual citizens through the popular media. This is what focused the drive for change and first made people vote against representatives of the morally corrupt old political elite. (Kegley, 1994: 24)

Each account answers the question 'Why did the Soviet Union change?'. At the same time, each produces a different narrative, emphasising different actors and events and a different time frame. The first asks: 'Why did the

Soviet Union *change?'*. The description begins in 1984 with a particular set of actions – a disinformation campaign on the part of the American government – that caused the Soviet Union to give up, submitting to the West rather than resisting as in the past. The second asks: 'Why did the *Soviet Union* change?'. Why did the Soviet Union lose its credibility or legitimacy in the eyes of its own people and the world community and cease to exist? Although less explicit in this brief presentation, the second account might be expanded into a story about the dissidents in Eastern Europe who sought to publicise the actions of the Eastern European governments in violation of the human rights provisions of the Helsinki agreements.

Embedded in each question, explanation and description are assumptions about when the Cold War ended, about the most important actors and about what it included. Each begins with a particular selection on the part of the analyst, that is, a naming of the significant variables in this context. The realist on the Right emphasises unitary states, and specifically superpowers, whose actions force the other to do what they otherwise would not do. The human rights explanation assumes that military force and power are not the primary criteria, that states are not necessarily unitary actors, but are dependent on the populations they represent for their power – a set of categories more compatible with the liberal tradition than the realist. Part of Kegley's critique is that most explanations represent a particular position, both theoretical and political, either realist or liberal, Right or Left. The bias is largely a result of an *a priori* act of naming the variables in this change. The criteria for determining the truth of a particular story do not belong to the reality which is the subject of study; the criteria belong to the theoretical lens through which it is observed.

The issue of multiple theoretical lenses might be resolved by adopting the argument of Thomas Kuhn (1970) about paradigm change. Kuhn's emphasis is changing paradigms within the scientific community, changing paradigms for explaining a reality that remains largely the same (Phillips, 1977: 95). However, the problem in this case is the difficulty, on the basis of existing theories, of coming to grips with dramatic changes in the world. Kuhn's argument allows us to recognise that Aristotle looked at a swinging rock and called it a swinging rock, while Galileo called it a pendulum; or Copernicus saw the Earth revolving around the Sun, while his contemporaries believed the reverse to be the case. Both are examples of scientists looking at the same phenomenon and seeing something different because they are looking through different lenses. The object stays the same.

Realists and liberals, after the fact, observed the end of the Cold War through different lenses and saw something different, but this does not represent a paradigm shift within the scientific community; in this case the world of international relations had changed and scientists, in response, were trying to work out how it happened and how its advent escaped their attention. Kuhn focuses on paradigm change within the natural sciences. In that case, the objects of study do not talk, act meaningfully or think; as a result, the natural scientist has a monopoly on conceptual definition in a way that the social scientist does not. In the context of this transformation, which eluded scientific prediction, there is a responsibility to take seriously the categories and meanings of the subjects whose actions constituted the change.

Kuhn's work demonstrates that scientists do not just look through a microscope at an objective world. He demonstrates the social nature of scientific practice and the possibility of multiple paradigms for viewing reality. Given the emphasis on *scientific* practice, Kuhn's argument does not go far enough. What need to be understood in this case are changes in the practices of political actors which neither realist nor liberal approaches have successfully addressed. One tradition that has shifted attention to the actors is hermeneutics, which emphasises understanding over explanation.

Understanding

Hermeneutic approaches rest on an argument that all social activity is dependent on rules, norms and language. Social analysis is distinct from natural analysis because of the importance of human meaning structures. According to Hollis and Smith (1991: 72), the central hermeneutic theme is that 'action must always be understood from within'. The context and conventions that structure action are important because without them we could not possibly understand the motives or intentions of an actor.

Hermeneutics has not had a major impact on international relations scholarship, except through the work of Weber (see George, 1994). There is a tradition of looking 'inside the mind', at the rational calculations of actors, but the link between individual and social context has been weak. The brief empirical analysis of Gorbachev's decisionmaking processes in Alex Wendt's 'Anarchy is What States Make of It' (1992) is a case in point.[3] Wendt begins with a powerful theoretical argument that processes of identity and interest formation by states are inherently relational. States construct their relations to one another through a process of interaction. Identity is always identity within a specific social world.

3 Wendt's work is not usually referred to as an example of hermeneutics. He draws more on symbolic interactionists such as Berger and Luckmann (1966), Blumer (1969) and Mead (1934), and structurationists such as Bhaskar (1979) and Giddens (1979). I use this example because his empirical analysis illustrates the tendency to revert to a subjectivist position. Adler (1997: 326) argues that constructivism is compatible with Weber's *verstehen* approach.

59

While his theoretical argument emphasises the importance of the intersubjective and the social, Wendt's brief empirical analysis shifts attention to processes 'inside the mind' of Mikhail Gorbachev. As he looks 'into the mind' of Gorbachev, the relational and intersubjective elements of the transformation largely disappear. Wendt describes a process in which new 'possible selves' are identified and in which 'Gorbachev wants to free the Soviet Union from the coercive social logic of the Cold War and engage the West in far reaching cooperation' (Wendt, 1992: 421). Later in the argument, the 'self' who has rethought 'one's own ideas about the self' tries to alter the identities of others who also sustain the system. It is as if Gorbachev develops something of a 'private language', his 'new thinking', which he then presents to the world. But this is contrary to the constructivist principle that 'meanings in terms of which action is organised arise out of interaction' (Wendt, 1992: 403). Based on this principle, we should expect not that Gorbachev engages himself in a process of rethinking but that he engages in a process with others.

Wendt asks under what conditions an actor, such as Gorbachev, could engage in critical self-reflection and make choices designed to bring about change. He names two preconditions. There must be a reason to think of oneself in novel terms, which is likely to stem from the presence of new social situations and, second, the expected costs of intentional role change cannot be greater than its rewards. If these conditions are present actors can engage in self-reflection and practice designed to transform their identities and interests.

Among the 'new social situations' Wendt includes a breakdown of consensus about identity commitments; this process is primarily internal to the state. He refers specifically to a breakdown in the Soviet consensus that relations between capitalist and socialist states are inherently conflictual. The source of the internal breakdown is exogenous, however; it stems primarily from the inability of the state to meet the economic, technological and military challenge from the West. Wendt reifies a distinction between internal and external. He adopts the 'theoretically productive analogy between states and individuals', which is an accepted practice of international relations. In the process, he brackets out non-state or transnational actors.

The analysis of Gorbachev's internal process of rethinking, tied to a cost–benefit analysis by 'one' self, is consistent with Wendt's focus on the state as rational actor. The sociality that is central to his theoretical argument, as well as the possibility of any kind of actor other than the unitary state, is missing, however. Wendt believes 'with realists that in the medium run sovereign states will remain the dominant political actors in the international system' (Wendt, 1992: 424). But if, as he concedes, the significance of states is declining relative to multinational corporations, new social movements, transnationals and international government, can an analysis of change and process in international life afford to focus only on states? Most problematic, in light of his larger argument, is that he does not adequately situate Gorbachev in an international context. The emphasis on Gorbachev as a single actor initiating change obscures a central point of his analysis, that is, that meaning is intersubjectively constituted between actors.

Wendt begins with mutually constitutive practices, moves to the thought processes of an individual, but then points out that this process of rethinking was actually caused by external factors, not least of which was the inability of the Soviet state to meet the technological and military challenge from the West. The result is an analysis of the interaction between an individual mind and an external environment. Gorbachev, caused to rethink his 'self' by the West, transforms the world.

Like the 'explanations' explored by Kegley, this account of the end of the Cold War is empirically suspect. Besides the fact that Gorbachev's rethinking is ultimately subordinated to an external cause, references to speeches and other kinds of text by which we might make some assessment of what Gorbachev himself thought, are noticeable by their absence; instead, this rethinking is cast in terms of rational calculation, based on a disciplinary convention employed by the scientist.

The previous section raised questions about the criteria for selecting facts from the complexity of the international system; this analysis raises questions about how we know what is really going on 'inside' any individual mind, by what criteria we assume the importance of any one individual's thinking processes over another, or how it is that a single individual could change the world.

In this case, the hermeneutic aim of understanding action from within is problematic in a more general sense. One can ask a question about Gorbachev's motives for acting, and many have. But the question in this case is broader than any one individual; it is rather about *social* processes that gave rise to the end of the Cold War. The hermeneutic task is to understand the motives or actions of an individual by situating him or her within a context of the rules of a game. The game metaphor is useful for thinking about two different questions and, therefore, two possible ways to structure a description. The observer of a chess match, for instance, might, on the one hand, ask a question about the reasoning behind a particular move. On the other hand, she might ask a question about the types of move that are possible within the larger game of chess. The latter shifts attention to a description of the rules themselves, and highlights the importance of knowing these rules in order to understand any movement within them.

Wendt refers to actors engaging in self-reflection and practice specifically designed to transform their identities and thus to 'change the games' in which they are embedded (Wendt, 1992: 419). Wendt implies that *Gorbachev* constructs the parameters of a new game. Given the social nature of the rules, and the importance of intersubjective understandings, one might, by contrast, argue that Gorbachev, as the leader of a superpower, was in a position to make moves within a new game. But games by definition rely on shared rules; as a result, there is no reason to believe a single actor could constitute the game itself. To understand the process by which new games became possible against the backdrop of the Cold War, analysis necessarily shifts to a description of the changing rules, rather than that of individual intentions.

Interpreting

Wendt provides a theory of the social construction of reality, but then describes processes 'inside the mind' of an individual. As a result, his empirical analysis collapses into a subjectivist account. Post-structuralists, by contrast, have demonstrated how dominant interpretations of a context constitute the possibilities for action, and how some voices are marginalised and silenced in the process. In contrast to realism, which posits a world of material objects, the existence of which is independent of ideas or beliefs about them, post-structuralists have argued that 'reality' is always dependent on interpretation and 'there is nothing outside discourse' (Campbell, 1993: 8).

While critics have reacted with alarm to suggestions that there is 'only language', David Campbell (1993) clarifies that this formulation misses the point. The point is that human actors do not understand reality on the basis of pure sense data; rather, knowledge of the world is dependent on language and interpretive practice. Within the world of foreign policy, interpretive practice has everything to do with power, and the major political move in constructing the dominant narrative of events such as the Gulf War or the end of the Cold War was to objectify a particular representation of these events as 'real'. As Campbell states, 'the Pentagon sought to objectify representations of engagements in ways that obfuscated their constructed and contested character' (Campbell, 1993: 12). Campbell emphasises interpretation, but these interpretations are neither purely individual nor derived from rational thought processes; they are instead dependent on intersubjective meanings. These meanings are the point of departure for action in the world.

Campbell argues, in the case of the Gulf War, that 'naturalisation' processes reinforced the 'necessity' of certain actions in a 'black/white' world. Simplistic oppositions, such as sovereignty versus anarchy, tyranny versus democracy and good versus evil were the stuff of this world. Against the background of the invasion, August 1990, cast in terms of a World War II script of blitzkrieg against an evil adversary, Campbell examines counternarratives of six episodes in order to illustrate the 'shades of grey' surrounding this conflict. He argues that the goal is not to offer *the* true account of the Gulf War that will 'pierce the veil of official propaganda', but rather to problematise the attempt by the Bush administration to 'make absolute and emphatic claims about agency, ethics, responsibility and sovereignty' (Campbell, 1993: 3).

Campbell analyses the public language of the US, exposing this 'true' account of the Gulf War as one interpretation that disguises a range of details. He demonstrates that counternarratives, emphasising other details in this context, such as the diplomatic potential for a resolution of the crisis, may have created space for other possibilities. The critical task is to demonstrate that other narratives could have and should have been constructed.

The critical activity of this project is somewhat different. The goal is not to analyse how a realist discourse was reproduced; instead, it is to ask how alternatives, originally thought to be unrealistic, became possible. Campbell, like the realists he criticises, emphasises the practices of states. This analysis, by contrast, embeds state actors in a larger context of changing games in order to understand their relationship to other types of actor.

Campbell highlights the distinction between different interpretations. One might, for instance, construct multiple narratives about the end of the Cold War, based on a peace movement account, or that of dissidents in the Eastern bloc, or that of NATO or Russia. By contrast, I present a method for constructing a multi-layered narrative, structured by the rules of a range of grammars shared by all of these actors. Participants who occupy different positions may engage in distinct and conflicting language games; however, in so far as they are acting and reacting to one another, they manoeuvre within a space, the boundaries of which are constituted by meanings held in common. The central act of states may have been to maintain the structures of the Cold War, while social movements sought to dismantle them, but both acts were meaningful within a shared grammar of structure.

Realist arguments that NATO or the West won the Cold War have become the conventional wisdom. However, if we trace the movements of diverse actors over time, based on the grammars shared between them, we end up with a different account of how this context unfolded. Consistent with Campbell's argument, 'the West won' is revealed as a single realist narrative, articulated by the powerful. This narrative, imposed after the fact, provides a partial and distorted picture, however. More importantly, when embedded in a series of transitions over time, the victory explanation can be understood as a single move in a process that continues to unfold. Campbell's argument lends itself to the conclusion that nothing has changed with the end of the Cold War.[4] The following analysis opens up

4 Campbell (1992) does in fact make this claim.

spaces for thinking about alternative futures.

Conclusion

Campbell (1993: 7) argues that in telling a story one establishes order and meaning. Each of the approaches to narrative presented here establishes order and meaning on the basis of a different set of criteria. For objectivist approaches, the criteria for selecting facts or events are determined by an *a priori* theory. Wendt's criteria for describing Gorbachev's internal process of rethinking rely on the assumptions of rational choice. In Campbell's interpretivist account, power determines which narrative will dominate and which details of a situation will be prioritised. The narrative that follows relies on different criteria, that is, the criteria of a grammar shared by a range of actors in this context.

This description is said to be better for a number of reasons. First, unlike the explaining or understanding approaches, as presented above, the criteria for selecting from the detail belong to the context itself rather than a set of *a priori* categories. Second, unlike Wendt's analysis, which looks inside an individual mind, this approach embeds the moves of any one actor in a larger context of changing rules. Third, in contrast to Campbell's story, which emphasises the marginalisation and silencing of alternatives, the story that follows demonstrates how states were enabled to move towards alternative policies as the rules of the dominant game were politicised by those outside the established structures of power in East and West.

The analysis of a grammar of structure in Chapter Five describes the transformation of the Cold War. All of the players, state and non-state, shared a naming of the Cold War as a structure. Each occupied a different position in this field of action and therefore was capable of moving in different ways, much as a queen and a pawn move differently based on the rules of chess. The starting point for the critical acts of social movements was the dominant grammars of the Cold War. States were maintaining these structures; social movements began to dismantle them.

Given a consistency in the moves of different types of actor, it is possible to identify a change on the part of the superpowers from acts of maintenance to acts which contributed to the eventual collapse of different parts of these structures. The analysis demonstrates a degree of coherence to the changes. The coherence is ordered by the narrative but the basis for the narrative is a shared grammar of structure. The coherence does not belong to a reality independent of human meaning. The changes were the result of acts by agents in the real world; the acts were invested with meaning by reference to a larger grammar.

5

Describing the transformation

Where does our investigation get its importance from, since it seems only to destroy everything interesting, that is, all that is great and important? (As it were all the buildings, leaving behind only bits of stone and rubble.) What we are destroying is nothing but houses of cards and we are clearing up the ground of language on which they stand. (Wittgenstein, 1958: para. 118)

THE FOLLOWING ANALYSIS is based on an archive of documents including texts from the Committee on the Present Danger (CPD), NATO, President Reagan, the Soviet Union, the Western European peace movements, Polish Solidarity and Charter 77.[1] The narrative establishes the context of the end of the Cold War as the collapse of a structure, and describes this process of transformation over a sixteen year period. The contours of the narrative are provided by a grammar of structure.

In Chapter Three, I explored a range of categories belonging to this grammar, such as maintaining, restoring, dismantling and building. Each time a category is included in the text, a few examples of the empirical source are provided in the notes. This represents a mere sampling of the data, to provide readers with a sense of the empirical basis for the narrative without overwhelming them with detail.[2] The point is that these are *shared* categories drawn on consistently by actors occupying a particular position. Given space limitations, only single examples will be included in Chapters Six to Eleven.

A distinction was made in Chapter Three between a grammar and a language game. A grammatical investigation is one that looks into the possibilities of phenomena; in this case, the possibilities belonging to a structure. States and social movements share a grammar of structure; their acts in relation to that structure differ, however. In this sense, a contestation of

1 On 7 January 1977, a call for civil and human rights to be respected in Czechoslovakia was issued in Prague. The declaration was published on 1 January 1977 and the informal association of its supporters was titled Charter 77.
2 Those titles from the *CDSP* or *CDPSP* without an author head off a larger piece which includes a compilation of articles from a variety of newspapers or journals on that subject. The original analysis was based on more than 650 documents. For an earlier version including further examples, see Fierke (1995).

language games is evident. The issue of contestation will be explored in Chapter Six.

The narrative is presented in four stages. The stages serve two functions. First, they break up the text into periods of three to five years. Second, they represent shifts in the locus of action. Stage One examines mutual acts of maintenance, and related problems, by the two alliances. Stage Two shifts attention to processes of erosion and undermining within each bloc. Stage Three makes a link between changes internal to each bloc and a change in the language games of the two superpowers. Stage Four covers the period from 1989 to 1991 when the structures of the Cold War visibly collapsed.

Stage One: maintaining a multidimensional structure

In the mid 1970s, at the height of détente, the two Cold War alliances were engaged in acts of structural maintenance. NATO provided a framework[3] that rested on the foundations of deterrence capability and transatlantic ties.[4] NATO was a political structure furnished with military means.[5] Its central task was the maintenance of deterrence, defence capabilities and political cohesion.[6] The framework of the Eastern bloc rested on the foundations of socialist production and the unity of the socialist countries.[7]

---

3 'For over twenty-five years, [NATO] has provided an irreplaceable framework for our collective security.' P. van den Boeynants, 'European Security in 1976', *NR*, 24: 3 (1976); 'In an environment of strategic nuclear equivalence, [NATO's strategy of flexible response] provides the essential framework for deterring the outbreak of conflict.' A. Haig, 'NATO: An Agenda for the Future', *NR*, 27: 3 (1979).

4 'Credible deterrence must rest on a triad of capabilities.' J. R. Schlesinger, 'NATO and Mutual Security', *NR*, 23: 3 (1975); 'The deterrent capacity of the Alliance is the foundation for the security of every member.' J. M. A. H. Luns, 'The Present State of East–West Relations', *NR*, 24: 2 (1976).

5 '[NATO] is a political organisation furnished with military means.' R. Strausz-Hupe, 'NATO in Midstream', *NR*, 25: 5 (1977).

6 'The Alliance must be under no illusions about the need to maintain a military balance.' Schlesinger, 'NATO and Mutual Security'; '[NATO has] to be willing to devote sufficient resources to maintain the credibility of the deterrent shield' [...] 'It is essential that the allies maintain a high degree of political cohesion.' Luns, 'The Present State of East–West Relations'; '[NATO] has maintained sufficient forces to deter any aggression.' Strausz-Hupe, 'NATO in Midstream'.

7 'The strength of our state lies in the fact that its economic foundation is socialist production relations, which have evolved on the basis of ... public ownership.' 'Why the Role of the State is Growing', *CDSP*, 27: 39 (1975); 'The foundation of foundations of our close cooperation is ... the indestructible military alliance of the Communist Parties of the socialist countries.' 'Brezhnev's Report to the Congress', *CDSP*, 28: 8 (1976); 'The social foundation of the USSR is the indestructible alliance of workers, peasants and the intelligentsia.' 'The New USSR Constitution', *CDSP*, 29: 41 (1977).

The socialist alliance was the cornerstone of relations between the Soviet Union and Eastern Europe.[8] Like NATO, maintenance was a central task of the Warsaw Pact; in this case the objects of maintenance were socialism, peace and equilibrium.[9]

Détente also provided a framework that needed to be maintained.[10] From the Eastern perspective, this framework had a solid foundation,[11] based on principles and mutual agreements within the CSCE, as well as arms control agreements between the United States and Soviet Union, such as SALT I and the Anti-ballistic Missile (ABM) Treaty. For the West, the Helsinki Final Act had produced a conceptual framework for judging the behaviour of states. Helsinki would provide the basis for future building and development.[12] Shared principles provided a framework within which East and West could coexist, but the stability of the structure remained in question for the latter. One problem was the need to find a common ceiling for the two military structures.[13] For the Eastern bloc, the permanence of the arms control regime had already been cemented in arms control agree-

---

8 'One of the cornerstones of our fraternal relations is the Treaty of Friendship, Cooperation and Mutual Aid.' 'Brezhnev Visits Czechoslovakia', *CDSP*, 30: 22 (1978).

9 'The solidarity of communists has been and remains a powerful factor in maintaining ... the great achievements of the forces of peace, democracy and socialism.' 'Prague Meeting Calls for Communist Unity', *CDSP*, 29: 17 (1977); 'Only in conditions of socialism has an army, for the first time in history, become ... a powerful means of restraining aggressive forces and maintaining peace on earth.' 'Ustinov Speech on Red Army's Birthday', *CDSP*, 30: 8 (1978).

10 'Détente will be maintained only by the continued assertion of vigilance ... based on strength ... and solidarity.' 'CSCE Ends, Some Views of Alliance Leaders', *NR*, 23: 5 (1975); 'The preservation of this balance is a sine qua non of détente.' Van den Boeynants, 'European Security in 1976'; 'The maintenance of détente requires more vigorous actions.' 'Arbatov Reviews U.S.–Soviet Relations', *CDSP*, 28: 13 (1976); 'The task [of US–Soviet relations] consists not only in preserving and consolidating what has been achieved but also in moving ahead, to new agreements and understandings.' 'More Pravda Comments on U.S. Policies', *CDSP*, 29: 28 (1977).

11 '[Relations of states in the CSCE] rest on a solid foundation of the principles of peaceful coexistence.' 'Gromyko Speaks at Warsaw Pact Fete', *CDSP*, 27: 20 (1975); 'The relations of participating states have been placed on a firm foundation of fundamental principles.' 'Brezhnev Speaks in Helsinki', *CDSP*, 27: 31 (1975).

12 '[The Final Act] will have produced a framework and standards for judging the behaviour of states in the future.' 'CSCE Ends'; 'The West European countries, within the framework of the CSCE, placed considerable emphasis on the quality and duration of the relationship to be built up with the USSR.' M. van der Stoel, 'East–West Relations: Limits and Possibilities', *NR*, 24: 6 (1976); 'The framework for the future development of the CSCE process is established.' T. Solesby, 'Helsinki to Belgrade – and Beyond', *NR*, 26: 3 (1978).

13 'A common ceiling would surely reflect the principle of equality that the USSR has so long expounded.' Schlesinger, 'NATO and Mutual Security'; '[The Warsaw Pact] has refused to accept a common ceiling on manpower.' W. Pabsch, 'Détente and Disarmament', *NR*, 25:

ments[14] and détente was the 'essence of everything that ought to make peace in Europe firm and unshakable'.[15]

Within the détente framework, the West faced several problems maintaining its own security structure. In the context of a deteriorating economy and relaxation of the superpower conflict, it had become difficult to convince Western publics of the need to continue to pay for defence.[16] Cracks had developed in the economic system and prolonged unemployment had become a powerful factor of social disintegration.[17] Despite the economic problems, no one yet believed that the welfare state, which was seen as a barrier to Soviet political intentions in Western Europe, could be dismantled.[18]

Détente had been a mixed blessing for the West. On the one hand, increased cooperation between East and West would potentially assist in the further breakdown of barriers separating the two structures in East and West. On the other hand, the combination of a relaxation of tensions and economic crisis had contributed to public unwillingness to pay for defence spending, which would potentially undermine the NATO deterrent. At the same time, NATO was concerned that the Soviet Union was building up its military potential[19] and attempting to undermine the internal politics of the

5 (1977).

14 'The first USSR–US agreements on strategic arms limitation were concluded in Moscow – the permanent treaty on the limitation of ABM systems.' 'The Soviet Stand on SALT Talks', *CDSP*, 28: 1 (1976); 'Present figures for the two weapon systems ... were established by mutual understanding between the US and USSR in the 1972 agreement.' 'Arbatov: Soviet Goal is Nuclear Parity', *CDSP*, 29: 5 (1977).

15 'Brezhnev Speaks in Helsinki'.

16 'Reluctance by the public to continue America's post-World War II role in maintaining security abroad is striking.' C. R. Foster, 'American Elite and Mass Attitudes Toward Europe', *NR*, 23: 3 (1975); '[Prolonged unemployment and persistent inflation] ... create a climate of insecurity for individuals, enterprises and governments which in the long run could undermine the organization of economic life and consequently the financing of the defence effort at a sufficiently high level to preserve its deterrent value.' 'Atlantic Alliance and Recession', *NR*, 24: 1 (1976).

17 'There is a dreary familiarity about the words inflation, recession and unemployment which pepper the language of the media. [The West] had begun to come to terms with the first of these phenomena ... when other cracks suddenly appeared in the system we were caught napping [...] Prolonged unemployment and persistent inflation can become powerful factors of social disintegration.' 'Atlantic Alliance and Recession'.

18 'No one among the leaders of the parties that now oppose the incumbent socialist regimes believes that the structure of the welfare state can be dismantled and the profound changes wrought by social democracy undone.' Strausz-Hupe, 'NATO in Midstream'.

19 'NATO devotes so much attention and effort to disarmament at a time when the Warsaw Pact is building up its military potential.' W. Paubsch, 'Security and Arms Control: A View from NATO', *NR*, 24: 1 (1976); 'Soviet theatre nuclear forces have been built up.' '25th Annual Assembly of ATA Told of Theatre Nuclear Force Modernization Needs', *NR*, 27: 6 (1979).

West.[20] It was believed that this combination of factors might make it possible for the Soviet Union to fulfil its ultimate objective of dismantling the NATO alliance and separating Europe from America.[21]

The Soviet Union was ready to dismantle the military organisations of both the Warsaw Pact and NATO,[22] which was precisely NATO's fear. Without NATO, the United States would be isolated from Europe and the Soviet Union would be able to fulfil its objective of an all-European security system, in which it would be the dominant player. In the first few years following the signing of the Helsinki Final Act, the Soviet Union expressed confidence that socialism was being built in Eastern Europe[23] and maintained a consistent policy that the military organisations of the two blocs should be dismantled. By 1977, however, the Soviet Union was becoming increasingly concerned that the Eastern foundations, as well as the framework of détente, were being undermined by the West.

One source of concern was the development of momentum in the United States to restore the deteriorating foundations of deterrence.[24] The restoration process was initiated by, among others, the CPD. The CPD argued that CIA estimates, which had provided the basis for arms control agreements between the two superpowers, had failed to account accurately for the build-up of Soviet forces at a time when Western defences were being dismantled.[25] In order to undertake the restoration, the United States had to build a fresh domestic consensus about the need to diminish the danger. The old consensus had

20 'Even if we leave aside this infiltration into the establishments of allied countries, the creeping enemy of subversion, whether directly Communist inspired or merely battening on a troubled situation, can easily sap our best military defences and undermine the political will of governments by inducing an attitude of mind where the Soviet threat is discounted and defence expenditure is cut, and cut again.' E. Peck, 'The Five Fronts of NATO', *NR*, 24: 3 (1976).

21 'The principal objective of the Soviet Union's European policies has been the dismantlement of the Atlantic Alliance.' Strausz-Hupe, 'NATO in Midstream'.

22 'The conference participants also reaffirm their readiness to dissolve the Warsaw Treaty Organisation, simultaneously with the dissolution of NATO and, as a first step, to dismantle their military organisations.' 'Warsaw Pact Leaders Meet in Moscow', *CDSP*, 30: 47 (1978).

23 'A developed socialist society has been built in the USSR.' 'Pravda Hits West's Defense of Dissidents', *CDSP*, 29: 6 (1977); 'Now a developed, mature socialist society has been built in the Soviet Union.' 'Brezhnev's Speech on Draft Constitution', *CDSP*, 29: 23 (1977).

24 '[The US] strategic deterrent ... is deteriorating due to aging and technological obsolescence.' 'Peace with Freedom', in Tyroler (1984); '[US] nuclear superiority has eroded.' 'Is America Becoming Number 2?', in Tyroler (1984); '[The US] must restore an allied defence posture capable of deterrence at each significant level.' 'Common Sense and the Common Danger' and 'Does the Official Case for the SALT II Treaty Hold Up Under Analysis?', in Tyroler (1984).

25 'Introduction', in Tyroler (1984: xv).

disintegrated in the aftermath of the Vietnam débâcle and the Watergate affair.[26] A new consensus would provide the backbone of the political will to restore the strength and coherence of US foreign policy.[27] Restoration was essential given the erosion of US nuclear superiority. In the absence of these steps, US alliances could also erode.[28]

Rather than a justified response to an unparalleled build-up, the Soviets viewed the Western restoration as an attempt to re-establish military superiority. The myth of a Soviet military threat was once again being mobilised in order to undermine an agreement on the limitation of strategic offensive arms, and the SALT II agreement in particular.[29] The CPD believed that the agreement should be amended; from the Soviet position such an amendment would undermine the principle of equality and equal security.

A second force undermining the Soviet foundation was internal.[30] Charter 77, whose activities were said to be orchestrated by the United States,[31] had exposed and publicised Czech violations of the human rights provisions of the Helsinki Final Act, which the Eastern bloc states had signed. A committee of the Warsaw Pact argued that Charter 77's acts represented interference in their internal affairs.[32] At the Belgrade review the West claimed that the dissidents were being persecuted. The Soviets responded with a charge that the Final Act's meaning was being distorted, which could

---

26 'The United States must build a fresh consensus to expand the opportunities and diminish the danger of a world in flux.' 'Common Sense' and 'Is America Becoming Number 2?', in Tyroler (1984).

27 'Political will is needed to restore the strength and coherence of [US] foreign policy.' 'Common Sense' and 'Peace with Freedom', in Tyroler (1984).

28 'Our alliances could erode.' 'Peace with Freedom', in Tyroler (1984).

29 '[The opponents of SALT] would like to "adjust" the agreement that is being drafted in such a way as to undermine the basic principle of equality and equal security for the two sides.' 'U.S. Blamed for Stalled Arms Talks', *CDSP*, 30: 6 (1978); '"Amendments" [to the SALT II agreement] would undermine the principle of equality and equal security.' 'SALT II: A Soviet Historical Perspective', *CDSP*, 31: 29 (1979).

30 'Charges may be brought against individuals who engage in anti-Soviet propaganda and agitation aimed at undermining or weakening the social and political system established in our country.' 'Pravda Hits West's Defense'; '[Dissidents] were guided by ... an aspiration to undermine the foundations of Soviet power.' 'Jewish Doctor Links Dissidents to CIA', *CDSP*, 29: 9 (1977).

31 'Newspapers, magazines, radio and television in many Western countries have raised an unprecedented furor over the so-called Charter 77, an anti-socialist lampoon fabricated by a group of right-wing counterrevolutionary figures [...] There can be no doubt that the synchronized nature of the articles in the Western press is a clear sign of a single conductor's baton.' 'Pravda Hits West's Defense'.

32 'Interference in the internal affairs of sovereign states is at variance with ... the explicit commitment made by states in ... the Helsinki Final Act to respect ... the right to establish their own laws and administrative regulations.' 'Warsaw Pact Leaders Meet in Moscow'.

only undermine efforts to strengthen European security and cooperation.[33]

The maintenance of the two structures in East and West, as well as the CPD's proposals for a Western restoration, relied on a logic of military power. The power of the dissident was of a different kind. Vaclav Havel, one of the spokespersons for Charter 77, argued that non-conformity was impossible within the politically ossified official structures of the Eastern bloc. Subsequently, the dissident became a subcitizen 'outside' the power establishment. The glue of this metaphysical order, which guaranteed the inner coherence of the power structure, was based on 'living a lie'. Living a lie meant that the population accepted appearance as reality; they accepted the given rules of the game. Without this glue, Havel argued, the structure would vanish, disintegrating into individual atoms. Ideology was an increasingly important component of this power; it was the pillar that provided it with both legitimacy and inner coherence. By breaking the rules, the dissident disrupted the game (Havel *et al.*, 1985: 40).

Charter 77 was silenced for the time being and many of its supporters were given lengthy prison terms. In the United States, the consensus desired by the CPD had, by 1979, failed to emerge. The Carter administration was attempting to counter the Committee, as well as the Coalition for Peace through Strength, with arguments that the collapse of the SALT process would make détente impossible. Despite this domestic division, NATO joined the restoration effort in December 1979, with its decision to deploy cruise and Pershing II missiles in five Western European countries. The Soviets saw this as a further step to undermine the foundations of peace in Europe, which signalled the collapse of détente.[34]

To summarise, during the first stage of the collapse, from roughly 1975 to 1977, NATO was concerned about internal disintegration due to economic crisis. There were problems maintaining deterrence in the face of a Soviet build-up, given weakening public support for defence spending during a time of relaxed tensions. In the United States, momentum was building to restore the deterrent. This debate threatened the future of SALT II, one of the pillars of détente. After 1977, the Soviet Union became obsessed with fears that its foundations were being undermined, both militarily and internally. In both East and West, signs of erosion or fears of

33 'The Belgrade Meeting Through Soviet Eyes', *CDSP*, 29: 42 (1977); 'All attempts at such interference in the internal affairs of sovereign states are actions aimed at undermining international cooperation.' 'Warsaw Pact Leaders Meet in Moscow'.

34 'The actions of [NATO's] bosses, who have set a course aimed at the further escalation of the race in nuclear missiles and conventional weapons ... are undermining the very foundations of peace in Europe, thereby assuming a heavy responsibility before the peoples.' 'NATO Decision on New Missiles Slammed', *CDSP*, 31: 50 (1979); 'We frequently hear voices in the West talking about [...] the near "collapse" of the effort to ease international tension.' 'Andropov: U.S. is Undermining Détente', *CDSP*, 32: 6 (1980).

undermining were attributed to the actions of the other bloc. Maintenance and undermining were two sides of the same coin. The former was an action undertaken by states; the latter was said to be orchestrated by 'other' states. Détente was a framework for breaking down barriers between the two sides, but it had also exacerbated the conflict. Western actors politicised arms control agreements, arguing that détente favoured the Soviet Union. Dissidents in the East challenged the distinction between the words and deeds of Eastern states, against the background of the human rights principles signed at Helsinki.

Stage Two: the collapse of détente

A number of events in 1979 inspired the conflicts that developed in Stage Two. NATO announced the double track decision. The Polish Pope, John Paul II visited Poland. The Soviets invaded Afghanistan. During the period that followed, roughly 1980 to 1984, the maintenance problems of Stage One were exacerbated, resulting in the collapse of détente. By looking inside the structures in East and West, a clearer picture of these developments as they relate to the détente framework emerges.

But first a brief step backwards. In 1976 the Workers' Defence Committee (Komitet Obrony Robotnikow; KOR) was formed in Poland. Like Charter 77, KOR was attempting to monitor Eastern compliance with the human rights provisions of the Helsinki Final Act. Also like Charter 77, KOR positioned itself outside the official structures of the party and the state. By offering 'solidarity with striking workers, with students holding a mass meeting, with protesting intellectuals', based on a strategy of 'social solidarity', KOR was undermining 'the acceptance of the government as the basic point of reference'.[35]

KOR provided the foundation for Solidarity, channelling public anger over a worsening economy into the construction of a movement. The development of Solidarity in 1980 was dramatic. The movement was initially successful in achieving an agreement with the government on the legal existence of the trade union. Sixteen months later, it was driven underground with the imposition of martial law. The progression of events has been examined in detail by others.[36] The goal here is to look briefly at the contesting games of the government and Solidarity based on a grammar of structure.

The two parties shared a language of restoration, dismantling and erosion. But the subject and object of these acts differed. The following is a good example of the relationship:

---

35 'A New Evolutionism', in Michnik (1985).
36 See, for instance, Ash (1983), Michnik (1985), Weschler (1982) and Zielonka (1989).

SOLIDARITY
Solidarity restores society
Solidarity dismantles totalitarianism
Eroding fear results in open resistance.[37]

THE GOVERNMENT
The Party restores order
Solidarity wants to dismantle socialism
Solidarity leaders are eroding the foundations of socialism.[38]

Solidarity was restoring a pluralist society in stages, and at the same time was, very slowly, dismantling totalitarianism. The government, on the other hand, applied a different name to the object of Solidarity's actions: it was not totalitarianism but socialism that Solidarity wanted to dismantle. The government and the democratic movement were at loggerheads, but Solidarity would only fight with peaceful means; the possibility of partnership would depend on the degree to which the government followed this rule. However, the restoration of civil society did contribute to the disintegration of government authority. Party attempts to restore order did not initially succeed.

The government identified both external and internal sources of the erosion of its power. Solidarity was one source of erosion. The working people, who were the foundations of socialism, were increasingly shifting allegiance away from official parties towards the trade union movement.[39] By the time martial law was imposed at the end of 1981, the 'enemies of socialism' were said to be shaking the foundations of the party and

37 'The essence of [Solidarity] lay in the restoration of social ties, self organization ... For the first time in the history of communist rule in Poland "civil society" was being restored and it was reaching a compromise with the state.' 'A Year Has Passed, August 1981', in Michnik (1985). '[Solidarity] gradually dismantles totalitarianism [...] Erosion of the threshold of fear has resulted in increasingly open expression of the growing general aversion to the government.' J. Kuron, 'Not to Lure the Wolves Out of the Woods', *Telos*, 47 (1981).
38 'There is no more urgent ... duty than leading the country out of its difficult situation, and restoring the normal rhythm of work and public life.' 'Strikes in Poland: The Soviet Coverage', *CDSP*, 32: 33 (1980); '[Enemies of socialism] want to dismantle, and as a result undermine and overthrow, Poland's socialist statehood.' 'Kania Warns Against Political Strikes', *CDSP*, 32: 49 (1980); 'Some Solidarity leaders ... are holding "warning strikes" and conducting other actions with a view to putting pressure on the authorities and eroding the foundations of the existing system.' 'Polish Leaders Begin to Assail Solidarity', *CDSP*, 33: 3 (1981).
39 In March 1981, Solidarity had 9.5 million members of about 12.5 million employees who were theoretically eligible. According to official figures, the Party lost 216,000 members between October 1980 and March 1981, bringing its total membership below 3 million. See Ash (1983: 155, 170).

destroying the foundations of peace in Europe.[40] Solidarity's activities were presented as characteristic of Western interference in the internal affairs of socialist states, and therefore a violation of the Helsinki Accords. From the Western position, repression in Poland had eroded the political foundation for progress on the East–West agenda.[41]

While martial law apparently destroyed Solidarity and restored the functioning of totalitarian institutions, illegal newspapers began to reappear and the process of reconstructing independent institutions continued.[42] The post-martial law strategy of Solidarity hoped for the 'slow disintegration of the system, together with progressive changes that may allow society to regain some influence over its destiny'.[43] It was predicted that a new rivalry would emerge between the military apparatus and the Party under conditions of martial law, and with it contradictions which would eventually result in a collapse of the structure.[44] In the meantime, underground Solidarity continued with its efforts to restore civil society, creating a basis for Polish democracy.

In the West, as the 1980s began, NATO was concerned about the eroding credibility of its deterrent and began a restoration effort with the decision to deploy cruise and Pershing II missiles in five European countries.[45]

---

40 'In the party itself there are unhealthy phenomena that are shaking its ideological foundations.' 'Poland: Solidarity's "Guidelines" Slammed', *CDSP*, 33: 20 (1981). 'Poland to get Economic Aid', *CDSP*, 32: 37 (1980); 'The process of the destruction of the postwar alignment of forces in Europe, and thus on a world scale, was supposed to have begun on Polish soil. Those who sought to bring about destabilization and attain a one-sided advantage put their stakes on destroying the foundations of peace in Europe, which is the Yalta and the Potsdam agreements.' 'Jaruzelski Reviews, Justifies Martial Law', *CDSP*, 34: 4 (1982).

41 '[Martial law] threatens to destroy the basis for reconciliation [...] The persistence of repression in Poland is eroding the political foundation for progress on the full agenda of issues which divide East and West.' 'Declaration on Events in Poland', *NR*, 30: 1 (1982).

42 Michnik (1985), 'The Polish War'. Also, 'It is widespread underground activity that will reconstruct society, spreading throughout towns and villages, factories and research institutions, universities and high schools.' Michnik (1985), 'On Resistance'.

43 W. Kulerski, 'The Third Possibility, Solidarity Debates Strategy', *LFEE*, 5: 3–4 (1982).

44 Z. Kowalewski, 'War of Position and War of Movement: On the Strategy of Solidarity', *LFEE*, 5: 3–4 (1982).

45 'Eroding NATO capability has prompted serious concern.' S. R. Hanmer, Jr, 'NATO's Long-Range Theatre Nuclear Forces: Modernization in Parallel with Arms Control', *NR*, 28: 1 (1980); 'Soviet defences have eroded our current advantage.' J. Nott, 'Decision to Modernise UK's Nuclear Contribution to NATO Strengthens Deterrence', *NR*, 29: 2 (1981); 'Western nations will ... do what is necessary to restore and maintain balance.' B. Goetze, 'Security through Arms Control: A New Realism for the 1980s', *NR*, 29: 2 (1981); '[NATO] has some years to go before restoring our LRTNF [Long-range theatre nuclear forces] deterrent.' B. Rogers, 'Increasing Threats to NATO's Security Call for Sustained Response', *NR*, 29: 3 (1981).

NATO's modernisation decision of 1979 has to be situated in the context of the revised American strategic posture, which had become known as the 'countervailing strategy'. The review of the requirements of a continued credible deterrent culminated with Presidential Directive 59 in September 1980, while Carter was still in office. The object of this directive was to increase the flexibility of American strategic forces by increasing the range of targeting options available, thereby reinforcing the credibility of extended deterrence. American policymakers had recognised that a posture of assured destruction alone was an inadequate basis for the American strategic commitment to Europe. In the face of an eroding deterrent, the Soviet build-up would emasculate deterrence based on mutually assured destruction (MAD).[46] The modernisation decision consisted of two tracks: deployments would only be necessary if a negotiated solution restoring the European balance could not be reached with the Soviet Union.

In the aftermath of the 1979 decision a mass peace movement emerged in Western Europe, particularly in the five NATO countries slated for the deployment of American cruise and Pershing II missiles. While stopping the deployments was the central goal of the movements, a rejection of deterrence lay at the basis of many of their proposals. NATO was moving away from MAD in favour of a countervailing strategy. Sections of the peace movement rejected MAD based on arguments that peace could only be built on trust.[47] In contrast to NATO arguments that nuclear deterrence preserves peace by preventing war, many were raising questions about whether the arms race was contributing to security or undermining it, given the increasing destructive power of nuclear weapons and movement towards a first strike capability.[48] While East and West accused one another of undermining activities, the peace movement argued that the arms race

46 'A posture of assured destruction alone is an inadequate basis for the American strategic commitment to Europe.' P. Buteux, 'Theatre Nuclear Forces: Modernization Plan and Arms Control Initiative', *NR*, 28: 6 (1980); 'The Soviets would have emasculated deterrence, which is based on MAD.' Goetze, 'Security through Arms Control'.

47 'The only possible route ... lies in the building of trust through gradual but *genuine* arms reduction.' R. Hinde and J. Hinde, 'The Case Against Deterrence', *END Bulletin*, 5 (1981); 'It is impossible to build security on weapons today.' Nej til Atomvaben, Denmark, 'Nuclear Free Europe', preparatory paper for the II Athens Conference for a Nuclear Free Europe, 10 August 1984', IKV Archives, no. 508, ISG, Amsterdam.

48 'For more than 30 years we have witnessed a continued growth in the arms race. Today we see an increase not only in the number but also in the killing capacity of modern weapons ... Nobody would question the right of nations and people to legitimate security ... But the question that should be asked is whether the arms race contributes to such security or undermines it.' 'Declaration of Pax Christi International on Disarmament and Security, June 1981', IKV Archives, no. 501, ISG, Amsterdam.

was undermining security and needed to be replaced by a political solution based on the construction of trust between East and West. The Western European movements were demanding small unilateral steps by either side to set a process of disarmament in motion. The challenge was addressed to both superpowers.[49] As stated in the 1980 END Appeal: 'The forces of both the North Atlantic and Warsaw Alliance have each had sufficient nuclear weapons to annihilate their opponents, and at the same time to endanger the very basis of civilised life.'[50] Civilised life, and not the military foundation of one side or the other, was to be the point of departure. The military foundation had contributed to a different sort of erosion in the West, an erosion of democratic systems.[51] The peace movement set out to build a new power base within Western European societies and, similar to Charter 77 and Solidarity, their energies were focused outside established political institutions. The Church was at the centre of these efforts. The construction did not take place exclusively in Western Europe. By 1982 and 1983 it had reached across the Atlantic, building links with the American nuclear weapons freeze campaign,[52] and to independent initiatives in Eastern Europe as well.

In 1981 a member of the CPD, Ronald Reagan, was elected President of the United States, and many members of the Committee came to occupy positions within the new administration. Reagan's goal, like the CPD's, was to restore the balance and American military might. He also wanted to restore the American economy by scaling back government bureaucracy. The two restoration efforts were connected.[53] In order to restore the

49 'A programme for a transcontinental peace movement can't be based on the perceptions and proposals of one-side only.' E. P. Thompson, 'Healing the Wound', *END Journal*, 1 (1982–83).

50 The END Appeal for a nuclear free zone in Europe was launched on 28 April 1980 in five European capitals of the deployment countries: and was initially signed by a wide range of prominent political, academic and scientific figures in East and West. 'A Nuclear Free Europe, END Appeal', *END Bulletin*, 11 (1982).

51 'In the West, the policy of nuclear deterrence has led to a gradual erosion of our democratic system of government.' Hinde and Hinde, 'The Case Against Deterrence'; 'Either democracy will destroy nuclear weapons, or nuclear weapons will destroy democracy.' M. J. Faber, 'We Have Challenged Faith in Nuclear Deterrence', *END Journal*, 6 (1983).

52 Unlike many of the Western European movements, the American Freeze Campaign did not reject nuclear deterrence. The hope, against the background of political momentum in the US for a first strike capability, was to freeze a situation of MAD as a first step, to be followed by mutual reductions.

53 'We have proposed a defence programme in the United States for the next five years which will remedy the neglect of the past decade and restore the eroding balance on which our security depends.' R. Reagan, 'U.S. Foreign Affairs Policy: Arms Reduction', *VSD*, 48: 4 (1981); 'By restoring America's military credibility ... we have strengthened our country's position as a force for peace and progress in the world.' R. Reagan, 'State of the Union 1982', *VSD*, 48: 9 (1982); 'Control over structures will restore growth in U.S. productivity [...] The program for economic recovery is not only designed to solve internal problems,

international balance, and America's position in the world, defence spending had to increase. A system antiquated through years of neglect had to be rebuilt, which would only be possible if the economy was restored. American alliances could not be restored without restoring confidence in the American economy.

The restoration effort was accompanied by rhetoric that the Soviet Union was an 'evil empire' and loose talk about the possibility of a limited nuclear war in Europe. Both exacerbated Eastern fears that the Soviet Union and détente were being undermined by those who wanted a return to the Cold War. It also fanned the flames of public opposition to the nuclear arms race. From the perspective of NATO and the US administration, the 'unilateralist' peace movement was now undermining and eroding Western foundations.[54] The Soviet Union, it was argued, would use these movements to its own advantage. Three fractures in the Western structure became evident. First, there was a split between what NATO referred to as the 'unilateralists', who argued that Europe would be safer without nuclear weapons, and NATO representatives, including President Reagan, who argued that, based on past experience, unilateral restraint would only encourage the aggressor. Second, NATO was increasingly split by the conflict between demands expressed in public opinion and the rhetoric of President Reagan.[55] Finally, the fear of nuclear war was attributed to a change of consciousness that was part of a psychological war waged by the Soviet Union against the West, aimed at undermining its will to preserve its way of life.[56]

Parallels to the Polish example are interesting. In both cases, domestic problems were attributed to a psychological war manipulated by the other side.[57]

however, but is viewed as part of an essential effort to restore the confidence of friends and allies.' R. Reagan, 'Address before a Joint Session of the Canadian Parliament, 11 March 1981', *DSB* (April 1981).

54 'By unilaterally abandoning our nuclear deterrent ... we might further contribute to the disintegration of the alliance ... which has been the basis for our security for the last four decades.' R. P. Bär, 'Views of Church Groups in the Netherlands on War and Peace', *NR*, 30: 1 (1982); 'Unilateral disarmament would ... undermine the basis of the alliance.' R. Dean, 'The Alliance and Nuclear Weapons', *NR*, 30: 6 (1983).

55 '[Public attitudes] can only undermine Atlantic cohesion and foster anti-Americanism.' G. Vaerno, 'A Public Opinion Strategy', *NR*, 31: 3/4 (1983); 'Breakdown of consensus has occurred in Alliance countries over the past few years ... Such a breakdown increases the potential difficulties of maintaining popular support for Alliance policies.' G. Flynn, 'Public Opinion and Atlantic Defense', *NR*, 31: 5 (1983).

56 'Psychological war, which has been waged by the Soviet Union against the West, ... is aimed at undermining the West's will to preserve its way of life.' W. Hofmann, 'Is NATO's Defense Policy Facing a Crisis?', *NR*, 32: 4 (1984).

57 'Psychological warfare centres in the West are helping the counterrevolutionary forces in Poland to stir up antisocial sentiments, destablise the situation and undermine the socialist system.' 'Poland: "Antisocialists" in Solidarity Scored', *CDSP*, 33: 17 (1981).

In both cases, a distinction was made between the legitimate concerns of a broader public and attempts by the other side to manipulate that public. The public demands focused on the foundation of each bloc. In the East, the worker was at the heart of the battle; in the West, deterrence. In both contexts, erosion at the basis became a source of division within established structures.

In April 1983, the year the deployments began in Western Europe, and five months after Nuclear Weapons Freeze proposals were passed in referenda in forty-four locations in the United States, Reagan announced the SDI. SDI was based on a rejection of deterrence and the possibility of building more peaceful relations with the Soviet Union. Reagan asked: 'What if free people could live secure in the knowledge that their security did not rest upon a threat of instant U.S. retaliation?' He proposed a technological answer to what was, in his words, a spiritual dilemma: 'I have become more and more deeply convinced that the human spirit must be capable of rising above dealing with other nations and human beings by threatening their existence.' Reagan presented a future where security would not rest on deterrence, but said, in the meantime, that the US had to remain constant in preserving and maintaining the Western foundation.[58]

The cruise and Pershing II deployments went ahead and Reagan was re-elected by a landslide, but the alliance was threatened with continued erosion. The concern in 1980 and 1981 about erosion due to Soviet actions was largely replaced by concern about the erosion of public support for deterrence.[59] The conflict was qualitatively different from past conflicts within the alliance – it was not merely a routine quarrel between states within NATO; rather, the post-war framework of debate over defence was crumbling.[60] The cruise missile deployments were underway, but the consensus that had previously underpinned alliance policy had all but collapsed. In light of these new threats, the maintenance efforts of NATO were increasingly geared to the maintenance of public support and adherence to the 1979 decision by governments.[61]

Part of the Western European peace movement, like NATO, had a two-

58 R. Reagan, 'Peace and National Security: A New Defense', *VSD*, 49: 13 (1983).
59 'Excessive rhetoric on the immediacy and seriousness of the Soviet threat has eroded NATO's self confidence and shaken public support.' T. Hitchens, 'NATO Parliamentarians Call for Increased Information Effort', *NR*, 30: 6 (1983); 'Public confidence in their elected leaders is eroded.' Vaerno, 'A Public Opinion Strategy'.
60 'We are witnessing a crisis of political elites that is both the cause and the result of the crumbling framework within which political battles were fought for most of the post-war period.' Flynn, 'Public Opinion'.
61 'The assembly urges member governments to maintain adherence to the 1979 decision.' Hitchens, 'NATO Parliamentarians'; 'A credible commitment to arms control and reducing the role of nuclear weapons ... would contribute to maintaining existing support [...] providing reassurance will be a precondition for maintaining the popular consensus.' Flynn, 'Public Opinion'.

pronged strategy. As deployments began, they shifted attention to the other part of this strategy. Before 1983 persuading national governments to refuse deployments had been the priority. The other objective, articulated in the END appeal of 1980, began with a renaming of the two mutually sustaining structures of the Cold War. It was not one side or the other that was maintained by the practices of the superpowers, but the Cold War itself. The objective was to break down the barriers dividing East and West.[62] While the central actions of the two superpowers, restoring, maintaining and undermining, were acts undertaken primarily with military tools, the dismantling actions of independent movements were directed more to the ideological structures of the Cold War.

END would dismantle the structure by beginning a dialogue with independent counterparts in Eastern Europe.[63] The significance of this act and the threat it posed to the structure have to be placed in context. First, the superpower relationship had deteriorated. Détente had collapsed. Second, within the Cold War, movements on the two sides were by definition at cross-purposes with each other; Western authorities saw the population as prey to a psychological war on the part of the Soviets relating to issues of peace; Charter 77 and Solidarity, according to the Soviet Union, were stimulated by a psychological war on the part of the West. The United States cheered on the latter; the Soviet Union the former. There was a direct relationship between the maintaining and the undermining efforts of each bloc. The dismantling effect of this dialogue can be understood within the framework of Vaclav Havel's argument that the dissident's act of breaking the rules disrupts the game itself; exposes it as a game, as convention, rather than permanent necessity.

The reaction of the Soviet authorities to the dialogue is interesting. In a written exchange between a spokesperson from END and the President of the official Soviet peace council, Yuri Zhukov, the latter claimed that END's concept of equal responsibility for the Cold War was undermining the anti-war movement.[64] Equal responsibility refers to the charge that both the

---

62 '[The new peace movements, East and West] have set themselves an astonishing objective: to break down, not in some distant future, but in the next ten years ... the Cold War itself.' E. P. Thompson, 'The "Normalisation" of Europe', *Praxis International*, 3: 1 (1983); '[END's objective] is to begin to break down the unnatural barriers which divide our continent and to prepare the way for ending the bloc system.' M. Beresford, 'An Open Letter to the Soviet Peace Committee, January 1983', *New Statesman* (21 January 1983).

63 Solidarity was, at best, a reluctant partner in this dialogue. See Zielonka (1989: 178) and Ash (1983: 332–3).

64 'We are firmly convinced that [the concept of "equal responsibility"] is aimed at ... undermining of the anti-war movement and is called upon to conceal and justify an aggressive militarist policy of the USA and NATO.' Yuri Zhukov, 'Letter to Peace Campaigners in the West, 2 December 1982', IKV Archives, no. 335, ISG, Amsterdam.

United States and Soviet Union had perpetuated the arms race. In the view of the Soviets, the concept was 'called upon to conceal and justify the aggressive military policy of the USA and NATO'. Zhukov suggests that END was promoting the policy of Reagan.[65]

END was undermining the anti-war movement by substituting the real mass movement of peace champions in the socialist countries with 'certain individuals passed off as allies who are active not in the struggle for détente and disarmament but in undermining the socialist system'. The attempt to develop a dialogue between Western peace movements – whose disarmament demands had been cheered on by the Soviet Union – and independent initiatives in the Eastern bloc, created a blurring of the distinction between friend and enemy.

Stage Three: collapsing images

In Stage One there was a clear relationship between the maintaining and undermining activities of each superpower. In Stage Two, with the collapse of détente, the relationship between the two superpowers deteriorated further due to domestic struggles originating outside established structures. While these struggles were presented in the framework of a psychological war by the other, the origin of the movements in sectors of the population identified with the fundamental values of the two sides, that is, the working class in Poland and the Church in the West, made the task of maintenance increasingly difficult. The boundaries between friend and enemy began to erode as citizens' initiatives in both blocs engaged in dialogue for the purpose of constructing a democratic and peaceful Europe. In Stage Three, the erosion continued. The actions characteristic of state players also began to shift.

During this stage, independent initiatives in East and West were engaged in the common activity of dismantling the Cold War itself. The point of departure for their actions was provided by the framework of détente, which had all but collapsed. One goal of the dialogue was to restore the Helsinki Final Act to its original meaning.[66] Although Helsinki had been interpreted as cementing the status quo and the Cold War division,[67] it also

---

65 The secret Stasi archives in the former East Germany made similar accusations that elements of the Western movements were engaged in destabilising anti-socialist activities. See 'Was Erich Mielke mit dem KGB-Chef streng geheim aushandelt?', *Frankfurter Rundschau* (1 February 1992), p. 10.

66 'The time has come ... to restore the Helsinki Agreements to their original meaning.' Charter 77 Document no. 13/84, *Palach Press Bulletin* (*PPB*), 25 (1984).

67 '"Peace" does not just concern weapons; nor must the necessary Detente be allowed to cement the division of Europe.' 'Letter from the Danish Peace Movement to Charter 77, 25 March 1986', *PPB*, 27 (1986); '[The Helsinki Accords] do not in letter or spirit cement the

contained possibilities for breaking up the bipolar structures. Helsinki did not cement the division of Europe, the movements argued, but rather opened the door for change towards a pluralistic Europe.[68] This would involve building a civil society that transcended national frontiers while dismantling the Cold War.[69]

As movements began to dismantle the structure of the Cold War, the military discussion shifted to SDI. In 1985 and 1986, NATO, the peace movements and the Soviet Union were all concerned that SDI was undermining arms control.[70] The Soviet Union had been worried for some time that ballistic missile defences would destroy the foundation for a normal relationship between the two, a foundation going back to the agreements of the early 1970s.[71] In early 1985, the Soviet Union began to talk of restoring the balance through reciprocal actions.[72] Reagan, on the other hand, became increasingly concerned that his plans were being undermined by domestic critics and particularly those who held the purse strings in Congress.[73]

bipolar structure of the power blocs.' *Giving Real Life to the Helsinki Accords: A Memorandum, November 1986*, (Berlin: European Network for East–West Dialogue, 1987); 'Helsinki contained the possibility of breaking up the bipolar structure of international relations.' D. Esche and C. Semler, 'Why we Should Not Dismiss Helsinki', *END Journal*, 26 (1987).

68 '[The Helsinki Accords] leave the door open for peaceful and gradual change towards a pluralistic Europe which can overcome the bloc structure.' *Giving Real Life to the Helsinki Accords*.

69 'Through our actions the Peace Movement is dismantling the ideologies and structures of the Cold War.' M. Kaldor and M. J. Faber, 'A Model for Détente', Pax Christi Netherlands Archives DB/87/142; 'A Europe which actually dismantled the structures of the Cold War ... could begin to play a really progressive global role.' M. Kaldor, 'A New Europe', *END Journal*, 30 (1987); 'Trans-frontier solidarity ... and cooperation between people and groups ... are an essential contribution to our common efforts to build a new peaceful and democratic Europe.' *Giving Real Life to the Helsinki Accords*.

70 'The resolution called on the US Government to refrain from taking any unilateral actions which would undermine the ABM Treaty.' R. L. Grant, 'NATO MPs Urge Improvement in Conventional Force Capabilities', *NR*, 33: 1 (1985); 'SDI would undermine the premises on which arms control has been conducted.' 'Reagan's Crazy Star War Plans', *END Journal*, 15 (1985); '["Star Wars" would undermine] the very process of arms limitation and reduction.' V. V. Shcherbitsky, 'Space Weapons Would Nullify All Arms Control Gains', *CDSP*, 37: 10 (1985).

71 'If the [ABM Treaty] lost its force ... the foundation on which talks are based would disappear.' 'Akhromeyev to U.S.: Leave ABM Peace Alone', *CDSP*, 37: 22 (1985).

72 '[The Soviet Union] will be forced to ensure the restoration of the strategic balance and to build up its strategic offensive forces.' 'Akhromeyev: Leave ABM Pact Alone'.

73 'This is the worst time to undermine vital defense programs and take away needed negotiating leverage.' R. Reagan, 'SDI: Promise and Progress', *Current Policy* (*CP*), 858 (1986); 'Each House action undermines our peace and security.' R. Reagan, 'Keep America Strong', *CP*, 869 (1986).

Reagan's SDI created new divisions in the alliance at a time when it had not yet recovered from the domestic battles over the cruise and Pershing II missiles. The NATO house was still suffering from an erosion in its consensus;[74] much of the unilateralist and anti-nuclear programmes of the peace movements had been institutionalised in the programmes of opposition parties to the Left, which was a 'serious blow to NATO'.[75] The alliance was threatened with erosion as the distance between the United States and Europe increased (in part because of SDI).[76] This erosion and deep cracks in the structure were recognised by the Soviet Union.[77] In addition, the image of the Soviet Union as a threat had begun to disappear, which was a further blow to NATO cohesion. As one author stated, 'Without a common perception every NATO activity is undermined'.[78] The common perception of a Soviet threat was fading among the Western public – a trend that Gorbachev encouraged – and, for many, the United States posed an equal threat. Gorbachev was undermining enemy images by taking unilateral steps, such as the eighteen month moratorium on nuclear weapons tests, and shattering old views about nuclear deterrence and balance of power politics.[79] In addition to the double burden of maintaining a deterrent and public consensus, NATO also increasingly had to be attentive to maintaining its image.[80] Further confusion emerged within the

74 'There is wide agreement that there has been an erosion in the consensus of member states.' E. H. van der Beugel, 'The Atlantic Family – Managing its Problems', *NR*, 34: 1 (1986); 'A poorly informed public debate may eventually erode the credibility of NATO's deterrence.' P. Corterier, 'The ATA and a New Approach to NATO Information', *NR*, 34: 2 (1986).

75 J. Dean, 'Can NATO Survive (Relative) Success?', *NR*, 34: 6 (1986).

76 'The issue is whether the process of distancing between United States and Europe will erode the power and authority of the Alliance.' Dean, 'Can NATO Survive?'.

77 'The Atlanticists' control has eroded.' 'Soviet Diplomacy Turns to Europe', *CDSP*, 38: 29 (1986); 'The current session of the NATO Council also testifies to deep cracks in "Atlantic solidarity" that can barely be concealed by facile final documents.' 'U.S. Refusal to Observe SALT II Hit', *CDSP*, 38: 22 (1986).

78 Beugel, 'The Atlantic Family'.

79 'When old views are shattered, resistance on the part of those whose political and material well being is linked to those views is bound to grow.' 'Gorbachev–Reagan Summit Meeting – III', *CDSP*, 39: 51 (1987); '[New thinking] undermines the "image of the enemy", and hence the ideological foundations of anti-Soviet and imperialist policy. That which so faithfully served reactionaries in past decades is collapsing.' 'Gorbachev Defends Restructuring to Party', *CDSP*, 40: 7 (1987); 'Progress in undermining enemy images has already been achieved by Gorbachev.' J. Steele, 'Loosening Superpower Bonds', *END Journal*, 32 (1988).

80 Preserving the perception [of our publics' determination to defend itself] becomes difficult when debate is marred by propagation of half truths, misconceptions and propaganda.' Corterier, 'The ATA'; 'A third problem concerns the seemingly exclusive preoccupation of NATO with military matters and arms control. The reality is of course different but the

alliance with the unexpected outcome of the Reykjavik Summit between Reagan and Gorbachev. As Karl Kaiser stated during an address at NATO headquarters in Brussels:

> No U.S.–Soviet summit has ever unleashed such an animated, confused and at the same time potentially momentous debate on the future of NATO strategy as the meeting between Reagan and Gorbachev in Reykjavik. Both leaders discussed disarmament and arms control solutions of radical and sweeping scope unprecedented in post-war East–West negotiation and yet failed to reach any agreement. In the aftermath, the public and intergovern-mental debate in the West treats the *theoretical* solutions of Reykjavik as if they were political *reality*. Depending on existing preferences, they are either depicted as an assault on the foundation of the post-war strategy of both Pacts, as a potentially disastrous blow to Western security, or as the greatest advance toward disarmament and progress ever seriously considered by world leaders.[81]

As the security consensus crumbled, Gorbachev made a move to rename the future contours of the European security structure by proposing to construct a European house, including both East and West, which was closely related to the restructuring of the domestic and foreign policies of the Soviet Union.[82] As discussed in Chapter Two, the Common House was a source of concern in the West because of the different meanings attached to 'house' or '*dom*'. The Soviet notion of a home is a structure with many entrances. This is consistent with Gorbachev's emphasis on pluralism and the idea that the rooms need not all be based on a Western model. But it is also consistent with the traditional stated goal of the Warsaw Pact: to dissolve and dismantle the blocs. Gorbachev reiterated this goal.[83] Pluralism, which was in the past associated with bourgeois thinking, was presented as a defence against the Western model.[84] Gorbachev wanted to

---

public image of NATO is of considerable importance [...] I plead for maximum efforts to restore in NATO – or at least in the image of NATO – the primacy of policy over what can appear to be the primacy of weaponry.' Beugel, 'The Atlantic Family'.

81 K. Kaiser, 'The NATO Strategy Debate after Reykjavik', *NR*, 34: 6 (1986).

82 'The all European house that we are building, a house in which everyone is equal, will not be safe or strong if deception, half truths and misinformation are mixed in the mortar that holds it together.' 'Shevardnadze Asks for Cooperation in Europe', *CDSP*, 38: 45 (1986); 'There is an opportunity to free our common European home from a large portion of the nuclear burden in a short time.' M. Gorbachev, 'USSR Asks Separate Euromissiles Pact', *CDSP*, 39: 9 (1987); 'The Soviet Union has sorted out the main thing, and that main thing is the basis of the policy of restructuring.' 'Gorbachev, Reagan Meet in Washington – I', *CDSP*, 39: 49 (1988); 'Success in restructuring is impossible without a foreign policy based on new thinking.' 'Gorbachev Defends Restructuring'.

83 M. Gorbachev, 'Gorbachev Suggests Wider Role for UN', *CDSP*, 39: 38 (1987); 'Gorbachev Addresses Council of Europe', *CDSP*, 41: 27 (1989).

84 'Pluralism vs. Proletarian Internationalism', *CDSP*, 39: 10 (1977).

restructure internally and to build a new structure internationally on the foundations of the CSCE. He planned to adapt socialism to a changing world. The old structure in the East could be preserved by making alterations.

NATO had since 1983 begun to emphasise a more European, as opposed to Atlantic, identity.[85] In 1984 attempts were made to breathe new life into the dormant West European Union and in 1985 Jacques Delors, Chair of the European Commission, launched a campaign for a new Europe free of borders. Two models of Europe were being discussed at this point in time: one building on Western institutions and the other, Gorbachev's house, emphasising a historical European culture that would transcend the East–West divide.

SDI was undermining arms control; the popular consensus which had underpinned NATO's deterrent in the post-World War II era was eroding; Reagan was concerned that Congress would undermine SDI; there existed blueprints for two different European structures. The peace offensive that emerged between the two superpowers must be understood against this background. Earlier in the narrative, the superpowers were doing the same things: maintaining and undermining. By 1986 they were both making moves in a different game belonging to the same grammar. Gorbachev was restructuring, an action that shares a family resemblance with restoring, but the building blocks were political rather than military. His peace offensive was launched against balance of power and deterrence thinking as a foundation of international relations. Reagan focused his offensive on breaking down the division of Europe, but the condition for this change was the technological and military solution of SDI. Both Reagan and Gorbachev, by this point, were breaking down the structure of the Cold War itself. Both leaders began to dismantle the foundations of traditional deterrence, emphasising the insecurity and fear upon which it was based.[86] Two different kinds of solution were offered: the technological solution of SDI and the political solution of Gorbachev.

The technological solution of SDI would create space for certain kinds of political action that had been unthinkable in the past, namely arms reduction and not only arms control. Reagan shifted attention away from

---

85 '[Europe] now needs to build a ... European security consciousness.' Lord Carrington, 'Lack of Consistent Political Strategy: A Cause of Friction', *NR*, 31: 2 (1983); 'The forthcoming difficult negotiations of Foreign and Finance Ministers ... are designed to review the building plans for Europe.' H. Kohl, 'Our Mandate: A Europe Strong and Able to Act', *VSD*, 49: 22 (1983).

86 'A lasting peace cannot be built on fear alone.' 'Gorbachev Proposes to US a Ban on Space Strike Arms', *CDSP*, 37: 40 (1985); 'Peace based on mutual fear cannot be true peace because staking our future on a precarious balance of terror is not good enough.' R. Reagan, 'Life and the Preservation of Freedom', *VSD*, 52: 3 (1985).

preserving deterrence to preserving human life.[87] Deterrence and human life became two alternative choices, rather than synonymous as in traditional NATO discourse. Reagan transformed deterrence, the stable foundation of the West, into a different kind of structure, a prison that had to be escaped.[88] Breaking down stereotypes and building coalitions for cooperation between East and West were complementary activities.[89] While there had been exchanges between the United States and Soviet Union for some time, Reagan wanted to launch a qualitatively new stage in the programme. In addition, in 1987 and 1988, he called on Gorbachev to tear down the wall separating East and West and to break down the artificial barriers between nations.[90]

Reagan, concerned about human rights, wanted to tear down the Berlin Wall and Gorbachev, focusing on disarmament, wanted to dissolve the two alliances. Neither was inconsistent with the past positions of their respective blocs. What had changed was the game within which these moves were embedded. The cross-beams which had kept the two separate parts of the Cold War structure standing side by side were shifting: Eastern advocates of human rights and Western advocates of peace, who had challenged the foundations of their respective blocs, were talking to one other and were doing so on the basis of principles agreed to by states within the framework of the Helsinki Final Act. That which was viewed as merely principle in 1975, given concerns about the possibilities for implementation, had become the backdrop for action. In this game, human rights and security, as well as a notion of détente characterised by cross-bloc citizen contacts, were no longer weapons in the superpower conflict, but a common frame of reference for actions aimed at dismantling the Cold War and building a democratic and peaceful Europe.

87 '[SDI] is not designed to kill people but to preserve human lives.' Reagan, 'Life and the Preservation of Freedom'.

88 'The United States seeks to escape the prison of mutual terror by research and testing [into SDI].' Reagan, 'Life and the Preservation of Freedom'; 'Nations could defend themselves against missile attack and mankind ... could escape the prison of nuclear terror.' R. Reagan, 'The Geneva Summit', *CP*, 766 (1985).

89 '[Exchanges] will help break down stereotypes, build friendships and provide an alternative to propaganda.' Reagan, 'Geneva Summit'; 'Exchanges can build in our societies thousands of coalitions for cooperation and peace.' R. Reagan, 'A Mission for Peace', *CP*, 765 (1985).

90 '[Reagan] urged ... Gorbachev to send a new signal of openness to the world by tearing down that wall.' R. Reagan, 'European Economic Summit Meeting', *VSD*, 53: 18 (1987); '[The US] challenged the Soviets to tear down the artificial barriers that isolate their citizens from the rest of the world.' R. Reagan, 'Reflections on U.S.–Soviet Relations', *DSB* (July 1988).

Stage Four: collapsing structures

By the beginning of 1989 change was in the air but an end to the division of Europe was not yet in sight, although there were hopes on both sides for a gradual effort to overcome the bloc division.[91] An infrastructure of cooperation was being constructed between East and West, in the form of treaties and accords both between the superpowers and within the Helsinki process. However, with the exception of Poland, where roundtable negotiations between Solidarity and the Communist Party had begun, and Hungary, the Eastern European communist parties, against the urgings of Gorbachev, were resisting change. As the Iron Curtain between Hungary and Austria was dismantled in September of 1989, thousands of East Germans made their way to the FRG via Austria.[92] Throughout the autumn the flow of East Germans to the West continued, as massive demonstrations developed, calling for the various East European communist regimes to be dismantled.[93]

As the Berlin Wall collapsed and remnants of the Iron Curtain were dismantled in November 1989, followed by the dismantling of the Warsaw Pact a little more than a year later, NATO was faced with the task of defining a new identity.[94] The collapse of the Eastern bloc also meant the dismantling of the Cold War structure within which NATO's *raison d'être*

91 'While the [Helsinki] process began and is still developing under the conditions of a Europe divided into military-political blocs and economic groupings, the construction of a common European home must lead gradually to the eradication of the division of the continent.' 'Common European Home Explained', *CDSP*, 41: 22 (1989); 'The chapter on *overcoming the division of Europe* is the heart and soul of the Declaration, a section that embodies the new hopes that attach to the momentous processes of change in the East.' H. Wegener, 'The Management of NATO's Anniversary Summit', *NR*, 37: 3 (1989).

92 'The flow of East German citizens, who have taken advantage of the dismantling of the Iron Curtain between Hungary and Austria to seek refuge in the FRG, has become a major political issue of the utmost importance to the future of inter-German relations.' T. Schreiber, 'The Soviet Union's European Allies: No Longer Satellites, Not Yet Partners', *NR*, 37: 5 (1989).

93 'President Gorbachev has so far not flinched from accepting the consequences of his policies: freedom of discussion and criticism in the Soviet Union, tolerance of nationalist dissidence, the dismantling of the regime of oppression within both the Soviet Union and its East European satellites ... and above all, the physical dismantling of the barriers preventing free intercourse between East and West.' M. Howard, 'Military Grammar and Political Logic: Can NATO Survive if the Cold War is Won?', *NR*, 37: 6 (1989); 'The incipient dismantling of the regime of the GDR and the opening of the border elicited obvious joy and were perceived as a clear signal of approaching "reunification".' 'Eyeing Eastern Europe's Historic Changes', *CDSP*, 41: 48 (1989).

94 'The collapse of the Wall has been presented as a triumph of America's policy of firmness and strength over many years.' 'Eyeing Eastern Europe's Historic Changes'.

had been defined.[95] In this sense, NATO had come full circle from the beginning point of this analysis in the mid 1970s. At that time, many were questioning the future need for the alliance in a context of relaxed tensions between East and West. NATO leaders wondered whether the alliance would survive in the absence of an enemy, but were clear that the organisation should not be dismantled.[96] Despite Soviet claims that both alliances should be dissolved, NATO argued that the Soviet Union remained a military power; therefore NATO had to remain intact.[97]

There was agreement about the need to build a European security structure, and a consensus that it should be based on the rule of law and human rights,[98] but the blueprint remained unclear. While Gorbachev continued to build support for a common European house,[99] NATO began to design a new European architecture.[100] The two general themes were distinguished, on the one hand, by a new structure encompassing all of Europe, and, on the other hand, the construction of additions on to the

95 'The entire framework within which we have for so long made our plans and conducted our policies is apparently disintegrating.' Howard, 'Military Grammar'; 'Social, economic and political structures that came into being as a direct result of World War II are breaking up.' 'Eyeing Eastern Europe's Historic Changes'.

96 'NATO is not being dismantled and for the time being it is useful for Moscow to keep the Warsaw Pact alive as a balancing factor.' R. McGeehan, 'The U.S. and NATO after the Cold War', *NR*, 38: 1 (1990).

97 'The secretary's vision cannot be faulted for lack of optimism, nor can any sensible observer want to disband the Atlantic Alliance regardless of whether the Warsaw Pact remains intact.' McGeehan, 'The U.S. and NATO'.

98 'Already in the preamble, the participating states "express their conviction that full respect for human rights and fundamental freedoms and the development of societies based on pluralistic democracy and the rule of law are prerequisites for progress in setting up the lasting order of peace, security, justice and cooperation that they seek to establish in Europe".' U. Ellemann-Jensen, 'The Copenhagen Meeting on the Human Dimension of the CSCE', *NR*, 38: 4 (1990); '"Our main goal," the Charter of Europe reads, "is to free Europe from the legacy of the past." Special emphasis was put on the observance of human rights and the principles of democracy and the supremacy of laws – the foundation on which the future Europe will be built.' 'The Paris Summit Ratifies the New Europe', *CDSP*, 42: 47 (1990).

99 'Participation in the construction of a "common European home" is a highly important area of our foreign-policy activities.' 'Gorbachev's Policy Speech to the Congress', *CDSP*, 41: 25 (1989).

100 'Secretary Baker, in an address in Berlin, outlined a blueprint for the "new era" in Europe. He called for creative arrangements and a new architecture to reflect developments in East Europe while retaining old foundations and structures which remain valuable, especially NATO.' McGeehan, 'The U.S. and NATO'; 'The often used concepts of European political architecture and European security architecture merge to provide a stable overall framework of peace in which military conflict becomes an increasingly unlikely hypothetical occurrence.' H. Wegener, 'The Transformed Alliance', *NR*, 38: 4 (1990).

Western framework.[101] Both the Common House and the architecture were meant to be multidimensional structures containing several different sections. Besides the greater connotation of intimacy suggested by the metaphor of a house, all the rooms in Gorbachev's home would be equal, although based on different societal models, of which socialism would be one.[102] By contrast, the proposed architecture would be designed on the basis of a Western model, with a Western European pillar at the centre.[103] The architecture would comprise a variety of interlocking institutions, drawing the former Eastern European satellites into dialogue and possibly future membership. The role of the Soviet Union in the architecture was ambiguous.[104]

The CSCE would provide the infrastructure of the common European home, while it would be a central, but not the defining, feature of NATO's architecture.[105] In 1990, the independent citizens' initiatives in both blocs institutionalised the cross-bloc dialogue, by creating a parallel citizen's parliament of the official CSCE process as a basis for developing a pan-European civil society. The blueprint for this parallel institution was formed in 1988 at a seminar in Prague, which was to be the eventual setting of the

101 'If [the heritage of Christianity and the Enlightenment] is to take its rightful place in the world, this heritage must now accommodate itself to a political structure, European Union, of which the Twelve of the EC constitute the solid foundation, and to a permanent alliance between Europe and America – an alliance resting not only on contingent historical situations but on a common cultural identity and a community of essential values.' J. Rovan, 'A Unified Germany in a United Europe', *NR*, 38: 6 (1990).

102 'The premise that the world should adopt some uniform standard, some single, standard design ... for the organization of differing societies, and that democracy can be built only and exclusively on the basis of Western standards and values ... is immoral and, moreover, dangerous ... [Soviet democracy] is laying at its foundations the Soviet peoples' own values.' 'Shevardnadze Addresses Paris Forum', *CDSP*, 41: 22 (1989).

103 'There is a growing appreciation of the need for a *European level of security*, that is, the development of a European security pillar.' L. Reychler, 'The Public Perception of NATO', *NR*, 38: 2 (1990); 'A related aim would be to build trust and transparency with regard to the military activities of all CSCE states, and finally the encouragement of a European security identity and defence role, reflected in the construction of a European pillar within the alliance, as a means of creating a more balanced and mature transatlantic partnership of equals.' M. Alexander, 'European Security and the CSCE', *NR*, 39: 4 (1991).

104 'Stability and prosperity in the new Europe can come only from a framework of interlocking institutions in which NATO, a European Political Union and the institutionalized CSCE process will be the principal actors.' M. Woerner, 'NATO Transformed: The Significance of the Rome Summit', *NR*, 39: 6 (1991).

105 'A new CSCE structure cannot substitute for the unique advantages which NATO offers in terms of collective defence and crisis resistance. The CSCE process, even though significantly strengthened, can only fulfil a complementary role.' Wegener, 'The Transformed Alliance'.

new institution. Jiri Dienstbier, one of the founders of this non-governmental institution, who after the Velvet Revolution became the Czech Foreign Minister, described the Helsinki Citizen's Assembly as 'typical of the dramatic pressure which has arisen due to the penetration of awakening freedom and responsibility into the ossified structures of the Cold War'.[106] The hope of the former Eastern European dissidents, many of whom had since become members of government, had been for the transformation of NATO as it merged into an all-European security structure, covering the whole of Europe, as well as North America and the Soviet Union.[107] In the aftermath of the collapse of the Council for Mutual Economic Assistance (COMECON), they approached Western institutions for support for the fragile democracies in Eastern Europe, whose economies were threatened.[108]

Both NATO and the former Eastern European satellites were aware of the possibility that forces in the Soviet Union might attempt to restore an authoritarian system,[109] a possibility exemplified by the failed coup against Gorbachev. Gorbachev, attempting to preserve the foundations of socialism while restructuring the framework, was pulled in two opposing directions by, on the one hand, the conservative forces of the old communist guard and, on the other, by demands for more dramatic market reforms. In light of the further disintegration of the Soviet economy and predictions of its breakdown,[110] his policies, both internal and external, were increasingly

---

106 J. Dienstbier, 'The Helsinki Citizen's Assembly', in Kaldor (1991).
107 'At the same time when the totalitarian systems in Central and Eastern Europe fell and democracy prevailed there ... everything appeared to us to be clear and simple: the Warsaw Treaty Organization ... would peacefully dismantle itself while the North Atlantic Alliance would proceed speedily to transform itself, so as to eventually merge in an entirely new security structure that would cover the whole of Europe and link it with the North American continent on the one hand and with what the Soviet Union would turn into on the other.' 'President Havel's Address to the NATO Council', *NR*, 39: 2 (1991).
108 'The democracies established [in Eastern Europe] are very fragile and therefore can be easily hurt, as everything in them is undergoing a fundamental transformation ... The thoroughly unnatural market based on compulsory exchange of poor quality goods which was maintained for years within the COMECON has collapsed.' 'President Havel's Address'.
109 'Those who fear an authoritarian backlash to restore order in an increasingly anarchic situation have ample precedents to justify them.' Howard, 'Military Grammar and Political Logic'; 'The conservative forces in [the Soviet Union] are obviously mobilizing in an effort to reverse the course of history and restore – against the will of citizens and peoples – a centralist authoritarian system. 'President Havel's Address'.
110 'The [socialist] ideology's destruction has deprived the peoples of a common future and caused an instantaneous growth in national ideas and beliefs, which are tearing us apart in irreversible centrifugal efforts.' 'Contemplating the Breakup of the USSR', *CDSP*, 42: 4 (1990).

viewed as a source of the Soviet Union's economic problems. In 1991, as the economy and the Soviet state further disintegrated[111] and the Soviet Republics began to dismantle the Union,[112] its collapse became inevitable.[113]

Conclusion

A shared grammar of structure makes it possible to trace the transition from a state of maintenance to one of collapse. This grammar included passive categories, such as deterioration and erosion, as well as categories related to human and state action, such as maintaining, undermining and dismantling. A further distinction is useful between any one actor's naming of their own activity and that applied to others. No actor claimed to be engaged in 'undermining'; this was a category applied to others in the naming of a threat and one's own response.

Erosion and deterioration connote natural cause rather than human agency, a change in the material conditions of a structure which requires some type of policy response. NATO's emphasis in the mid 1980s on erosion of the public consensus underlying its deterrence policy related to a long-term process of disintegration which was visible in the mid 1970s, at a time when the elite consensus was still intact. Gorbachev also referred to deterioration, erosion and decay, both economically and morally, as the starting point for the new policy of restructuring. The implication of both was that states act in response to deteriorating conditions; furthermore, these state actors – with the exception of Gorbachev[114] – were unable to recognise action *outside* the state, except in terms of manipulation by another state or, specifically, the other superpower. In both blocs, the same

111 'Very few realize how far the process of the state's disintegration has progressed in the past month.' 'Tsipko Urges Yeltsin Pullback to Save Union', *CDSP*, 43: 39 (1991); 'The convulsions of a disintegrating Soviet Union could set off a chain reaction of unrest, disorder and potential aggression throughout the area.' O. Pick, 'The Demise of the Warsaw Pact', *NR*, 39: 2 (1991).

112 'Republics Act to Dismantle Central Power', *CDSP*, 43: 44 (1991).

113 'It seems that everything possible was done to protect Party and state structures from destruction. But today the prosecutor's office has sufficient grounds to dissolve [Communist Party of the Soviet Union] agencies [...] The coup thwarted the signing of the Union Treaty, but it could not destroy the Republic's desire to build a new union. The collapse of the totalitarian empire has become irreversible.' 'Congress Votes Away its Powers', *CDSP*, 43: 37 (1991); 'The new structures in which the collapsed administrative empire will be resurrected in the form of departments of the Interstate Economic Committee are still only hazily visible.' 'Republics Act to Dismantle Central Power'.

114 Gorbachev attributed many of the ideas underlying new thinking to the influence of social movements. See interview with Mikhail Gorbachev, Moscow, 18 May 1988, *Washington Post*, 22 May 1988, p. A33.

categories of erosion and undermining were attached to the other super-power and their own domestic opposition or public.

Maintenance was the central act of states, and for NATO, consistently across the time span of this analysis. While states claimed to maintain deterrence or socialism, depending on their position, social movements named the objects of maintenance to be the status quo involving both blocs or, in Poland, the totalitarian order. Dismantling or breaking down were used by social movements in both blocs to attribute meaning to their own actions, and were central to the definition of their objectives. Both NATO and the Warsaw Pact claimed in the mid 1970s that the division between the blocs should be broken down or the military alliances should be dismantled, respectively; however, these did not correspond to the central acts of maintenance by both sides, until Reagan and Gorbachev began to negate the foundations of deterrence, in different ways, and break through the political barriers distinguishing East and West. While maintenance most often related to a military object, the dismantling activities of the social movements and later the superpowers were political in nature. Once deterrence was politicised in the early 1980s, NATO became preoccupied with the maintenance of a public consensus and its own image as well.

Restoring was an action category employed by all actors at one time or another. The CPD, NATO and President Reagan restored the eroding nuclear deterrent, actions which the Soviet Union referred to as an attempt to restore American superiority. Solidarity attempted to restore civil society while dismantling totalitarianism, and the government in response attempted to restore order. Independent movements in East and West attempted to restore the meaning of the Helsinki Final Act while dismantling the Cold War. Gorbachev, on the other hand, engaged in restructuring, which shares a family resemblance with restoration. The difference between the actions of NATO, Reagan and Gorbachev, on the one hand, and the social movements, on the other hand, was that the former were restoring or restructuring their own structure on the basis of an existing foundation, while the latter were dismantling the existing foundations of the Cold War and rebuilding the collapsed framework of the Helsinki Accords. In the last half of the 1980s, attention shifted to the construction of a new European house or architecture while the two frameworks in East and West remained standing.

This chapter began with an argument that one can trace this process of change by analysing the grammar of a structure. The structure was not a monolithic block, however, and its contours were named in different ways by the various actors over time. This multidimensionality suggests that parts of the structure can collapse before the entire edifice falls to the ground. In fact, several stages of collapse structure this story. At the end of the 1970s the moral authority of the Polish government collapsed with the visit of Pope John Paul II. In the early 1980s détente collapsed with the renewed psychological war between East and West. Domestic battles related to nuclear weapons and human rights became weapons in this war. By the mid 1980s, the foreign policy consensus in Western Europe was collapsing, after several years of living within a crumbling framework, and deep cracks in alliance solidarity were evident. As Gorbachev introduced new thinking and action, the enemy images underpinning East–West antagonism began to collapse. The meeting in Reykjavik was another disastrous blow to the foundations of post-war strategy in both blocs. As further cooperation developed between the superpowers and conditions in Eastern Europe opened up, the Berlin Wall and the Eastern European communist parties began to collapse in 1989, followed by Eastern European structures such as COMECON, the Warsaw Pact and finally the Soviet Union in 1991. Along with these dramatic events, the basic assumptions underlying the analysis of East–West relations crumbled.[115] Both the academic community and the politicians who predicted the permanence of both the Soviet Union and the Cold War system were taken by surprise.

115   Reychler, 'The Public Perception of NATO'.

PART II

Changing games

6

Denaturalisation and emancipation

Play by the rules of another's fight ... and you end up strengthening the very rules that favour the opponent. Change the rules and you are playing *your* game. (Rubin, 1997: 8)

THE PURPOSE OF the last section was to explore the methodological tools for describing a context of change. Chapter Five put them to use in an analysis of the end of the Cold War. I argued that a 'better' description of this context of change would reveal how actors occupying different positions in social and geographical space employed the rules of a shared grammar as they interacted with one another. The description was said to be 'better' in so far as it embedded the moves of each player in a larger intersubjective context, structured by rules, and identified key points of transition.

While the previous chapter examined a shared grammar of state and non-state actors, in this section I shall explore the *contestation* between games played by states and critical actors, and the mechanisms by which a transition between two different games became possible. Actors positioned outside the dominant rules of the game transformed the meaning of the Cold War, opening up spaces for alternative choices. One step in this process was to *denaturalise* the 'objective' basis of the dominant game in order to convince others that multiple games were possible.

Rules and rules

The International Society tradition has long emphasised the social nature of interstate relations and 'rules of the game'. Constructivists and critical theorists have argued that the actions of states belong not to an objective order but are rather constructed and therefore capable of change. Critical theorists have most often argued that alternatives to the dominant rules are possible in the context of a critique of *state* action. To understand how alternatives became possible in an actual context of change, it is necessary to analyse more explicitly the relationship between the rules of states and those employed by social movements. Social movements did not merely disrupt the rules of the dominant game; their moves can also be situated in a different kind of game, with its own history.

What kind of game? After a seminar discussion of this approach to games, a distinguished professor made an interesting point.[1] He agreed that there might be multiple games going on at the international level at one time. He referred to these with analogies to boxing, football and snooker. He made the point that most of these were 'guy' games and then asked 'Where are the girl games?'. What would a 'girl' game look like in a system that has been dominated by competition and war?

Harriet Rubin's book, *The Princessa: Machiavelli for Women* (1997), provides a partial answer to this question. She argues that women cannot succeed by following the rules of the male game; first, because they are not her rules, designed to enhance her strengths, and second, because no one wants her to succeed. The best strategy is, therefore, to transform the game so that others *want* to play by different rules. A combination of disrupting the dominant game, by flaunting the rules and acting as if alternatives were possible, transforms the conflict.

'Girl' rules rely on a different type of power than 'guy' rules. Guy rules seek power through control. Girl rules empower by refusing to be controlled or to control others; the actor in a girl game controls only her response to the other, by acting rather than reacting. As the similarity with nonviolent direct action suggests, these are not guy or girl rules by nature. In fact the latter are rules that have been employed by emancipatory movements of various kinds, including both men and women, who have recognised that those *outside* established circles of power cannot win by playing the dominant game because it is not their game.

'Guy' and 'girl' games

Realism is the ultimate 'guy' game and, from that perspective, the only game. Machiavelli was one of the first to outline its rules. Given that his rules provide the point of reference for Rubin's 'Princessa' strategy for waging war, a brief contrast is useful for thinking about the distinction between the two.[2]

---

1 The question was raised by Professor Ken Booth, Department of International Politics, University of Wales, Aberystwyth.
2 *The Princessa* is not an academic text but, like Machiavelli's *Prince*, a guidebook. Given the historical importance of Machiavelli for international relations, the contrast is interesting. For this reason I have structured the comparison around Rubin's argument rather than the literature on nonviolent action. Rubin is not providing an interpretation of Machiavelli's *Prince*, but rather an adaptation for women and others outside dominant power structures who 'play with a losing hand'. For more background on nonviolent strategy, see Bell and Kurtz (1992), Bondurant (1988), Boulding (1989), Gregg (1966), Holms (1990), Program on Nonviolent Sanctions (1992), Sharp (1973), Wehr, Burgess and Burgess (1994), Woehrle (1992) and Zielonka (1986).

Most often Machiavelli's name is a term of derision and contempt. The common perception is that the prince rules by deception, force and oppression. But a closer reading of *The Prince* (1975) reveals a more nuanced picture. The prince seeks control above all else, to consolidate and maintain his power. However, based on the maxim that 'it is better to be feared than loved', it is often assumed that fear does most of the work for Machiavelli. If one looks more closely at the detail of his argument, the significance changes dramatically. He says: 'From this arises the following question: whether it is better to be loved than feared, or the reverse. The answer is that one would like to be both the one and the other but because it is difficult to combine them, it is far better to be feared than loved if you cannot be both' (Machiavelli, 1975: 96).

One would like to be both feared and loved in the best of all worlds. If a choice has to be made it is better to be feared, since it is easier to keep one's subjects in line with fear than with love. One must not go too far to one extreme or the other, however: 'The prince should nonetheless make himself feared in such a way that, if he is not loved, at least he escapes being hated' (Machiavelli, 1975: 97).

Being hated is the worst possible outcome. Being loved and feared is the best. The wise prince maintains a tension between the two. He is capable of cruelty when necessary, but only when necessary; he lies and deceives when necessary but, to keep from being hated, he must present the appearance of being all things good:

> A prince, therefore, need not necessarily have all the good qualities I mentioned above, but he should certainly appear to have them. I would even go so far as to say that if he has these qualities and always behaves accordingly he will find them ruinous; if he only appears to have them they will render him service. He should appear to be compassionate, faithful to his word, guileless, and devout. And indeed he should be so. But his disposition should be such that, if he needs to be the opposite, he knows how [...] So let a prince set about the task of conquering and maintaining his state; his methods will always be judged honourable and will be universally praised. The common people are always impressed by appearances and results. In this context, there are only common people, and there is no room for the few when the many are supported by the state. (Machiavelli, 1975: 100–1)

To be loved, and to avoid being hated, requires that one present an appearance of compassion, faithfulness, devotion. The purpose of the appearance is to impress common people. Impressing the common people is key because it is fundamental to the prince's power.

In the previous chapter we saw that states within the Cold War were primarily involved in 'maintenance' activities. In particular they were maintaining a structure. The structural metaphor is interesting in so far as building fortresses is one of the ways that princes consolidate control. The combination of a solid structure and solid support from the population is the strongest fortification: 'A prince who has a well-fortified city and does not make himself hated cannot be attacked' (Machiavelli, 1975: 72).

Machiavelli does not say that fortresses are advisable in all situations. Although fortresses can be useful in some circumstances, they can be harmful in others. The most important thing is the relationship to one's people: 'The best fortress that exists is to avoid being hated by the people. If you have fortresses yet the people hate you they will not save you' (Machiavelli, 1975: 119). The best thing is to be loved and feared; the worst is to be hated. One must avoid being hated because the power of the prince rests ultimately in the people.

The strategy and power of Rubin's Machiavella mirrors that of Machiavelli. However, where Machiavelli seeks to control the game, Machiavella's power is in subverting and changing it to her own ends. Machiavelli consolidates his power against enemies through manipulation and fear; Machiavella's power is the power to take command of her own actions and to make the opponent react to her: 'Power neither commands nor controls. It marches you into the fray, keeps you open and unarmored in the face of whatever comes: your vulnerability is your power. Your own desires are ultimately more powerful than any designs or traps or attempts at sabotage you may contemplate against the enemy' (Rubin, 1997: 53). Her power is 'implied power', the power to stand tall, with dignity, even though one is weak. This represents a form of 'acting as if'. When Rosa Parks sat in the front of the bus, she acted as if she had the power and dignity to sit where she liked in the bus, despite laws that forbade it. Her act sparked the Montgomery Bus Boycott, one of the most significant campaigns of the US civil rights movement.

While Machiavelli maintains the tension between love and fear, Machiavelli's strength is the tension between love and war. First she exacerbates the tensions in a situation, creating a conflict in which the enemy is forced to react to her on her own terms. She does this by seeing, hearing and knowing the enemy: 'A princessa watches her enemy. Often it is in his smallest, most innocent gestures that he gives himself away. An enemy, an opponent, always gives himself away' (Rubin, 1997: 27).

In knowing the enemy, she discovers the difference between his appearance and his reality, his strengths and his weaknesses. By seeing beyond his strategy, she is not forced into reacting. She acts in a way that makes the prince respond to her.

She recognises that he is playing the only game he knows or the only game he thinks possible, that his acts are weapons of self-defence. She allows the tension to build, not to assume control over others, but to master the

97

tension among them. She finds the prevailing assumptions in a situation and then 'acts as if' they 'were cast not in stone but in sand' (Rubin, 1997: 69). She uses contradictions, combining opposites, being both tough and soft, both flexible and firm. Through the use of tension, she disarms her opponent. He may not even realise what is happening or that he has been introduced to a new set of rules, her rules. 'An antagonist, opponent, straggler or naysayer, may not even know he's been conquered and won over by her agenda' (Rubin, 1997: 27). If a prince's power is built on appearance, the princessa must get underneath the appearance, prying open a space, so that both he and those he controls may be freed from the constraints of a game that limits them both. If the prince's power is dependent on the appearances he presents to the common people, the princessa reveals the appearance in order to convince others that change is possible. In so doing, she frees the prince so that they can join in a fight together and win a larger battle.

Her strategy is a strategy of manoeuvre, based not on armies or weapons that hurt, but in small gestures, in acting on the perceptions of others. Her moves orchestrate others' moves by transforming the battlefield. She does not try to defeat the enemy but to win him over through 'besting':

> Machiavelli's prince could destroy his opponents and be secure in his triumph. Sun Tzu could play footsie with his enemy and humiliate him with his ingenuity. But the princessa cannot cripple the enemy. She must make her opponent an unwitting ally. This means neither hurting him nor eroding his confidence ... For the princessa, who is always fighting a come-from-behind war, besting is the only way to win because it means winning with a losing hand. Anyone can win with a winning hand. Only the princessa can win with less. (Rubin, 1997: 90)

Besting is a tactic designed to provoke a positive counteraction in the opponent. It is a means of demonstrating to him that your win is also his win. The princessa plays with a losing hand, from a position of weakness. She does not expect overt success in the short term. Her war is one of protracted conflict. The battle is not won immediately, but over the long run. In the end the prince can claim the victory as his own:

> By showing him she understands the power spinning across this table she is on her way to winning an ally and a war. How does she get what she ultimately wants? ... She saves that for another time ... She trusts that she will prevail in getting what she wants. Thus she is spared from reacting. React to another's fight and you get caught up in your enemy's war, not your own, which means you do not play from a position of strength. To rush a win would be to scare him; and it is clear that this man is already frightened of many things – especially good things. She does not need to walk away with a clear victory now. Each advance like this builds her strength, increases her resilience for the next campaign. (Rubin, 1997: 34–5)

Machiavella does not seek to defeat another. She seeks to win over, not only the prince, but first and foremost those who provide the foundation of his power. The victory is not immediate. The victory is not one of personal glory, as it is for the Machiavelli; the victory is in having changed the rules of the game, in having made the unthinkable not only thinkable but possible.

Rubin's guidebook is written for women about struggles involving the most intimate relations. But her examples dig deeply into the history of nonviolent resistance, from Gandhi to Martin Luther King.[3] The rules of Machiavella are the rules of those who are outside the dominant structures of power, of those who resist what is, believing that the impossible can be made possible. The tactics of Machiavella were the tactics of independent social movements and initiatives in both East and West. In this chapter, I analyse the first steps to change the games. In the next chapter, I explore the exacerbation of tensions, as the battle mounts, and the first steps by the superpowers into newly opened spaces. In the final chapter of this section, I illustrate the power of 'acting as if' in transforming the Cold War game.

Knowing, seeing and hearing

In the early 1980s, emancipatory movements in both East and West explicitly located themselves *outside* the established political structures of their societies, arguing that those within were trapped by the rules of a game that defined their identities. They set out to open up a space for a new game to be played. The first step was to know the rules in order to denaturalise them and to expose their social and conventional nature. An alternative game would only be conceivable once the 'objective' nature of the dominant rules had been drawn into doubt. The second step was to begin to change the meaning of the state-level game. The distinction between guy and girl games is particularly salient in a context where the task was one of emancipation from a structure of alliance families.

In both East and West, citizens' initiatives identified and analysed a logic of necessity as one of the central features inhibiting any kind of change. In Poland, in the early 1970s, Leszek Kolakowski published a seminal article in which he examined a frequently repeated argument about the structure of communism.[4] Because of its rigidity, reforms within the

---

3 Gandhi asked his friends to call him 'mother' as a recognition of his desire to fight like a woman. He distinguished 'Satyagraha' (brave cowardice) from the 'manly' fight that left some people brutalised and turned others into enemies for life. See Rubin (1997: 21).

4 L. Kolakowski, 'Hope and Hopelessness', *Survey*, 17: 3 (1971). According to Zielonka (1989), this seminal article was disseminated at the beginning of the 1970s and was adopted by the majority of the Polish opposition, and in particular the KOR.

framework of communism could not be institutionalised without destroying the entire system. A particular conclusion was often drawn from this type of argument, that is, that change was impossible without the total and simultaneous destruction of the structure.

Kolakowski argued that the thesis of the total rigidity of communism was incorrect. In fact, it was often used to convince people living under it of the futility or danger of attempting to bring about change. Hope was the necessary condition for change. As long as the structure was assumed to be permanent and unchangeable, it would be impossible to inspire people to action. A particular way of reasoning convinced people that reforms were dangerous, which informed their actions and made it possible for the game to continue. If Machiavelli's power is dependent on convincing populations that a particular appearance is necessary, Machiavella must expose the appearance as a first step in convincing populations that other alternatives are possible. As Kolakowski said:

> To what extent a movement ... is possible depends to a considerable degree ... on the extent to which society believes that it is possible. As the nature of a given society is dependent *in part* on its own self-image, there cannot be in social change a pure potential concealed in material circumstances alone and independent of the degree of awareness of potentialities by people. Thus in the countries of socialist despotism, those who inspire hope are also the inspirers of a movement which could make this hope real – just as in society's attempts to understand itself, object and subject often coincide. The belief that socialism in its present form is totally inflexible and can only be destroyed in one fell swoop and therefore that no partial changes are in essence changes in its social nature, easily lends itself to justifying opportunism and pure knavery.[5]

Adam Michnik took the argument a step further in 1976.[6] He examined how the structure of communism inhibited efforts at change by those contained within it. Past efforts at reform had originated within the Party, he argued. Since reformers were part of the existing structure, they were inevitably forced to conform with the powers that be or they would not survive; individuals who did not conform would be eliminated from positions of power and influence. Michnik concluded that gradual reform, to be at all successful, had to begin *outside* the established structure of power, and be geared less to influencing the position of the Party than the actions of those in society who provided the foundations of Party power. It was those outside state structures, in society, who ultimately would determine the parameters of correct behaviour for state leaders. A gradual opening up of spaces within Polish society might be possible by organising nonviolent

5 Kolakowski, 'Hope and Hopelessness', p. 51.
6 'A New Evolutionism', in Michnik (1985).

actions outside the Polish state directed towards changing the actions of individuals within society.

The Polish activists argued that Party members in the East were incapable of changing their behaviour because their own survival was at stake. In an analysis by the Dutch Interchurch Peace Council (Interkerkelijk Vredesberaad; IKV), the same logic was said to structure the relationship between the two superpowers in the security dilemma: individual states which tried to introduce change would do so at their own peril.[7] In the end, they would either conform or cease to exist.

Both the Polish and Dutch analysts concluded – independently – that state leaders were trapped by a particular logic, which in both cases constituted the boundaries of possibility in terms of a security dilemma for individual units. In the Dutch analysis, it was argued that neither the superpowers nor their allies were able, on their own, to find a way out of the deterrence game:

> We concluded that as long as you accept the principles, the implications and the rules of the 'deterrent game', you can't come up with a workable solution. The reason why it is so difficult while remaining mentally and politically *within* the ideology of the deterrence system, to find a way out – which has been tried for twenty years – is, in our opinion, because the most powerful drives or motors behind the arms race can be hidden behind balance of power reasoning, the perpetual type of argument which dominates the security discussion in our country. (emphasis added)[8]

Balance of power or deterrence belonged not to an objective reality, but rather represented a particular way of reasoning by which states knew 'how to go on' and which constrained action. IKV concluded that it was necessary to 'raise a new power within society' in order to press the political centre to change its policies. A radical rejection of deterrence and 'all its rules and implications' was fundamental to this effort. The Dutch movement argued that a solution to the arms race could not be found so long as one accepted the principles, implications and rules of the 'deterrence game'. Leaders, whose identities were constituted within this game, were trapped by its logic; societal actors, by contrast, were capable of stepping outside the dominant rules and beginning to play a different game. The Church was called on to be a leading force in the search for 'new ways of thinking and new approaches in the field of disarmament'.[9]

---

7 This realist assumption has also been articulated in theories of international relations. See, for instance, Waltz (1979).

8 B. ter Veer, 'Speech to the Presidium of the Christian Peace Conference', Noordwijkerhout, the Netherlands (24 October 1981), IKV Archives, no. 472, ISG, Amsterdam.

9 'Declaration of Pax Christi International on Disarmament and Security' (June 1981), IKV Archives no. 501, ISG, Amsterdam.

The analyses in East and West denaturalised two interrelated state-level games within the Cold War. Demonstrating the conventional nature of state-level arguments was a first step in beginning to act as if there were alternatives to the seemingly permanent logic of the Cold War.

Transforming the battlefield

The first step in bringing about the change was to denaturalise the rules in order to convince populations that change was possible. To convince someone an argument must be stated in meaningful terms. As a result, the dominant rules of the game, widely understood to be necessary and objective, were the point of departure for acts of critique. In Chapter Five, I demonstrated the relationship between acts of maintenance by the two superpowers and acts of dismantling by social movements. While the two expressed a common grammar of structure, each belonged to a distinct language game. The purpose of the second part of this chapter is to explore the latter point.

The structures of the Cold War were occupied by a particular type of identity, that is, families. Acts of commitment reproduced this game of permanent families. In the early 1980s, social movements began to challenge the meanings attached to these families and to engage in acts belonging to an emancipation game. Both rely on a second grammar of relationship for their meaning.

Language games of family structured the public texts of both alliances within the Cold War in slightly different ways. Both relied on a grammar of intimate relations but the structuring rules of each family were different. The following story illustrates the structure of alliance relationships at the beginning of the 1980s. Given space constraints, it is only possible to provide a single textual source, although the analysis was drawn from a much larger archive of examples.

NATO discourse in the early 1980s constructed the alliance as a family. The nuclear family of the West was built on a commitment between a stronger partner and a weaker one. The title of one article in the *NATO Review*, 'The Atlantic Family – Managing its Problems',[10] named the metaphor directly. This family included partners whose stable relationship was characterised by commitment, faithfulness, duties, responsibilities, common burdens and obligations.[11] The stronger partner had gotten into the habit of

10 E. van der Beugel, 'The Atlantic Family – Managing its Problems', *NR*, 34: 1 (1986).

11 '[Europeans] remain committed to the alliance.' S. Sloan, 'Crisis in NATO: A Problem of Leadership?', *NR*, 30: 3 (1982); 'The United States is also faithful to its alliances.' R. Reagan, 'U.S. and U.S.S.R. Negotiations', *VSD*, 51: 1 (1984); 'Whilst safeguarding the special responsibilities of the [nuclear] powers ... this thus demonstrated the interdependence

making most of the decisions,[12] partly because of its more global respons-ibilities, in contrast to the primarily domestic responsibilities of the other.[13] This relationship, which 'is now an old one', had become no less intense over the years.[14] The partners were bound by what bound them forty years ago and would not feel safe if they could not rely on each other. As one partner described it, 'their safety and ours are one'.[15] 'We were with you then; we are with you now. Your hopes are our hopes, your destiny is our destiny.'[16]

The stable and secure relationship of NATO's nuclear family was based on a foundation of values and friendship,[17] as well as inequality, since the two differed in capabilities.[18] The one, being stronger, offered protection and ensured the security of the weaker, who could not feel secure on her own, in the face of the Soviet Union, who wanted to isolate the two, making the feminine partner docile, productive and supportive.[19] The main objective of

between responsibility, rights and risks for all members in the Alliance.' P. Corterier, 'Modernization of Theatre Nuclear Forces and Arms Control', *NR*, 29: 4 (1981); 'Every alliance involves burdens and obligations.' Reagan, 'U.S. and U.S.S.R. Negotiations.'

12 'The truth is that, over the years, [Europeans] have all got into the habit of leaving ultimate decisions, and ultimate responsibilities, to the Americans.' Lord Carrington, 'Lack of Consistent Political Strategy: A Cause of Friction', *NR*, 31: 2 (1983).

13 'I have often discussed with European friends the different requirements for a nation with global responsibilities to those with more regional concerns.' L. Eagleburger, 'The Transatlantic Relationship – A Long-Term Perspective', *NR*, 32: 2 (1984).

14 'The American relationship with Europe is now an old one ... [The US] has been fully joined with Western Europe in the security process.' W. T. Bennett, Jr, 'The U.S. and the Atlantic Community', *NR*, 31: 2 (1983); 'Our transatlantic friendship and alliance ... has certainly not become less intense in recent years.' A. Levi, 'Western Values and the Successor Generation', *NR*, 30: 2 (1982).

15 'The ... interests of the two partners are too closely bound together to be unravelled, however exasperating and frustrating each may find the other.' C. Rose, 'The 1982 Summit and After: A Personal View', *NR*, 30: 4 (1982); 'Neither the United States nor Western Europe would be safe in a world where one could not rely on the other.' F. Lewis, 'Alarm Bells in the West', *Foreign Affairs*, 60: 3 (1981); 'Their safety and ours are one.' R. Reagan, 'Peace and National Security: A New Defense', *VSD*, 49: 13 (1983).

16 R. Reagan, 'Remarks at the U.S. Ranger Monument, Pointe du Hoc, France, 6 June 1984', in Reagan (1989).

17 'Only as partners can we defend the values of democracy and human dignity we hold so dear.' R. Reagan, 'East–West Relations: Reduction of Nuclear Arms', *VSD*, 48: 16 (1982).

18 'Structural inequality is a feature of the Atlantic Alliance, the military capabilities of the United States being of a different order than those of its European partners.' G. de Carmoy, 'Defense and Détente: Two Complementary Policies', *NR*, 30: 2 (1982); 'Many disputes arise from differences which are ineradicable – differences of size ... and economic circumstance.' Rose, 'The 1982 Summit.'

19 'We Europeans need the alliance because we cannot protect ourselves.' G. Vaerno, 'A Public Opinion Strategy', *NR*, 31: 3/4 (1983); 'The USSR does not want to destroy Europe but [to] isolate her from the US. Anything that separates the US from Europe is bad for the

the Soviet Union was to split or decouple the partners.[20]

The neighbouring enemy to the East also referred to its unit as a family, although based on different values. It was a very masculine family, 'fraternal' and attached to a 'fatherland', where everyone was said to be equal.[21] A particular kind of individual was protected by the fraternal family, that is, the labourer, and the socialist system in which he laboured.[22] Like NATO, the Soviet Union was concerned with preventing a shattering of the unity of this family by an 'interference' in its domestic space.[23] Poland, in the early 1980s, was a key concern precisely because it was the place where this interference was said to be most evident, and a space most vital to the maintenance of international security. Actors in both households were concerned that their unity was being shattered; both were protecting a set of values. This difference in values was said to be the cause of conflict between them.

In the West 'security' was inseparable from the need to secure the space of Western Europe, the securing of a feminine object by a masculine subject. The relationship was consensual, based on a shared history and culture, was less imposed by the Americans than desired by the Europeans[24] – although the balance between these two was precarious – but the relation-

alliance.' T. Hitchens, 'NATO Parliamentarians Call for Increased Information Effort', *NR*, 30: 6 (1983); '[Soviet policy] would undoubtedly prefer to turn [Western Europe] into a docile, productive and supportive buffer area.' K. Rush, B. Scowcroft and J. Wolf, 'The Credibility of the NATO Deterrent', *NR*, 29: 5 (1981).

20 'To "decouple" Europe from North America has always been a primary objective of the Soviets.' J. M. P. Villas-Boas, 'Public Perceptions and Nuclear Morality', *NR*, 32: 2 (1984).

21 '[The socialist commonwealth] is not simply founded on the common state interests of a group of countries, it represents a fraternal family of peoples guided by Marxist-Leninist parties and united by a common world view.' 'Brezhnev Speaks at Polish Congress', *CDSP*, 27: 49 (1975); 'Acting as a united family, the peoples of the socialist countries are affirming relations of peaceful coexistence in the international arena.' 'Pravda Hits West's Defence of Dissidents', *CDSP*, 29: 6 (1977); 'The Soviet Union has no need to expand its state borders; its main goal is to protect the socialist fatherland.' D. Ustinov, 'Military Leaders Assail "Hostile" U.S. Policy', *CDSP*, 34: 19 (1982).

22 '[The combat potential of the Soviet armed forces] serves the noble cause of protecting the peaceful constructive labour of the Soviet people.' D. Ustinov, 'Ustinov Cites Imperialist War Threat', *CDSP*, 33: 25 (1981).

23 '[Those who run the US] are not abandoning hope of creating a split in the international workers' and Communist movement, driving a wedge between the USSR and the countries of the socialist commonwealth, and breaking up their unity.' Ustinov, 'Military Leaders'; 'The United States is resorting to unceremonious interference in the affairs of other states, imposing the American way of life on them.' 'Andropov Asks Warhead Equality in Europe', *CDSP*, 35: 18 (1983).

24 'The European powers had pleaded strongly with the Americans for a much more far reaching and automatic commitment than the United States at the time was ready to give.' Vaerno, 'A Public Opinion Strategy.'

ship, nonetheless, involved the securing of a larger continental space by an external power.

While the Warsaw Pact also presented itself as a family, the Soviet Union actually focused its gaze, like the United States, on Western Europe and its relationship with the United States. The Soviet Union transformed the hierarchical commitment and need expressed by NATO into the imposed obedience of Western Europe to the *diktat* of the United States.[25] For the Soviet Union, the Western alliance was a form of imprisonment, done by people 'overseas', not present, not part of the European continent.[26] While Western Europe held each superpower's attention, Eastern Europe lacked any identity whatsoever, largely invisible, historically abandoned, visible only as a domestic space in which the West should not interfere.[27] The two family spheres in East and West, as well as the security dilemma constituted between them, were mutually reinforcing, a family feud in which the 'other' was not to be trusted because of the lack of correspondence between words and deeds.

The family metaphor constituted each alliance as a safe place, even though these structures were buttressed by the threat of nuclear war. In the early 1980s, both East and West were consumed by the need to keep their families together in light of a renewed threat from the 'other' and the activities of a 'younger generation', which was questioning the fundamental values at the foundations of each family. The naming of emancipatory movements as a 'younger generation' was particularly evident in NATO documents,[28] in which the Western peace movement was characterised, among other things, as 'immature, naive, and irresponsible'.[29] The connotation of this particular label was that these movements were made up of rebellious 'kids' reminiscent of the 1960s.[30] Participants in the peace movements were

25 '[NATO's West European participants] obediently supported the decisions that had been prepared in advance in Washington.' 'NATO's Tough Stand on Nuclear Arms Hit', *CDSP*, 33: 19 (1981).

26 'People overseas are again talking about the acceptability of "limited" nuclear war in Europe.' Ustinov, 'Ustinov Cites Imperialist War Threat.'

27 'This applies to in particular "the other Europe", the one that we have forgotten under Soviet hegemony.' G. Defois, 'The Church and Deterrence', *NR*, 32: 3 (1984).

28 'The older generation's span of public activity is about to reach its end ... [There are] doubts about whether the most cherished values and ideals, whose defence was so dear to the older generation, will still be upheld by the younger one.' Levi, 'Western Values.'

29 This, among other things, includes claims that they 'may be in need of being reminded' of basic Western values; have become something of a problem because they 'call everything into question' and reason 'simplistically'. See Levi, 'Western Values'; F. W. Baer-Kaupert, 'Peace and the Nuclear Paradox', *NR*, 33: 2 (1985); Villas-Boas, 'Public Perceptions.'

30 Interestingly enough, if one looks back at NATO documents from the 1960s, the 'younger generation' is handled in a much different way, at least within the European context.

not necessarily young, however, as various opinion polls have demonstrated.[31] This labelling effort on the part of NATO communicated a particular image of these movements and what they were about, that is, overturning a set of values by which peace had been maintained in Europe since World War II. While Eastern European 'dissidents' were cast in less familial terms by state officials, the conflict has been discussed by many as the difference between the World War II generation and those who grew up in the relative wealth and security of the post-war period.[32]

While the two families were concerned with providing security for their domestic spaces, the younger generation in each house was attempting to emancipate itself from the destructive practices of each family.[33] While Machiavelli presents the appearance that his practices are a source of security, Machiavella, in changing the battlefield, transforms the *meaning* of these practices. In this sense the critical movements took these language games of security very seriously: while the families claimed to provide security, the emancipatory movements exposed or renamed these security practices as a source of insecurity. Their actions drew on the same grammar of relationships, but involved a different move in an alternative emancipation game, which began with a renaming of the relationship. 'Emancipation', and the cluster of concepts belonging to it, can relate to families,[34] but is not within the realm of possibility in alliance games based on the permanence of a particular family structure. The structuring role of

Texts from the time focus on grooming future leaders who are praised for making certain kinds of distinction between East and West against the background of the Soviet invasion of Czechoslovakia. See, for instance, Fifth Atlantic Conference of Young Political Leaders: 'An Alternative Policy for the West', *NR*, 16: 7–8 (1968); K. Sandegren, 'The New Generation and NATO', *NR*, 17: 9 (1969).

31 Opponents of the cruise and Pershing II deployments were in fact distributed across the age spectrum. For figures in different countries, see Flynn and Rattinger (1985).

32 An internal document of the Polish Communist Party expressed concern about 'the negative influence of the current situation on the ideological formation and personality of the younger generation.' 'Letter from the Secretariat of the Gdansk Provincial Party Committee to the Central Committee', signed by Henry Bartkowski, 24 August 1980, *LFEE*, 4: 1–3 (1980). Waller (1993) discusses the emergence of a generational cleavage in Eastern Europe which favoured development of 'anti-politics'.

33 'A wave of emancipation has been spreading over Europe, in some countries faster than others. People are becoming aware of the chains that hold them down ... Two examples of this emancipation process that have been in the news are the international peace movement and Solidarnosc.' 'Europe for the Europeans', IPCC Paris Meeting, September 1982, IKV Archives no. 504, ISG, Amsterdam; 'For none of us was it just a question of material conditions ... History has taught us that there can be no bread without freedom. We also wanted justice, democracy, truth, freedom of opinion, a reconstructed republic.' 'The Programme of Solidarnosc, October 1981', *LFEE*, 5: 1–2 (1982).

34 One need only think of the women's movement.

these concepts is evident in the texts of Solidarity and the Western European peace movement.

The central value of the Eastern house was protecting workers in the process of building socialism. Yet as the protector became a source of threat to workers, the KOR, and later Solidarity in Poland, attempted to reveal, to expose abuse by the Party and state of those rights which the latter had promised to protect,[35] both in its own constitution and in signing the international Helsinki Accords. The younger generation was revolting against the oppressive control of the family over all spheres of life.[36] It wanted to open up a dialogue with the government so that society could take its fate into its own hands, speak with its own voice, and develop its own self-governing and independent institutions.[37]

In the West the alliance partners claimed to be protecting the Western family, but the acquisition of more and more sophisticated weapons, as well as heightened tensions between the two families, was making many feel insecure.[38] While the family named the neighbour as the source of threat, the peace movement named the arms race as the primary threat.[39] Like Solidarity, the Western peace movement was exposing a distinction between the words and the deeds of the older generation.[40]

Social movements in both houses were calling for emancipation from a particular form of politics that had become a source of insecurity. At the international level, 'talk' between the two households, at the time, served

35 'The ruling party is in the dock: being judged by the class from which it allegedly derives its pedigree and in whose name it pretends to govern.' 'Solidarity Strike Bulletin, No. 5', *LFEE*, 4: 1–3 (1980).

36 'The authorities have much to learn before they understand that a dialogue with society includes neither brandishing a truncheon nor a monologue on the television screen.' 'A Time of Hope, 1980', in Michnik (1985).

37 'It is no longer possible to postpone essential reforms [including among others] to enter into dialogue with society at large [...] The people, having taken the hitherto prevailing policies of the authorities to the limit, are now taking their fate into their own hands.' 'Solidarity Strike Bulletin, no. 4', *LFEE*, 4: 1–3 (1980); 'Society must have the right to speak aloud, to express the range of social and political views.' 'The Programme of Solidarnosc, October 1981.'

38 'To get into a negotiation about balance is to accept both the argument of adversary posture and the notion that any of these weapons could make us more secure. They do not ... If the cruise and Pershings come, Europe will be immensely more insecure.' M. Foot, O. Palme and E. P. Thompson at Craxton Hall, 2 September 1981, *END Bulletin*, 7 (1981–82).

39 'Whereas before, the arms build-up of the opposing side appeared as the main threat ... now articles depicted the arms race as the main threat.' R. Holmes and U. Stehr, 'Two Germanies ... A Common Theme', *END Bulletin*, 9 (1982).

40 'We have stripped the veils of consensus from our nuclear predicament and made it visible to all ... [Our movements] have made visible not only the weapons but also the premises of the Cold War.' E. P. Thompson, 'Beyond the Blocs', *END Journal*, 12 (1984).

only to fix the antagonistic relationship between them.[41] The main function of this antagonism, and the negotiations by which it was preserved, was, in their view, to 'discipline' the younger generation and the alliance partners.[42] That which the alliance named a relationship of security and protection, the Western European peace movement renamed a relationship of dependence and submission.[43] It called on Europeans within each alliance to reclaim responsibility for their own lives by taking a more independent role, disengaging from the military side of the relationship and liberating themselves from the ideology of the Cold War.[44] Common security between East and West required loosening the hold of the two families and opening up spaces for more voices to speak.[45]

The foundations of each bloc enclosed two different kinds of family, neighbours who could not get along because of a difference in values. In both houses the 'younger generation' began making different moves which transformed these family games, pointing out the distinction between the claim to provide security and protection and the practice of creating insecurity.

41 'There is a danger that the negotiations will fix such a Euro-strategic balance.' 'Common Statement of IKV in the Netherlands and Action Reconciliation in the FRG, 26 November 1981', IKV Archives no. 500, ISG, Amsterdam; 'The negotiators talk over the heads of the people concerned, about preserving the status quo and legitimising each side's argument.' 'New Initiatives for Disarmament and Détente, accepted at the Paris meeting of the IPCC, 9–11 June 1983', IKV Archives no. 503, ISG, Amsterdam.
42 'Arms negotiations between East and West have a disciplining function within each alliance.' IKV and Pax Christi, 'The Future of Europe: Armed Security or Political Peace?', 15 December 1984', IKV Archives no. 508, ISG, Amsterdam.
43 'It is precisely because cruise and Pershing II have come to symbolize Western Europe's dependence that we have to win in 1983.' 'A Strategy for 1983', *END Journal*, 2 (1983).
44 'The answer has to lie in an increased readiness of Europeans to act independently from the superpowers.' 'Nice Smiles ... ', *END Journal*, 19 (1985–86); 'Europe [should] become more and more militarily and politically disengaged from the two superpowers.' Wim Bartels, 'Address to the 12th Special Session of the United Nations, June 24, 1982', IKV Archives, no. 548, ISG Amsterdam; 'The aim [of this vision of a Europe of diversity] is not to find some new oppressive unity in Western or Eastern or even all of Europe, but rather to eliminate the unifying hold of the Cold War on European politics and culture ... The most important contribution we can make to that vision is to liberate ourselves from the ideology of the Cold War.' 'Liberating Ourselves from the Cold War', *END Journal*, 10 (1984).
45 'We wish, not to revise the frontiers of Yalta, but to throw these frontiers more open. We wish to enlarge in every way communication and informal exchanges between citizens ... We are calling for a "thaw" in human relations between the blocs. E. P. Thompson, 'Contribution to the Panel Discussion on "The Actual Crisis in Europe," Athens, Greece, 7 February 1984', IKV Archives, no. 337, ISG Amsterdam.

Conclusion

Cold War language games of security were paradoxical. While the American promise to use nuclear weapons in defence of Europe was an expression of potential violence and destruction, it was framed in a context of family, commitment and protection. In this semantic disarrangement, properties conventionally ascribed to one form of life, families, were metaphorically attributed to another, a military alliance. In this act an otherwise abstract experience of promise binding populations on two distant continents was described in the more understandable everyday language of the protection provided by families. The act was not simply one of description, however; it also replaced the destructive fearful emotions associated with nuclear war with positive emotions of safety and belonging. The language of family reinforced an appearance that was constitutive of alliance power *vis-à-vis* its population.

On a symbolic level, the conceptualisation of the two Cold War alliances as families resembles Geertz's (1973) interpretation of the Balinese cockfight. Geertz presents betting on the cockfight, a cultural practice of the Balinese, as a form of 'deep play'. Deep play – a concept going back to Jeremy Bentham – means that the stakes of a conflict are so high that it is irrational, from a utilitarian standpoint, to engage in it at all. While depicted as a rational strategy, a game involving nuclear weapons can be thought of in this way. Both parties were in over their heads, engaged in a relationship that would potentially bring greater pain than pleasure if the outcome were nuclear war. Bentham makes an argument about the immorality of deep play for this reason. Geertz, by contrast, makes the point that, despite the logical force behind Bentham's analysis, 'men do engage in such play'. Geertz argues that the explanation, for the Balinese, lies in the fact that deep play is a symbol of moral import. Much more is at stake than material utility: namely, esteem, honour, dignity and respect.

One might argue, similarly, that the cultural force of 'protecting the family' goes far beyond any material gain or pleasure but relates to some of the deepest moral values of a society. Language games of nuclear families connect us with one of the few forms of life that one can imagine people taking action to preserve, regardless of the stakes. The language of 'better dead than red' communicates the same sense of ultimate stakes, but the family is more powerful as a symbol in so far as it has been considered sacred. Understood as a willingness to engage in deep play – with weapons capable of destroying that which was the subject of conflict – this contest is revealed as one between two forms of life, a contest over the organisation of the state, laden with the symbolic meaning of the more basic unit of family life.

The 'guy' games of the Cold War relied on the appearance that nuclear weapons or state control was a source of safety and stability rather than destruction. The appearance was necessary in order to convince the 'common people' in each bloc that a particular game was necessary. The game constituted a relational field occupied by two permanent and committed families. The emancipatory movements began to transform the battlefield by questioning this necessity, by situating these acts within a social game rather than an objective order.

Traditional game theory has been criticised for trivialising life and death experiences at the international level by drawing on game metaphors. By contrast, the language games explored here were not 'mere games' but rather acts by which we were connected and reconnected with a particular kind of experience. At the same time, these acts organised and constructed the identity of NATO or the Warsaw Pact, creating and sustaining these 'imagined communities' as well as their practices of threatening nuclear annihilation. The emancipatory acts of social movements reversed the paradox, exposing the violence and dependence underlying the external images of commitment and protection, just as the women's movement in Western culture exposed the prison of dependence and/or violence that the nuclear family can sometimes become. As in the Balinese cockfight, these are games less in the sense of winning and losing than in showing us something about the contents of our lives.

7

Immanent critique

The use of tension disarms opponents; more important, it makes them react to you. Use contradiction. Find the prevailing sentiment or law in any situation and act as if it were cast not in stone but sand. (Rubin, 1997: 70)

L ANGUAGE OFTEN ISN'T taken seriously at the international level because it is assumed that the words of state actors cannot be trusted. Alliance identity may have been given meaning within a language of family, but alliances are not really families after all, and this 'soft' language merely makes an otherwise horrific possibility palatable. The language of family is a mere appearance that can be distinguished from the destructive reality of nuclear weapons. Realists assume that the words of state actors disguise other interests. The purpose of this chapter is to raise a question about what happens if the disguise is exposed. Moving to the next stage of a Machiavellan strategy, I explore the exacerbation of tensions as the battle-ground was transformed. Processes of immanent critique by independent initiatives in the two blocs opened up spaces of opportunity for both Reagan and Gorbachev to move towards alternative policies.

Clothing state power

Realists and Marxists assume that the everyday language of international politics acts as a disguise for more real interests in power. E. H. Carr (1964) analysed the British doctrine of Harmony of Interests in these terms. Britain, as the dominant world power at the time, clothed its particular interest in the guise of a universal interest. Carr argued that the moral arguments of the strong play an instrumental role in maintaining their power. The point is not that moral argument has no role in international politics, but rather that this role is somewhat more opaque than is often assumed. Morality is not a guide to state action, based on universal moral principles, as the idealists argued. Morality is instead a tool for justifying actions that serve the political interests of those in power. Moral language acts as a disguise for other interests.

A disguise is similar to a lie. It is a cover that hides something. If language is potentially a disguise, the central issue is its truth or falsity. But lying is also a particular kind of language game which is dependent on rules. Wittgenstein (1958: para. 249) states that 'lying is a language game that needs to be learned like any other one'. We are not born liers, but learn how to lie. We learn the types of context that require acts of lying and 'how to go on' in this way. Diplomacy, as a board game and as an historical practice, is an example of a context in which lying is a constitutive rule of the game. One of the reasons why language is not taken seriously by realists is because diplomats or politicians are known to lie. We cannot trust what they say, therefore language should be approached as pure rhetoric.

This assumption is over-simplified for two reasons. First, as John Vincent (1991: 121–2) pointed out, such assumptions fail to ask why people bother with the disguise at all, if pure interests are doing the work. The need to lie, to devote large resources to the public justification of acts, implies that these justifications play a role in constituting the power to realise interests. Second, if the disguise constitutes the power to act then it is not the truth of the claim itself that is most significant, that is, whether a particular individual is lying or telling the truth; rather, it is the ability to *persuade* with this language that is key. Language is convincing if it is meaningful to the listener and if it appears to be reasonable and true.

The language of disguise may be directed at the enemy, but it is also one's own population that must be convinced of the rightness of acts, since they supply the resources and troops which make state power possible. As Hannah Arendt (1958: 57) said in her analysis of the Pentagon Papers, 'concealment, falsehood and the deliberate lie' were aimed less at the enemy than at domestic consumption and Congress in particular.

As the lie enters the public realm it may become difficult to distinguish it from the truth – the lie becomes a rule that constitutes 'reality'. Adam Michnik, from the Polish KOR, identified the power of communism in Poland with success in imposing a language, a power that lost its force once 'workers made their own voices heard'. He states:

> What do I mean when I say that the Polish allowed themselves to have a language imposed upon them after 1945? ... [One] example is the attitude toward the German question. The role of Stalin in the annexation of territories, and in the victory over the Germans was only mentioned positively. To do so was to accept a language that was compromised. One was free to say many things of Stalin – whether it was true or false was irrelevant – as long as the rhetoric was positive. To be sure, those who played this game (journalists, for example) understood full well that it was a game with rules. Their readers, however, were not always so well informed. Due to the long habit of covering Stalin's real face with a mask, the mask seemed more real than the reality.[1]

1 A. Michnik, "What We Want to Do and What We Can Do', *Telos*, 47 (1981), pp. 70–1.

Michnik's point is that these language games did not by definition involve lies, although they could; rather, playing the game involved knowing the rules and what could and could not be said in relation to any particular subject.

On the one hand, political language is often a matter of knowing what can and cannot be said in a given situation, of knowing which language game to play. On the other hand, the words of state leaders do not necessarily correspond to what is being done. In this case, it is possible to reveal the discrepancy between lie and truth. It may be that in most cases the discrepancy is accepted or ignored. But when it isn't the effect can be powerful.

Think of the story of the emperor's new clothes (Anderson, 1993). The emperor was convinced by two wicked men, parading as weavers, that they could make a special magic cloth that could not be seen by a foolish person. The emperor, impressed by this new prospect, asked to have a suit from this magic cloth. The emperor provided the weavers with gold thread and they pretended to make a magic garment. When the prime minister was sent to find out whether the cloth was ready, he could not see a thing, but ran off to tell the emperor that he had never seen such beautiful cloth, for fear of being thought stupid. When the emperor tried the new suit on, the weavers exclaimed gleefully that it was a perfect fit. The emperor, looking in the mirror, could not see a new suit at all, but did not want to seem foolish, so he remarked on its magnificence. By this time, everyone in the land had heard about the new suit and were sure *they* would be able to see it. The emperor led a grand procession in his new magic suit. The crowds were surprised when they could not see the suit; however, as soon as one person in the crowd praised the cloth for its beauty, everyone started to make a similar claim, each of them anxious not to seem more foolish than the rest. But one small boy laughed out loud and shouted, 'Look! The emperor has no clothes on!' At once people around him began to laugh as well. The emperor gasped, realising he had been the most foolish of all.

This story reveals several points about language. First, it demonstrates how easily the rules of what can be said and not said in a particular context can be adopted and repeated, even in the case of an obvious lie. There was initially an agreement in judgement that the emperor's new clothes were beautiful.

Second, the judgement was maintained, in the face of observations to the contrary, because of a social environment in which no one wanted to be seen as foolish. Because we live in a fundamentally social world, we depend on others for recognition of our identities. This is even more true of politicians or emperors since they cannot lead without the support and recognition of populations.

Third, recognition can be taken away. The grown ups were all willing to engage in the game of praising the emperor's new clothes. It only took a small child to point out the discrepancy between what they were saying and the emperor's nakedness. At that point, the crowd quickly turned around and began to laugh with the little boy.

The story of the emperor's new clothes is a useful point of departure for thinking about the concept of immanent critique. The Frankfurt School of critical theory understood critique to be a tool for finding and heightening the tensions between that which exists – for instance, our concepts or theories for defining the world or structures of material or social relations – and the potential for change within it (Calhoun, 1995: 23).[2] Critique does not happen in a vacuum but in relation to a set of historical conditions. The contradictions of a context can serve as the starting point for critique. The little boy in the crowd recognised a contradiction between the rule that people wear clothes in public, his observation that the emperor had no clothes on, and the claims of others that he was wearing a magnificent garment. The little boy's exposure of this contradiction transformed the situation.

Immanent critique does not necessarily involve exposing a lie. Immanent critique can also be used to situate the meaning of a particular practice within an alternative language game. Nathan Stoltzfus (1997) revealed an interesting example from Nazi Germany. He recounts the story of February 1940 when hundreds of unarmed German women engaged in a seven day street protest in Berlin, demanding the release of their Jewish spouses. The Nazi authorities responded to their protests, not only by releasing the Jews in question but by returning those who had already been transported to Auschwitz. The secret of this small success story, in the face of a totalitarian power, was that the spouses exposed the contradiction between a doctrine of family life, espoused by the Nazis, and acts which separated family members from one another. Hitler was aware that his policies had to have the backing of public opinion. Goebbels shaped that public opinion. Wives, who had been fed the doctrine of family life, used it to defend their Jewish spouses.[3]

Nazi discourse about family provided a point of departure for a critique of Nazi practices towards Jewish husbands. The contradictions of this context related to a material reality, of Jews being arrested and deported, but immanent critique was revealed in the contest between language games of family, mobilised by German wives, against a background of a conflicting game which constructed bigotry towards Jews.

2 See also Bernstein (1979); Hoy and McCarthy (1994).
3 As cited in J. Bakewell, 'In 1940 Germans Took to the Streets to Demand the Release of Jews. Why Didn't They Keep it Up?', *The Observer* (16 February 1997).

Why would the exposure of a lie or a contest between conflicting language games have a transformative power? If individuals or states are understood to be purely self-regarding egoists, the discrepancy is not problematic since the maximisation of one's own interests, regardless of others, is key. It becomes extremely important, however, if one's identity and ability to act are understood to be fundamentally social and, therefore, dependent on the recognition of others. The shame or disrespect that comes from failure to live up to previously stated norms or ideals is only experienced in relation to others' recognition that normative expectations have been dashed. As Honneth (1995: 259) points out, it is not in the positive affirmation of these norms that one's constitutive dependence on recognition from others is evident, but in the inability to continue with action once confronted with the discrepancy. Recognition, and its withdrawal, are expressed in language. The ability of states or alliances to act is as dependent on the positive recognition of identity as it is for individuals. Both rely on some measure of acceptance of an alignment between ideals or moral argument and practice.

Removing the cloak

In the previous chapter I examined a process of denaturalising the 'objective' rules of the Cold War game and efforts by independent social movements to 'emancipate' Europe from the Cold War families. In both Eastern and Western Europe, citizens' initiatives took a further step, engaging in acts of immanent critique to expose the contradictions of the Cold War order. The following analysis reveals the tension between conflicting language games by states and citizens' initiatives. As analyst, I am not making a claim about the greater 'truth' of one position or the other, but instead am exploring the dynamics of the contestation between them.[4] In both cases, reasoning about 'correct' action relied on distinct language games. Both movements and states were involved in naming a crime and morally right and wrong behaviour, but each constituted a different set of identities and moral reasons for action.

The next layer of this thick description demonstrates that the language of the Cold War provided the background for processes of immanent critique involving alternative moves that changed the nature of the game as contradictions were exposed. The structure of the two stories is provided by a third grammar of moral discourse, which reveals the creation of 'spaces of opportunity' for an alternative to state-level games, alternatives introduced by Reagan and Gorbachev in the mid to late 1980s.

4 The relationship between truth and contesting language games is a tricky one which is discussed in greater detail in Chapters Nine and Twelve.

Identifying the crime

The construction of the two Cold War alliances as committed families was inseparable from a naming of the 'other' as a threatening neighbour. Accusing the other of criminal behaviour was a pattern in the relationship between the two superpowers, which was exacerbated in the early 1980s with the election of Ronald Reagan to the US Presidency. In 1981, he accused the Soviet Union of reserving itself the right to commit any crime, to lie and to cheat. This behaviour was most evident within the Eastern bloc, where the Soviet Union 'kept its own people imprisoned', which was most visible in Poland. The accusations also related to Western Europe, however, which the Soviet Union was said to hold hostage to its nuclear weapons.[5] The Soviet Union also accused the United States and NATO of a whole range of crimes, from sabotage to blackmail, to slander and poisoning. These accusations related primarily to the US response to martial law in Poland and to the US attempt to hold Western Europe hostage to its nuclear policy.[6] Both superpowers focused on Poland and the nuclear relationship to Western Europe. Both emphasised the criminal acts of the other.

As analysed in the previous chapter, in the early 1980s moral questions began to surface about a contradiction between the claim to protect or to provide security and the actions of the 'older generation'. In the West, members of the alliance family began to feel more threatened by the weapons themselves than the 'other', given the heightened tension between the two and the acquisition of a new generation of weapons. In Poland, moral objections were raised because weapons were being used to discipline and abuse family members rather than protect them.

In both cases, the identification of a contradiction corresponded with a renaming of the crime and the criminal Other. In Poland, the KOR, a group of Polish intellectuals, came together in 1976 to defend the rights of workers persecuted by the Polish government. KOR positioned itself metaphorically as an agent of the law who was unmasking the lawlessness of the government, which had been contradicting legally codified principles of human and civil liberties in its everyday practice.[7] KOR set out to inform the public of the growing rate of criminal behaviour on the part of authorities. This was done, on the one hand, by reference to existing law,

5 See notes 12–14, Chapter Two, p. 39.
6 See notes 15–19, Chapter Two, pp. 39–40.
7 'It is the workers who are the agents of law and order in Poland today.' 'Solidarity Strike Bulletin, no. 5', *LFEE*, 4: 1–3 (1980); 'There are increasingly frequent signs that those designated to guard the public order and binding norms are employing methods which not only contradict the law but incur the abhorrence and condemnation of the whole of society.' 'Appeal by Wladyslaw Bienkowski, October 1976', *LFEE*, 1: 1 (1977); 'We have won the ability to unmask lawlessness.' A. Michnik (1985), 'A Time of Hope.'

both national and international. On the other hand, the group relied on legal metaphors to make an extended moral critique of government action.

In Western Europe, a few years later, peace movements also renamed the crime; it was not an act by one superpower or the other, but the continued growth of the arms race for over thirty years. Europe, both East and West, had been taken hostage by those pursuing the arms race.[8] Guilt rested with both superpowers, rather than one or the other.[9] At the beginning of the 1980s, the urgency of freeing Europe, the hostage, and enforcing détente increased due to the greater technological possibility and political plausibility of confining a nuclear war to the same space as hostage Europe.[10] By contrast, the peace movement hoped to confine nuclear weapons to the territories of the two superpowers.[11]

In each space, the naming of the crime became the focus of a battle between those inside the established centres of power and social movements which positioned themselves 'outside'. The *shared* naming of each contest as a battle suggests the gravity of the situation. The battle represented more than a simple disagreement about peripheral matters; rather, it challenged the values at the foundation of each family.

Wielding the strike weapon

About four years after KOR's renaming of the crime, Solidarity emerged and with it a battle with the government that escalated in several stages. KOR played an important role in preparing the way for Solidarity. KOR was composed primarily of intellectuals and former members of the 1968 student movement. By defending protesting workers against violations of their civil and human rights, the group managed to bridge the historical distrust between intellectuals and workers. By forming an alliance between

---

8 'The all too mighty nations in their spiralling mutual hostility use our peoples in Europe as hostages, at a time when we ourselves have become so free from aggressive impulses.' 'Alva Myrdal's Blueprint for END', *END Bulletin*, 7 (1981–82).

9 'The peace movements do not wish to apportion guilt between the political and military leaders of East and West. Guilt lies squarely with both parties.' 'A Nuclear Free Europe, END Appeal', *END Bulletin*, 11 (1982).

10 '[The peace movement's] objectives must be to free Europe from confrontation, to enforce détente between the United States and Soviet Union and, ultimately, to dissolve both great power alliances.' 'A Nuclear Free Europe, END Appeal.'; 'Many Europeans have come to believe the U.S. motive for deployment of the LRTNF is to make possible a limited nuclear war confined to European soil.' C. J. Lamb, 'Public Opinion and Nuclear Weapons in Europe', *NR*, 29: 6 (1981).

11 '[Peace movements have] the united aim of confining existing nuclear weapons to the territories of the nuclear powers.' Wim Bartels, 'Address to the 12th Special Session of the United Nations, June 24, 1982', IKV Archives, no. 548, ISG, Amsterdam.

117

workers and intellectuals, it overcame one of the traditional barriers to any kind of mass movement.[12]

The defence effort was organised around four principles: trust, openness, truthfulness and autonomy. This policy of 'militant decency' was later adopted by Solidarity.[13] The moral element of the defence plan was strengthened by the central role of the Church in Poland, as the only independent institution in society. The Church became both a tacit ally of Solidarity and an arbiter or mediator between the opposition and the state. The visit of the Polish Pope, John Paul II in 1979 inspired hope within Polish society, which was the other necessary condition for a mass mobilisation.

The battle began with an assault on living standards, which was part of a unified attack on society by the government.[14] Workers responded by mobilising in Gdansk and wielding what would become their most effective weapon: the strike.[15] The weapon was used to force the government into negotiations and compromise.[16] The threat to launch a strike became an important tool for ensuring the compliance of management with the Gdansk Accords, the agreement reached with the government in August 1980, recognising the right of Solidarity to exist as an independent trade union. The agreement, originally signed by the government in the hope of containing the independent union to the coastal cities, became the inspiration for nation-wide strikes in September 1980.[17] The strikes forced the government to accept an independent trade union covering the entire country.

After Solidarity launched its strike, the government responded with a call to battle, which it intended to win.[18] The terrain over which they

---

12 'The demands for bread and for freedom have fused in a single movement of struggle, and an alliance between workers and intellectuals has at last been achieved ... the two groups play quite distinct roles in social relations, and the interests they express are different. Hence the difficulty of forming an alliance.' 'Activists Debate Strategy', *LFEE*, 1: 6 (1978).

13 Jonathan Schell, 'Introduction', in Michnik (1985: xxvii).

14 'All other assaults on the standard of living have evoked sharp opposition within society and explosions on a more or less local scale. The current attack is the largest so far ... These decisions formed a unified attack on the whole of society.' J. Kuron, 'The Situation in the Country and the Programme of the Opposition – Some Notes', *LFEE*, 3: 3 (1979).

15 'Strikes are the workers' most effective weapon.' 'Strike Bulletin Solidarnosc, No. 1', *LFEE*, 4: 1–3 (1980).

16 'One of the duties of a free labour union is to force the authorities to talk, to negotiate.' A. Michnik and J. J. Lipski, 'Some Remarks on the Opposition and the General Situation in Poland', in Michnik (1985).

17 'The avalanche unleashed by the workers of the coast can only be contained by a radical change in the attitude of the state towards the workers.' 'Solidarity Strike Bulletin, No. 9', *LFEE*, 4: 1–3 (1980).

18 'Our party [has] been also called to a battle. This battle we have to win.' 'Letter from the Secretariat of the Party Central Committee, 19 August 1980', *LFEE*, 4: 1–3 (1980).

fought was public opinion.[19] Solidarity was fighting for human rights in a general sense and an independent trade union in particular. Its objectives were more moral than political and it initially – and eventually – succeeded because it was defending those the state claimed to protect, that is, the working class.[20] The objective of the government, on the other hand, was political, that is, to maintain its hold over Polish society. Subsequently, it faced the task of winning back credibility.[21]

For the Party, the battle represented a threat to the security of Poland. A connection was made between the acts of the criminal 'other' outside Poland, that is, the United States, and 'anti-socialist elements' within Poland. Both presented a threat and both were enemies.[22] Solidarity – and KOR before it – was explicit in positioning itself outside the Party, as a way of claiming independence. The Party, by contrast, located part of the movement outside in the camp of the Western 'other', who was attempting to inspire a psychological war against Poland and interfere in its internal affairs.[23] Both sides in this conflict accused the other of criminal behaviour. The Party was cautious, however, making a distinction between anti-socialist elements and the strikers as a whole.[24] The distinction made sense given the goal of winning back credibility among the population. As it was, the attack on 'anti-socialist elements' enhanced the image of KOR in the public mind, lending it 'a greater moral and political authority than its capabilities actually warrant'.[25]

19 '[The Polish United Workers' Party Central Committee] plenary session is taking place in conditions of an acute struggle for public opinion.' 'Moscow Assails Solidarity's Congress', *CDSP*, 33: 36 (1981); 'The workers are not surprised by the vile methods of psychological warfare carried out by the authorities aiming to provoke and mislead public opinion.' 'Statements Nos 1 and 2 of the Interfactory Strike Committee', *LFEE*, 4: 1–3 (1980).

20 'Solidarity represented a deadly threat to the government, for it challenged the chief principle of communist ideology, which is that the party represents the working class.' Michnik (1985), 'The Polish War.'

21 'The government must gain credibility – not in its old role of dictator but in that of partner.' Michnik (1985), 'Hope and Danger, 1980'; 'The authorities have no credibility in society.' 'Poland on the Eve of the Coup', *LFEE*, 5: 1–2 (1982).

22 'It is no secret that Solidarity has become a target of active penetration by the open enemies of socialism.' 'Polish Leaders Begin to Assail Solidarity', *CDSP*, 33: 3 (1981).

23 'U.S. reactionary circles are continuing to step up their interference in the internal affairs of socialist Poland.' 'Polish Leaders Begin to Assail Solidarity'; 'This anti-socialist organisation has enjoyed the support of foreign subversion centres ... that are waging "psychological warfare" against the socialist countries.' 'More Tension in Poland: Jaruzelski In', *CDSP*, 33: 6 (1981).

24 'The opponents of socialism who have infiltrated Solidarity make up a small segment of this trade union association, but they are playing on people's emotions and trying to use the current mood to win over workers to their side.' 'More Tension in Poland.'

25 Michnik (1985), 'Hope and Danger.'

In addition to imposing a blockade on information,[26] the government actively constructed a public image of the internal enemy. This image was consistent with the naming of a context of battle. The internal enemy was, according to the government, engaged in a range of war-like acts, including penetration, escalation, threatening, operating under cover, holding warning strikes, shifting to a frontal attack, maintaining strike readiness, unleashing a war, disarming the Polish people, arming themselves, launching attacks, and waging an open offensive and combat.[27] The objects of action were metaphoric in nature, however, in so far as Solidarity was 'escalating demands' or 'maintaining strike readiness via the media'.

As martial law was declared, these military acts were combined with accusations that Solidarity was actually using violence, for instance by setting up commando groups at enterprises or creating combat groups to safeguard Solidarity's security.[28] Solidarity was also accused, in the month preceding martial law, of 'having military detachments of the storm trooper variety' and of frequently using brute force. It was also said to be attempting to overthrow the socialist state and spread conflict to other socialist states.[29]

Just prior to the step up in the campaign for public opinion, the Party, by its own reports, was losing the battle. Acts of the trade union were increasingly identified as a threat not only to Poland but to the Eastern bloc as well. As advances were made into the Party itself, and as the economic structure became increasingly unstable, Jaruzelski adopted the weapons of war in a literal sense. He justified his actions with arguments that Solidarity

26 '[The work of KOR was] undertaken with a view to break through the officially imposed blockade of strike information.' 'Statement and Appeal from Social Self-Defence Committee "KOR", 25 August 1980', *LFEE*, 4: 1–3 (1980).

27 See, respectively: 'Strikes in Poland: The Soviet Coverage', *CDSP*, 32: 33 (1980); 'Poland: Focusing on New Trade Unions', *CDSP*, 32: 47 (1980); 'Kania Warns Against Political Strikes', *CDSP*, 32: 49 (1980); 'Poland: Pravda's Comments Get Tougher', *CDSP*, 33: 1 (1981); 'Polish Leaders Begin to Assail Solidarity'; 'More Tension in Poland'; 'Poland: "Anti-Socialists" in Solidarity Scored', CDSP, 33: 17 (1981); 'Kania, Jaruzelski Visit Brezhnev in Crimea', *CDSP*, 33: 33 (1981); 'Moscow Assails Solidarity Congress'; 'Soviet Workers Join in Blasting Solidarity', *CDSP*, 33: 37 (1981).

28 'Polish television reports that leaders of local Solidarity organisations have begun setting up "commando groups" at enterprises. Instances of the theft of weapons and explosives from state storehouses have been noted.' 'Poland Declares Martial Law', *CDSP*, 33: 50 (1981).

29 '[Solidarity's extremist leaders] are seeking to deepen the atmosphere of antisocialist and anti-Soviet psychosis so that in this situation ... they can make further attacks on socialism with the aim of seizing power in Poland.' 'Soviet Workers Join in Blasting Solidarity'; 'The so-called "appeal to the peoples of Eastern Europe" ... can be assessed in no other way than as a direct call to overthrow socialism not only in Poland but also in other socialist countries.' 'Soviet Attacks on Solidarity Continue', *CDSP*, 33: 38 (1981).

was planning to take over the state. The United States and NATO were identified as accomplices in this effort.

Solidarity referred to the imposition of martial law as a 'coup'. Normally, martial law is the administration of law by military force, invoked by a government in an emergency when the civilian law enforcement agencies are unable to maintain public order and safety. A *coup d'état*, on the other hand, is most often the violent overthrow or alteration of an existing form of government. Solidarity's use of *'coup d'état'* communicated that an existing authority had been replaced, an authority that possessed a legitimacy that the military government lacked. The coup had replaced a 'sovereign society' with its 'delegitimised authorities'.[30]

Solidarity's immanent critique of the distinction between the Polish government's claim to protect workers and its acts of repression against a workers' movement, gave rise to a contest between two conflicting language games regarding the place and authority of the worker within Polish society. While martial law was an apparent defeat, a new stage of the battle emerged as Solidarity was pushed underground. A different strategy, adapting the decentralised structure of Solidarity to the conditions of martial law, emphasised 'being what you want to become'.[31] If the Polish people continued to act as if they were free, even under martial law, then the government might have won the battle but it would eventually lose the war. As Adam Michnik noted:

> Regardless of what may be written in their newspapers, they know that they did not win this war, but only a single battle, in which an army of a few thousand men battled against defenceless workers. But they lost something that every government wants most; they lost their credibility and all hope of credibility. No one believes them now and no one will believe them in the future. The last hope for communism to take root in Polish society lies buried with the bodies of Wujek miners.[32]

Freeing the hostage or containing the prisoner

Solidarity and the Polish government engaged in a battle for public opinion and the credibility to defend the working class. In the West, another battle surfaced between a peace movement engaged in developing an alternative transatlantic alliance,[33] and a transatlantic alliance which claimed to be the

---

30 A. Michnik, 'What We Want to Do'.
31 Weschler (1982: 56).
32 Michnik, (1985).
33 Kaldor stated that, 'In effect, the peace movements have begun to create an alternative Atlantic alliance based on cooperation and common interest instead of fear.' See M. Kaldor, 'Alternative Alliance', *New York Times* (15 December 1983).

real peace movement.[34] The battle broke out in the aftermath of the 1979 decision by NATO to deploy cruise and Pershing II missiles in five Western European countries unless a balanced agreement could be negotiated with the Soviet Union. While guilt for the arms race was attributed to both super-powers, the NATO decision provided a pretext for an initial confrontation on the Western front.[35]

In this context, language games of security and crime were closely intertwined. Deterrence was a family place, but also a prison of mutual terror, shared with the Eastern bloc, a prison which, like the security dilemma, was inescapable. NATO was a committed partnership but also the prison guard, vigilant in maintaining the balance of terror. Without the prison, the West would be insecure since the Soviet Union would not be dissuaded from its desire to dominate Western Europe. The security of the Western family was inseparable from the existence of a prison of terror, and this prison was inescapable.

The Western European peace movement situated this reversible image within an alternative game, which transformed the moral logic of nuclear weapons and what should be done with them. The greatest threat was not from the Soviet Union, as articulated by state leaders, but the nuclear weapons themselves, which were or had become a source of insecurity.[36] The cruise and Pershing II deployments did not enhance protection; they symbolised Western Europe's dependence on the United States.[37] The prison hostage was not the people of *either* Eastern or Western Europe, but *all* of Europe and the Europeans, who needed to be liberated from the Cold War.[38] Nuclear weapons had to be confined to the territories of the superpowers in order to free Europe from nuclear weapons and the nuclear prison. Not the prison, but responsibility for these weapons and their use, could not be escaped.[39]

NATO emphasised that the prison could not be escaped. The peace movement stressed the need to free Europe and the world from nuclear

---

34 'NATO had demonstrated its deterrence value for over 35 years and in doing so, had proved itself to be Europe's most successful peace movement.' Lamb, 'Public Opinion and Nuclear Weapons'.

35 'On every front, the Western European peace movement finds itself facing momentous challenges. On the Western front ... the first is to take the political initiative and to keep the missile issue firmly on the electoral agenda.' 'Curiouser and Curiouser, Editorial', *END Journal*, 3 (1983).

36 See discussion in the family section of Chapter Six, p. 107.

37 'A Strategy for 1983', *END Journal*, 2 (1983).

38 M. Kaldor, 'Liberating Ourselves from Cold War Ideologies', *END Journal*, 10 (1984).

39 'As either voters and/or taxpayers ... we cannot escape responsibility for these weapons or their possible use.' Robert and Joan Hinde, 'The Case Against Deterrence', *END Bulletin*, 5 (1981).

weapons if civilisation and future generations were to survive. Each side in this conflict claimed a moral position. The question of the potential use of nuclear weapons was pivotal to both. The strategy of nuclear deterrence was the key to NATO's modern theology of war. It had blessed Europe with an otherwise inexplicable period of peace.[40] Deterrence rested on the threat to use nuclear weapons in order to prevent any kind of war; this presumed a clear distinction between the threat and actual use. From the perspective of NATO, the strategy was morally superior for this reason. The tremendous destructive power that would potentially be released in the case of nuclear war made actual use unthinkable. If the stakes were so high, neither side would cross the line and any kind of war would be averted.

The peace movement, with a growing number of Churches in its ranks, challenged this logic, calling into question the morality of a strategy that threatened the destruction of civilisation and the world itself. Besides the existing overkill capacity of both sides, they argued that developments in the early 1980s – technological, strategic and political – were moving in the direction of a first strike capability and fighting a limited nuclear war confined to Europe.[41] Some also argued that the threat to use nuclear weapons implied their possible use.

At the height of the debate, a third position was adopted by a number of Church authorities, including Pope John Paul II. He argued that deterrence 'may still be judged morally acceptable', but only on a temporary basis. 'Deterrence can't be an end in itself, but must be a step on the way towards progressive disarmament.'[42] This position provided a temporary justification for efforts to maintain the nuclear deterrent. However, given the emphasis on 'temporary', it undermined NATO's argument that the prison of deterrence was 'inescapable', which implied its indefinite maintenance.

The peace movements formulated the problem in terms of liberation from the Cold War rather than an escape. A solution to the problem had to be political in nature, as opposed to military. It had to involve freeing Europe, and eventually the world, of these weapons. While both NATO and

40 'Deterrence is the key to a modern theology of war.' J. M. P. Villas-Boas, 'Public Perceptions and Nuclear Morality', *NR*, 32: 2 (1984); 'It is highly probable that this strategy [of deterrence] has been responsible for Europe being blessed with an otherwise inexplicable period of peace.' W. Hofmann, 'Is NATO's Defence Policy Facing a Crisis?', *NR*, 32: 2 (1984).

41 'Fear of nuclear war has inspired the huge public protests ... Some of those campaigning for Western disarmament have suggested that the new NATO weapons will upset an existing parity, increase the likelihood of nuclear war limited to Europe, give the United States the ability to launch a "first strike" against the Soviet Union, and make the territory of European states accepting them a target for Soviet nuclear attack.' R. Dean, 'The Alliance and Nuclear Weapons', *NR*, 31: 1 (1983).

42 Dean, 'The Alliance.'

the peace movements claimed a morally superior position, the contest was potentially lethal for NATO, since political cohesion was necessary for the working of the deterrent.[43] A divided public would undermine the credibility of the threat. The European public was increasingly divided, given a growing perception that the United States was forcing weapons on Europe and the absence of any perception of immediate danger from the Soviet Union.[44]

NATO's fear of losing the battle for public opinion emerged as early as 1981, but the language of battle became a structuring feature of NATO discourse in 1983, the year the deployments began.[45] The decision to proceed was on the surface a victory for the alliance; however, continuing conflict within NATO was evident from inconsistent reports on the battle. In one account, peace movement 'unilateralists' had seized the high ground in the debate. In another, they were moving onto the defensive and retreating, although they were far from rerouted. The alliance had fought a hard parliamentary battle and won, on the one hand; on the other hand, it was witnessing a crisis of elites. This crisis was both the cause and the consequence of the crumbling framework within which political battles had been fought for most of the post-war period. One element of consensus remained, however; security policy in Western Europe had been politicised and democratised during the cruise and Pershing debates.[46] In contrast to the 1970s, when questions of defence were primarily dealt with in secret, the debate was now taking place in the public realm.[47]

43 'By questioning the moral aspect and also the legitimacy of deterrence, representatives of [the Church] may endanger its effectiveness in no small way.' Hofmann, 'Is NATO's Defence Policy Facing a Crisis?'

44 The growing public perception is that the US is forcing nuclear weapons on Western Europe.' Lamb, 'Public Opinion and Nuclear Weapons'; 'Immediacy is absent in popular perceptions of the Soviet menace.' G. Flynn, 'Public Opinion and Atlantic Defense', *NR*, 31: 5 (1983).

45 Lamb, 'Public Opinion and Nuclear Weapons'; R. Giradet, 'Neutralism and Pacifism: Improving Public Understanding of Alliance Objectives', *NR*, 30: 5 (1982); Dean, 'The Alliance'; T. Hitchens, 'NATO Parliamentarians Call for Increased Information Effort', *NR*, 30: 6 (1983); A. Fontaine, 'The Future of Détente', *NR*, 31: 1 (1983); Lord Carrington, 'Lack of Consistent Political Strategy: A Cause of Friction', *NR*, 31: 2 (1983); Flynn, 'Public Opinion'; A. Levi, 'NATO: Key to Peace and Security', *NR*, 31: 6 (1984).

46 'Public opinion is in fact being "democratised" as well as "politicised".' Villas-Boas, 'Public Perceptions.'

47 'The task of enlisting and even maintaining public support is particularly difficult for an international organisation operating mainly in the confidential and often secret areas of defence and political consultation. The debates in NATO Council, even at the Ministerial level, do not take place in public like those at the United Nations or [European Community]. For useful consultation, rapid decisionmaking and effective action are the advantages, but there is a price to be paid insofar as public opinion is not directly and immediately involved.' F. Roberts, 'Voluntary Societies in Support of NATO', *NR*, 23: 6 (1975).

As in Poland, a battle had apparently been won, but the larger outcome of the war was not yet decided. Leaders were suffering from a credibility problem before their own publics.[48] This credibility problem related to the survival of the alliance, since 'the best way to kill an alliance is to make it controversial'.[49] It also related to the credibility of the threat itself, given its dependence on an image of unity. As in Poland, the 'other' superpower was said to be engaged in psychological warfare directed at public opinion in the hope of influencing the outcome of the battle.[50]

Spaces of opportunity

In the same year that the European battle climaxed, Reagan's position within the war shifted. He was confronted with his own domestic battle in Congress over a nuclear weapons freeze resolution.[51] At the beginning of March 1983, he tried to counter the influence of the Nuclear Weapons Freeze campaign with his 'Evil Empire' speech before a group of Evangelical Christians.[52] The speech was one of his most pronounced characterisations of the Soviet Union as criminal. Two weeks later, he introduced the idea of SDI, which marked the beginning of a change in both tone and emphasis. While the Soviet Union was previously *the* threat, nuclear weapons moved to centre stage with Reagan's argument that they must be rendered 'impotent and obsolete'.[53] In the Evil Empire speech, he warned his listeners 'to beware the temptation ... to ignore the facts of history and the aggressive impulse of an evil empire, to simply call the arms race a grand misunderstanding and thereby remove yourself from the struggle between right and

48 Flynn, 'Public Opinion.'
49 Flynn, 'Public Opinion.' See also 'The forces [sapping the alliance] do not have to take over countries; it is enough for them to reach a certain critical mass to produce enough turmoil and division to make governments tremble and alliances totter.' A. Levi, 'Western Values and the Successor Generation', *NR*, 30: 2 (1982).
50 'The current phenomenon of fear is indeed primarily due to a change of consciousness. A German opinion pollster ... attributes this development partially to a psychological war which has been waged by the Soviet Union against the West ... which is aimed at undermining the West's will to preserve its way of life.' Hofmann, 'Is NATO's Defence Policy Facing a Crisis?'
51 Most speeches from this time include arguments about the dangers of a Nuclear Weapons Freeze, for instance: 'The Freeze concept is dangerous because it would preserve today's high, unequal and unstable levels of nuclear forces.' R. Reagan, 'Arms Control: A Plea for Patience', *VSD*, 49: 13 (1983).
52 As Oberdorfer (1992: 24) states, 'The main purpose of the international section of the [Evil Empire] speech was to enlist the Evangelicals in the administration's fight against the nuclear freeze movement ... The nuclear freeze, which was backed by many American churches, was under intense debate in Congress.'
53 R. Reagan, 'Peace and National Security: A New Defence', *VSD*, 49: 13 (1983).

wrong and good and evil.' As the SDI idea developed in 1984 and 1985, the arms race became a grand misunderstanding. Reagan wanted to escape the prison of nuclear deterrence which held nations hostage to nuclear terror and to identify common interests with the Evil Empire.[54] With the announcement of SDI, Reagan began to name the same threat as the peace movements, that is, the nuclear weapons themselves. Security was redefined as neutralising these weapons, which, he argued, would make the world, and not only the West, sleep more securely.[55] After this point, Reagan engaged in two conflicting language games at the same time. He continued to emphasise the need to 'maintain deterrence' until such a time that SDI could be developed, given the evil nature of the Soviet Union. He also pointed to nuclear deterrence as the central problem and to SDI as the solution that would make cooperation with the Soviet Union possible.

Reagan had shifted attention to the same threat as the peace movement, but offered a different solution. The peace movement proposed liberating the hostage and freeing Europe from nuclear weapons; Reagan wanted to escape the prison of deterrence, which was in conflict with NATO's position that the prison was inescapable.[56]

The Soviet Union, prior to Gorbachev, dramatised the crimes of the United States, and particularly its efforts to hold Western Europe hostage to its policy. Gorbachev, like Reagan, shifted the parameters of both the crime and the solution. He began to implicate both superpowers equally, rather than pointing to the criminal acts of the other. Instead of escaping the prison, he argued the need to destroy the guillotine. In a speech to the International Forum for a Nuclear Free World, he said:

> With the stockpiling of nuclear weapons, the human race has lost its immortality. It can be regained only by destroying nuclear weapons. We have rejected the right of the leadership of any country whatsoever, be it the USSR,

---

54 'Nations could defend themselves against missile attack and mankind at last could escape the prison of nuclear terror.' R. Reagan, 'The Geneva Summit', *CP*, 766 (1985); 'We should always remember that we do have common interests. And foremost among them is to avoid war and reduce the level of arms ... Today, our common enemies are poverty, disease and, above all, war.' R. Reagan, 'U.S.–Soviet Relations: A Policy of Credible Deterrence', *VSD*, 50: 8 (1984).

55 'Surely, the world will sleep more secure when these missiles have been rendered useless, militarily and politically.' R. Reagan, 'Life and the Preservation of Freedom', *VSD*, 52: 3 (1985).

56 According to Flynn, the switch to SDI caused considerable complications in the European context. In addition to the fear that SDI would decouple the US from Western Europe, 'SDI, following the [intermediate-range nuclear forces, INF] discussion, presented a new challenge to the management of security policy consensus by Western governments.' Flynn, Moreton and Treverton (1985: 8).

the United States or any other, to pass a death sentence on mankind. We are not judges, and billions of people are not criminals who must be punished. It is necessary to break the nuclear guillotine. The superpowers should step out of their nuclear shadow into a nuclear free world. In doing so, they will put an end to the alienation of politics from the norms of morality common to all mankind.[57]

The superpowers, which had hidden behind balance of power reasoning, should step out of the shadow. Instead, they should reason on the basis of norms of human decency. Like the peace movements, Gorbachev wanted to free not only Europe, but the world, of nuclear weapons.[58] Rather than escaping the prison, he proposed destroying the guillotine. Like the peace movements, he suggested a political solution that recognised the interdependence of humanity as the basis for a new form of international relations, new habits of acting. He argued the need to get rid of outdated ideas and theories that no longer fit the reality of the world.[59] His 'new thinking' was inseparable from domestic changes within the Soviet Union, including greater openness and decency in both domestic and military affairs, as well as economic reforms which, like Solidarity, began with self-governance.[60]

It is not the case that language games of this kind had never before come from the mouths of politicians. However, given the politicisation of domestic reforms in Poland and the politicisation of deterrence, these games had acquired a broad basis of public support which they had not enjoyed at earlier points in the Cold War. The two superpowers were competing for international and domestic opinion; the public was divided over the moral justification for particular forms of action by state leaders. Both superpowers moved outside the presumably inescapable constraints of the Cold War game. An alternative course of action internationally and domestically, within the Eastern bloc, which in the past would have threatened their survival, at least temporarily restored the popularity of both.

57 M. Gorbachev, 'Gorbachev Talks to Moscow Peace Forum', *CDSP*, 39: 7 (1987).
58 'We proceeded from the need to clear the way to détente in Europe, to free the European peoples from the fear of a nuclear catastrophe, and then to go further toward the elimination of all nuclear weapons ... Europe deserves to be freed from nuclear weapons, to stop being a nuclear hostage.' 'Gorbachev Hits Reagan on Reykjavik Failure', *CDSP*, 38: 42 (1986).
59 'Europe's security cannot be ensured by military means, by armed force. It is a completely new situation, one that marks a break with tradition, a way of thinking and a way of acting formed over the centuries, even millennia.' 'Gorbachev Proposes to U.S. a Ban on Space Strike Arms', *CDSP*, 37: 40 (1985).
60 Gorbachev (1987: 33).

Conclusion

The coincidence of a moral challenge to the practices of states in both East and West provided a *space of opportunity* for the two superpowers to manoeuvre in ways that were partially consistent with previously articulated interests. The peace movements and Churches presented a moral challenge to the logic of the deterrence game in general, but also pointed to a contradiction between this logic and what they viewed as new practices. The morality of deterrence rested on arguments that it would prevent any kind of war; NATO and Reagan continued to articulate this argument while moving towards a warfighting strategy by the same name. Reagan resituated the general attack on deterrence, and the public fear of nuclear war, in an argument for SDI. While ingenious on one level, this move also put him in conflict with his NATO partners.

The Soviet Union recognised that Poland could not be ruled by force for ever and that Polish ideas were seeping into Eastern Europe. It saw an opportunity to attach face-saving reforms to the international momentum for disarmament in such a way that the Soviet Union, with a charismatic new leader, could seize the initiative. The basis for this claim will be analysed in more depth in the next chapter. The central point is that the possibility of this change has to be situated in the context of a widespread change in public judgements regarding 'correct' behaviour. As Kratochwil (1989: 12) has pointed out:

> Most of our arguments concerning policy or rights are not so much about the determination of the likely result, *given* a certain distribution of 'preferences', as they are debates over which preferences deserve priority over others, which ones ought to be changed, and which judgements deserve our assent. Here the overall persuasive 'weight' of claims rather than their logical necessity or aggregation is at issue.

Morally correct action was defined in a social context. As the tensions in this context were exacerbated and as meanings were situated in alternative language games, new possibilities, such as disarmament, became thinkable. The conflict in Poland was over the meaning of the state/society relationship and, in particular, the identity of the worker in a workers' state. Once a new set of meanings began to take hold within populations, and affected the actions and practices of a large number of people, the old way of reasoning began to lose its hold.

The moral challenge pointed to a distinction between state argument-ation and action, and was threatening precisely because of the public basis of power. In both blocs, the challenge arose out of a growing articulation of a distinction between what states claimed to do, that is, to provide security, and actions that were generating an increased sense of insecurity. Gorbachev's 'new thinking' became possible against the background of a breakdown in the public consensus regarding nuclear weapons internationally and domestic reforms in the Eastern bloc. Given the taboo against defensive systems in both blocs, going back to the 1970s, it was by no means given that Reagan's 'surprise' announcement of SDI would take hold in public discourse. It did so against the background of an increasing fear of a nuclear war and widespread questions about the moral rightness of nuclear deterrence. Disarmament became possible in a context of changing games.

8

Dialogue

Oppose power, don't *fight it directly. Rely on the tactic of As If. Act* as if *the power you seek is already yours.* (Rubin, 1997: 105)

DISARMAMENT AND RESTRUCTURING became possible against the backdrop of battles for the allegiance of public opinion in each bloc. The end of the Cold War was also about the breakdown of the division of Europe. The maintenance of this division was dependent on the antagonistic relationship not only between East and West, but between human rights and peace or disarmament as well. It is not incidental that I have focused on a peace movement in the West and initiatives in the East, defined in part by their exposure of human rights violations. The two battles took place within each house, and were not on the surface related, except for the fact that in both cases social movements were understood by states to be pawns in a psychological war manipulated by the 'other'. As long as the two were defined in mutually exclusive terms, these internal battles only hardened the divisions of the Cold War.

The 'battles' for public opinion, explored in the previous chapter, opened up spaces of opportunity for Reagan and Gorbachev to consider alternatives which had previously been understood to be unrealistic. The purpose of this chapter is to analyse more explicitly the rationality of moving towards a new game in which the identities and practices of the superpowers changed. I shall explore the transition from a game of 'other minds' involved in negotiations to one of 'human beings' engaged in dialogue.

The 'other minds' problem

The crucial point of the 'other minds' problem is the inability to know the particular thoughts of individuals. Unlike an engine, which can be taken apart in order to examine its internal workings, it is impossible to look inside the mind of another (Hollis and Smith, 1991: 172). However, as Martin Hollis (1994: 142–62) suggests, the significance of the problem changes if one shifts from the model of the individual actor to an analysis of social rules. To return to the chess metaphor, an observer cannot look into the mind of Kasparov, but she can see the possibilities available to him from a particular position on the board and she can see the outcome, that is, how he in fact moves. It is impossible to answer why he moved as he did without knowing the context and how this context constrained or empowered him to move in particular ways.

An emphasis on rules, as opposed to the 'mental processes' of individuals, is particularly significant for two types of analysis. First, it is useful for understanding a context in which individual minds are less the issue than collective ones, which are 'other minds' only by analogy. Given the collective nature of international politics, one can question whether the central issue is one of looking inside individual minds or, subsequently, individual lies, since the 'other' in this case is a collective entity rather than a single individual.

Second, it is useful for the analysis of change from one game to another, in which case identifying the rationality of possible moves is dependent on the *a priori* identification of a new game. Given the intersubjective nature of games, one can ask whether, ultimately, the *motives* of one side are more important for understanding outcomes than the more public *interactions* between the two sides. Because East and West, or Gorbachev and Reagan, were acting and reacting to one another, it may be more significant for understanding the outcome to situate these acts within the context of a changing game than to understand *why* one side acted as it did. One might argue that Reagan's gestures of friendship towards Gorbachev were a reflection of the 'other minds' problem, in so far as these acts were part of another agenda. Either of them may have had motives other than friendship. But which is more important: the real motive underlying Reagan's actions or what became possible as a result of these acts, that is, the outcome of friendship and subsequent changes in policy? Top officials in both administrations noted, after the fact, the significance of this development.

In February 1993 two teams of former high-ranking officials from the United States and the Soviet Union met at Princeton University to analyse the diplomatic and political episodes of the mid 1980s prior to the collapse of the Cold War. Throughout these discussions, participants articulated a recurring theme that is rarely mentioned in conventional accounts of changing superpower relations.[1] Actors on both sides expressed a sense of surprise that Gorbachev and Reagan, not to mention the other members of their negotiating teams, began to deal with one another as human beings. Chernayaev, the personal adviser on foreign affairs to General Secretary Gorbachev, reflecting on the 1987 Washington Summit, stated that

1 The exception is Oberdorfer (1992).

'perhaps for the first time we understood so clearly how important the human factor is in international politics'(Wohlforth, 1996: 8). In a speech to the Politburo, Gorbachev himself said that 'policymakers, including the leaders of states, of governments, if they really are responsible people, they also represent purely human qualities, the interests and aspirations of common people, and that they can be guided by purely normal human feelings and aspirations' (Wohlforth, 1996: 8). George Shultz said he felt that 'Gorbachev laid it on the line and so did Reagan. And that one reason they respected each other was that both could see that the other guy was saying what he thought ... It was real' (Wohlforth, 1996: 9). Finally, Besmertnykh, the former Soviet Foreign Minister, concluded that the Cold War 'was ended by human beings, by people who were dedicated to eradicating this part of history' (Wohlforth, 1996: 9).

The Cold War was ended by human beings sitting down together and talking face to face. This is a very different conclusion than the conventional wisdom that Reagan or the West 'won' by pressuring the Soviet Union to change. We have become used to thinking about the end of the Cold War as the latter; yet top officials involved at the highest levels seem to be saying something different. How do we account for a transition from a military stalemate based on a game of 'other minds', which no one seriously expected to end in the foreseeable future, to Reagan and Gorbachev sitting down together as human beings? The two represent quite different forms of life and relationship.

Other minds and other games

The 'other minds problem' within the Cold War can be approached as part of a game which relies on certain kinds of distinction by which players knew 'how to go on'. Playing the game reproduced a division of space populated by 'others' who disagreed or could not be trusted. In this context, the spatial division between two households established the boundaries of self and other. In playing the game, the two sides made similar moves that hardened the boundaries between them, making any kind of 'agreement' next to impossible.

Language games involving 'other minds' were evident in two forums established for the purpose of improving communication between the two blocs. The first goes back to the mid 1970s and involved efforts, within the context of détente, to institutionalise communication between the members of each bloc. The hope was to ameliorate the misunderstandings that had given rise to tensions in the past. The culmination was the signing of the Helsinki Final Act in 1975. The Final Act was signed by members of both blocs on 1 August 1975 after several years of negotiations involving diplomats from thirty-five participating countries.

132

The Helsinki process was not intended to overcome the spatial division between East and West, at least in the short term; only to improve the conditions for dialogue between the two sides. However, as the process developed, the hoped for dialogue disintegrated into a competition between two fixed positions, based on different interpretations of the document, as representatives from East and West struggled to 'realise their main policy purposes' (Bloed, 1990:6).

The two sides interpreted the Final Act selectively. The Eastern bloc drew on Helsinki to emphasise the primacy of 'external' issues of peace, as articulated in the security basket, as well as peaceful coexistence based on non-interference in internal affairs.[2] The words 'human rights' rarely appeared in their interpretations. The West, on the other hand, focused on the violation of commitments regarding human rights and fundamental freedoms.[3]

Misunderstanding began not with misperception but with two mutually exclusive interpretations of the document. The conflict was exacerbated as Charter 77 and the Polish KOR exposed the distinction between the act of signing by Eastern leaders and their own persecution for pointing out this inconsistency. The initial effort to improve communication broke down over different interpretations of the meaning of human rights and the significance of the document as a whole.

A similar fixing of positions developed out of the interaction between the two superpowers in the years prior to their sudden reconciliation. The distance between the two grew as arms control became a site of conflict. At the end of the 1970s, a movement was afoot to restore the military capabilities of the West, based on the conclusion that 'talk' over the past decade had benefited the Soviet Union. The West did nothing to improve its military capability during this time, it was said, and détente provided a screen behind which the Eastern bloc had rearmed.[4] Talking with the Soviet Union would only be possible once Western capabilities were restored.

Western language games relied on assumptions about the requirements of effective communication, based on a means–end logic. States, like politicians, may need to engage in less than pure acts in order to achieve a good

---

2 See, for instance, *For Peace, Security, Cooperation and Social Progress in Europe: On the Results of the Conference of the Communist and Workers' Parties of Europe, Berlin, June 29–30, 1976* (Moscow: Novosti Press Agency Publishing House, 1976).

3 See *Texts of Final Communiques, 1975–1980*, Volume II, issued by Ministerial Sessions of the North Atlantic Council, the Defence Planning Committee and the Nuclear Planning Group. Brussels: NATO Information Service.

4 'From the beginning of SALT ... the Soviet objective has been to extend its gains in relative posture while encouraging maximum restraint upon U.S. programmes.' 'Where We Stand on SALT', in Tyroler (1984).

end. The build-up of military hardware was understood to be the necessary condition for communicating with the other and persuading him to disarm. A restoration of military strength would provide an incentive for the Soviets to come to, and stay at, the bargaining table.[5]

This means–end approach hardened the boundaries between two collective selves. One had to present a united front in constructing a military force that would convince the other to come to the bargaining table. When the two sides did meet, during negotiations regarding intermediate-range nuclear forces in Europe, they occupied two distinct and fixed spaces, from which movement was difficult, if not impossible. The context was one of bargaining between representatives.[6] Each side proposed solutions that were presented to the other, who most often rejected or placed obstacles in the way of the other's plans.[7]

Each side made claims about the distinction between the words and deeds of the other,[8] about their own sincerity and commitment to negotiate in good faith,[9] and about the greater seriousness with which they had

5 'As a result of NATO demonstrating the resolve to modernise its [theatre nuclear forces], the Soviet Union has been persuaded to put on the negotiating table, for the first time, nuclear forces that threaten the allies.' R. Burt, 'NATO and Nuclear Deterrence', *DSB* (November 1981).

6 'In a negotiation impatience can be a real handicap. Any of you who have been involved in labour–management negotiations, or any kind of bargaining, know that patience strengthens your bargaining position.' R. Reagan, 'Arms Control Policy: A Plea for Patience', *VSD*, 49: 13 (1983).

7 For the immediate future, I am asking my [Strategic Arms Reduction Talks] negotiating team to propose to their Soviet counterparts a practical, phased reduction plan.' R. Reagan, 'East–West Relations: Reduction of Nuclear Arms', *VSD*, 48: 16 (1982); 'The proposals that [the Soviet Union] placed on the negotiating table with the United States last year ... express a readiness to discuss and resolve the question of limiting and reducing medium range nuclear arms in Europe.' 'NATO's Tough Stand on Nuclear Arms Hit', *CDSP*, 33: 19 (1981); 'In our negotiations on INF, when the Soviet leaders adamantly refused to consider the total elimination of these weapons, the United States made a new offer. We proposed, as an interim solution, some equal number on both sides between zero and 572. Once again, the Soviets refused an equitable solution and proposed instead what might be called a "half zero option".' R. Reagan, 'United States' Commitment to Peace: An Equitable and Verifiable Arms Limitation', *VSD*, 49 (September 1983); 'The United States not only has refused to eliminate the obstacles created by the deployment of the new American missiles in West Europe, it is continuing to deploy them.' 'Chernenko Sees Hope for Better U.S. Ties', *CDSP*, 36: 42 (1984).

8 'Cooperation and understanding are built on deeds, not words.' R. Reagan, 'U.S.–Soviet Relations: A Policy of Credible Deterrence', *VSD*, 50: 8 (1984); 'Reagan's "peace-loving" rhetoric is essentially nothing more than a verbal wrapper that camouflages Washington's true aims with respect to the unrestrained buildup of U.S. arms.' Y. V. Andropov, 'Andropov Takes Tough Stand on U.S. Policy', *CDSP*, 35: 39 (1983).

9 'We intend to negotiate in good faith and go to Geneva willing to listen to and consider the proposals of our Soviet counterparts.' R. Reagan, 'US Foreign Affairs Policy: Arms

presented possible solutions. The two negotiators were doing the same thing; both proposed solutions and accused the other of rejecting their proposals or placing obstacles in the way of an agreement. The result was immobilisation, which destroyed any possibility of an arms control or arms reduction agreement.

Against this background, citizens' groups within each bloc launched an initiative to 'break down the barriers' dividing Europe. This 'dialogue from below', between independent movements in the two blocs, was said to be necessitated by the inability of the 'other minds' to communicate. In 1982, at a time when the arms control negotiations had broken down, the Russian, Yuri Medvedkov, stated the following:

> Today the top leaders of the two camps are not on speaking terms; they are not ready even to 'tango' as one of them put it. It means it is up to us to provide alternative forms of constructive East–West dialogue in order to shorten the time needed for the business-like attitude of the politicians to the settlement of their disagreements.[10]

Against the background of states bargaining from two fixed positions, against the background of domestic battles in each house, in which social movements on each side were believed to be pawns in a psychological war instigated by the other, those positioning themselves 'outside' the established structures in their respective blocs began a dialogue across the division of Europe, given the immobilisation of negotiations and the incapacity for dialogue at other levels.

Negotiation and dialogue

Taylor (in Dallmayr and McCarthy, 1977: 116) and Pitkin (1972) have respectively made arguments that 'negotiation' and 'dialogue' are distinct forms of life. Each is constituted by particular language games and rules. Taylor points out that 'negotiation' is inseparable from 'the distinct identity and autonomy of the parties, with the willed nature of their relations; it is a very contractual notion'. Pitkin argues that dialogue belongs to the realm of 'moral discourse', which also relies on a vocabulary with rules. This tradition focuses more on a context in which one party has been injured and seeks redress as well as the healing of a relationship. She quotes Cavell (Pitken, 1972: 150–2), who says of dialogue and moral discourse:

Reduction', *VSD*, 48: 4 (1981); 'The complex of Soviet proposals, which convincingly demonstrate our political will to do everything in the name of lasting peace, has been placed in the centre of the agenda of international life.' I. Aleksandrov, 'U.S. Arms Buildup Assailed', *CDSP*, 33: 12 (1981).

10 I. Medvedkov, 'Independent Soviet Group: "Our Aim is to Build Trust"', *END Journal*, 2 (1983).

It provides one possibility of settling conflict, a way of encompassing conflict which allows the continuance of personal relationships against the hard and apparently inevitable fact of misunderstanding, mutually incompatible wishes, commitments, loyalties, interests and needs, a way of healing tears in the fabric of relationships and maintaining the self in opposition to itself and others.

Each language game had its own logic. Each took place within a different spatial field, involving different types of identity, following different rules in relation to one another. A few distinctions between the two types of game as played in this context may make the significance of the following description more clear.

First, negotiations reinforced the distinctions between 'us' and 'them', so that each could speak with a single voice. By contrast, an initial act in the cross-bloc dialogue was a *renaming of self and other*. In his essay, *Protest and Survive*, E. P. Thompson (1980) discussed the relationship between the naming of the other and the 'thinkability' of nuclear war. The thinkability of nuclear war, he argued, relies on a language that makes possible the 'disjunction between the rationality and the moral sensibility of individual men and women and the effective military process' (Thompson, 1980: 26). In Thompson's argument, a particular vocabulary effects a closure which habituates the mind to nuclear holocaust by reducing everything to the level of normality. This reduction makes it possible to 'kill each other in euphemisms and abstractions long before the first missiles have been launched' (Thompson, 1980: 26). Nuclear war was unthinkable for the West, but the idea came quite easily as long as it was to be inflicted on the enemy, defined as an 'other', as Asians, Marxists, non-people. Moving beyond the logic of deterrence or the logic of nuclear arms required an act of renaming, of giving an identity to the people of Eastern Europe.

Second, the negotiations consolidated two family spaces whose boundaries cut through the middle of Europe; by contrast, the dialogue began with commencing 'to *act as if* a united, neutral and pacific Europe already exists' (emphasis added).[11] Commencing to act as citizens of Europe, no longer distinguished by East and West, involved challenging the dichotomies of the Cold War. The barriers separating the two halves of the continent would be overcome through a process of meeting. A first step in eliminating the division of Europe was dismantling a range of conceptual categories into which all had been socialised.

Third, negotiation involved proposing and rejecting, and attempting to reach a formal compromise. The hope of dialogue, by contrast, was that the identity of each side would grow and be transformed as they confronted an 'other' whose views were not their own. In the process of dialogue, the

11 'A Nuclear Free Europe, END Appeal', *END Bulletin*, 1 (1982).

weakness of one's own reasoning is exposed. As Andrew Linklater (in Smith, Booth and Zalewski, 1996: 286) has said, 'true dialogue exists when moral agents accept that there is no a *priori* certainty about who will learn from whom and when they are willing to engage in a process of reciprocal critique.' Dialogue is a reciprocal exchange through which both parties grow and change. While weapons are subject and object of speech at the negotiator's table, it is the meaning of words, knowledge of one another's position and the stakes of the relationship itself that constitute dialogue. Negotiating and entering into dialogue, in this context, represented the juxtaposition of two contrasting forms of self/other relationship: the one secured two mutually exclusive spaces of secrecy and militarism; the other involved an engagement with the other in a process of making public and opening spaces.[12]

After decades of having been enclosed within two bloc spaces, each side in the dialogue brought a different understanding of the world to their interactions. For Eastern Europeans, 'peace' and 'disarmament' were slogans that had lost their meaning and were at best a tool of government propaganda. For Western peace activists, human rights were often subordinated to the goal of disarmament. Overcoming the division of Europe and constituting a Europe free and whole meant dismantling the mutually exclusive terms in which peace and human rights were defined in the Cold War. In the beginning, this tension was no less evident in the political positions of the movements than those of their governments.

A final difference between these two games relates to the means–end strategy of negotiating with weapons. The notion of acting 'as if' one were a citizen of a whole Europe began with a very different principle. Acting 'as if' is the process of constructing the future by acting as one would act in such a future. In acting 'as if' dialogue were possible, the means and the end of the act are simultaneously realised. The point is to demonstrate a form of life that belongs to the realm of human possibility but which is not yet a defining feature of a particular context. The power of acting 'as if' is in disrupting and politicising the injustice underlying the constitutive categories of the dominant game.

Many saw these acts of 'talking' as potentially destabilising to the Cold War order and therefore dangerous.[13] In the end, they were destabilising in so far as these ideas seeped to a broader range of citizens in Eastern Europe

12 'This calls for open and public negotiation. We must fight tooth and nail to prevent talks going on behind the backs of the public and disarmament matters eluding public control.' J. Sabata, 'The Struggle for Peace and Eastern Europe', *LFEE*, 6: 1–2 (1983).
13 See, for instance Schell, 'Introduction', in Michnik (1985), on the destablising effect of Solidarity's actions.

and transformed the thinking of 'official' elites who were involved. In the short term, the violence of the barbed wire division was exposed as peace activists were thrown out of Eastern European countries for simple acts of attempting to 'talk' with their independent counterparts in the East. The 'dialogue from below' represented a hope that a wider and wider circle in both East and West would be drawn into the process until the division and finally the physical walls and barbed wire, as well as the missiles by which they were maintained, would be dismantled.

Dialogue

What follows is a reconstruction of different 'meeting places' of the dialogue between dissidents in East and West. While negotiators reinforced 'obstacles' standing in the way of an agreement, the dialogue attempted to break down the barriers between 'us' and 'them'. Besides END, an international network based in Britain, the dialogue involved Charter 77 in Czechoslovakia, members of the International Peace Coordination and Cooperation Network, based in the Netherlands, the European Network for East–West Dialogue, the Hungarian Group for Dialogue, the Moscow Dialogue Group for Trust, groups associated with the Protestant Churches in the two Germanies, Solidarity in Poland (albeit reluctantly) and, finally, the official peace councils in the different East European countries. Given the conversational nature of these passages, I have largely written in the present tense in order to reinforce the quality of this narrative as a dialogue in process.

Place One: peace and human rights

As the dialogue began in the early 1980s, participants from the two halves of Europe spoke from very different political and historical positions. Interactions, like the state-level forums, were characterised by a tension over the relationship between human rights and disarmament. In an exchange of letters between Vaclav Racek of Czechoslovakia, and E. P. Thompson of Britain,[14] the Czech stated that 'any disarmament movement is meaningful and hopeful only in the sense of the realisation of its objectives as a human rights movement'. He refers to the 'opposite method' of his British counterpart which was, he claimed, similar to a 'mechanical notion of détente' in that it assumes that 'the increasing rate of armament is the cause of suppression of human rights'. While this may have been true

---

14 Vaclav Racek, 'Letter to E. P. Thompson, 12 December 1980', in *Human Rights and Disarmament: An Exchange of Letters Between E. P. Thompson and Vaclav Racek* (London, 1981); E. P. Thompson, 'Letter to Vaclav Racek, 29 March 1981', in *Human Rights and Disarmament*.

in the West, the Czech argues that the suppression of human rights in the East manifests itself in the increase of armaments, as well as militarism. In his view, the disarmament movement, operating on the basis of this mechanical notion of détente, is 'an influential force which works unconsciously in the interest of a totalitarian system whose aim is world domination'.

Thompson responds that this position assumes that there must be some contradiction between the cause of peace and the cause of liberty. 'You clearly suspect that those who work for the first cannot be in earnest about the second.' This separation of peace and liberty, in the view of the Englishman, comes from a tendency in Eastern Europe 'to construct in their minds a wholly illusory view of the other world, made up from Radio Free Europe' and from the habit of believing always the opposite of whatever official communist propaganda states to be so. If reports from 'less partial observers' were to get through, the East European would 'find a picture more complex than that of a free world here and a totalitarian [i.e. communist] world there'. Each writer accused the other of a one-sided approach to the Cold War.

Place Two: disuniting or healing?

Place Two was typical of the early interactions between the official Eastern European peace councils and a section of the Western European peace movement, represented in particular by END, which was developing contacts with human rights initiatives in the Eastern bloc. The voice is that of Yuri Zhukov, the President of the official Soviet Peace Committee.[15] The Peace Committee was a public organisation in the Soviet Union which promoted the Soviet government's policy and mobilised the 'masses of peace-loving Soviet people for peace'.[16] The subject of his letter is the END Convention, an annual gathering of the Western nuclear disarmament movement, held in a different European city each year. The END Convention was also intended to be a meeting place for the dialogue between East and West.

The extension of invitations to the Eastern bloc was a highly political matter, given tensions between the official peace committees and the independent initiatives or 'dissidents' in the East. The one supported the policy of the government and the other, not specifically concerned with peace, at least as meant by the officials, did not. According to Zhukov, the

15 'Letter to Western Peace Campaigners from Yuri Zhukov, President of the Soviet Peace Committee to END', 2 December 1982, IKV Archives, no. 335, ISG, Amsterdam.

16 Jiri Hajek, former Foreign Minister of Czechoslovakia, said of these peace councils that they 'are being appointed from above and are nothing but "transmission belts" of the Stalinist and neo-Stalinist political system, which has its centre at the summit of the Communist Party apparatus, the only institution authorised to take any initiative whatever.' J. Hajek, 'View from the East', *END Journal*, 9 (1984).

two cannot occupy the same space. An invitation to the 'dissidents' is, by definition, discrimination against the former and, as stated elsewhere, makes the official committees into 'second-class citizens' of the peace movement.[17] The extension of an invitation to the 'dissidents' makes the conference into a Western European, as opposed to a European, operation.[18] The Western peace movement is subsequently an extension of the 'aggressive and militarist policy of NATO and Reagan'. There is only space for two voices in the Cold War. Either one fits into the category of the real peace movement of the Soviet Union or the militarist policies of the West.

Meg Beresford, one of the END organisers, responded to Zhukov's letter.[19] Zhukov accuses END of attempting to disunite the global peace movement, but, she argues, END is trying to heal the division of Europe. She points out that Zhukov assumes the peace movement should align itself with the Soviet Union, and not to align itself is to be identified with NATO, which, on the other hand, takes every occasion to accuse the peace movement of being a 'servant of Moscow'. It is precisely this logic that END wants to overcome, that is, the idea that any voice is by definition partisan, aligned with one side of the conflict or the other. This is the logic of the Cold War which END wants to break down. As this conflict shows, the division of Europe is not only geographical. Bitter arguments and divisions have constructed barbed wire in people's minds and hearts. This barbed wire, which relates fundamentally to human beings and not only to ideology, can only be dismantled by meeting one another face to face, coming to know one another as human beings who communicate and tolerate difference, rather than as enemies. Barbed wire through the heart and through the continent has left Europeans and Europe wounded, in need of healing. Governments, possessed by deep suspicions of one another, will not undertake this type of action in the absence of efforts by ordinary citizens.

Place Three: talking away the division

In 1982 E. P. Thompson spoke to an intimate group in a small apartment in Hungary.[20] He made a distinction between what politicians do, that is, 'behave', 'argue about numbers', and what citizens do, that is, 'act', 'follow a code of conduct', 'assume responsibility', 'engage in difficult and uncomfortable arguments' without 'a mask'. He encouraged the audience to act 'as if'

17 Tair Tairov, 'Eastern Peace Councils Decide Against Conference Participation', *Disarmament Campaigns* (July–August 1985).

18 Zhukov, 'Letter to END.'

19 Meg Beresford, END Coordinating Committee, 'An Open Letter to the Soviet Peace Committee', *New Statesman* (21 January 1983).

20 E. P. Thompson, 'The Normalization of Europe', *Praxis International*, 3: 1 (1983).

they were citizens of a healed continent, as if the Cold War was already over. The divided continent is a symbol of the Cold War. The Cold War is 'artificial'. It is 'ideological' and constructs a 'chasm' across which communication is broken and voices cannot be heard. If the chasm is artificial, not natural, it can be removed, and removed now, by acting as European citizens would act in its absence.

There was a practical political reason for the Western peace movement to join hands across the chasm. The chasm constructed a particular kind of ideological and political barrier that had begun to take its toll on the Western movement. So long as there was no voice in the East critical of Soviet weapons, Western peace movements, the critics argued, were *de facto* unilateralist, no matter what they claimed, because equal pressure was not brought to bear on Eastern governments.[21] The only way to break through this barrier and bridge the chasm was to clasp hands with another truly independent group in Eastern Europe. The rationale was not purely political, however; it was fundamentally human, that is, to talk as human neighbours rather than fighting as ideological ones. Talking is a form of defiance – it defies the barriers: national security and ideological. It is also natural, unlike the unnatural chasm, given the common history and culture of Europe. The only thing stopping the engagement of talking citizens is not something outside, a geography, but a range of conceptual distinctions by which Europeans have, unnaturally, come to think of themselves as divided. But this division, which Thompson names a form of segregation or apartheid, has become obscene. The Cold War is an unnatural state, like a disease that has overcome Europe. To act as if Europe were whole and the Cold War is over is to commence with the healing process, and a return to the natural state of health.

Sometime later, a young Hungarian, Janos Laszlo, who had been present at the lecture of Thompson, reflected on the experience.[22] A sentiment repeated by Eastern Europeans is the meaninglessness of the word 'peace' after decades of forced demonstrations organised around related slogans. Peace is at best 'uninteresting, nice, abstract', and at worst a cover-up for the foreign policy of the government. In any case, it is simply too abstract, too risky to bother getting involved, unless it somehow relates to the day to day, the tangible, that is, the 'reality of the Cold War'. Laszlo's text is full of awakenings, of *realising* that peace is inseparable from

21 See, for instance, as articulated in the American context: 'The Freeze would also make a lot more sense if a similar movement against nuclear weapons were putting similar pressures on Soviet leaders in Moscow. As former Secretary of Defence Harold Brown pointed out, the effect of the freeze "is to put pressure on the United States but not the Soviet Union".' R. Reagan, 'Arms Control Policy'.
22 J. Laszlo, 'I Do Have A Right To Have My Voice Heard', *END Journal*, 3 (1983).

freedom, that changes *might be possible*, contrasted to its prior unthink-ability: 'We have got used to a divided Europe; it has become too much a part of our consciousness, and it does not even occur to us that it can be changed.' A cross-bloc exchange requires making the Cold War an enemy rather than human beings on the other side. Once meeting face to face and the 'other' can no longer be a beast, can no longer be killed, because one does not fight friends; one enters into dialogue with friends.

At the same time, a confidential Hungarian government document expressed concern that 'imperialists' had launched 'an attack on a wide front against the anti-war movement' by trying to 'stimulate opposition forces in some socialist countries to step out with slogans in defence of peace' in order to legalise them and broaden their base.[23] Independent voices in Eastern Europe were concerned about losing the autonomy of an independent movement if their position on peace was not sufficiently distinguished from that of the government. The government, by contrast, feared that these 'hostile, oppositional groups' were using issues of peace to 'strengthen their influence and power base'. This interest is not genuine, according to the author; it is rather 'an anti-Soviet disguise'. The opposition had changed its ways; it no longer fit into the comfortable dichotomies of the Cold War, which constituted a hierarchical relationship between human rights and peace. The hierarchy still existed, however, since these 'hostile groups' have simply put on a peace movement 'disguise'; what they say and what they are doing do not correspond. They remain anti-Soviet: 'this is a tactical change to disorient the peace movement in Hungary which was formerly free of oppositional influences'.

The same year, the Hungarian government began to take action to redraw the tight boundaries, to reinstate the hierarchy. A Western peace activist addressed a polite but direct letter to the Hungarian Minister of Home Affairs after being 'expelled' from the country along with others who shared the common purpose of 'talking' with members of the Dialogue group.[24] The writer points out the contradiction in the government's response. The Dialogue group is fully supportive of the Western peace movement, which has the same goal as the Hungarian government: preventing the stationing of new NATO weapons of mass destruction in Western Europe. There is no way to explain the government's exaggerated response to efforts to talk with a group that respects the law of the country and a visit undertaken in all 'openness'.

23 Central Committee Section for Party and Mass Organisation, Hungary, 'New Phenomena Appearing in the Peace Movement. Proposal for Future Action' (Hungary: Samizdat Publishing House, 1984).
24 C. Voute, 'Letter to Dr. Horvath Istvan, Minister of Home Affairs of the Hungarian People's Republic, 15 August 1983.' This was not an isolated occasion. See also, L. Jones, 'A Time for Change', *END Journal*, 28–29 (1987).

'It must be known in advance that such actions will serve the ends of NATO propaganda by reinforcing Western Cold War prejudices', he states.

Place Four: a united and democratic Europe

Against the backdrop of two warring families, the 'younger generation' began to redefine their relationship to one another. In a 1984 text from Charter 77 to the Western movement,[25] the former points out that it is different from the peace movement; it has a different basis and a different mission, but is nonetheless open to peace issues. Despite differences, the two find the same situation intolerable, that is, a Europe that continues to be 'artificially divided' forty years after World War II. Because of this shared intolerance, Charter 77 can say 'we feel close to you'. Given a common interest in a new Europe, 'your hopes are our hopes and vice versa'. This same language game was played by Reagan towards NATO at a given time. In that context it cemented the transatlantic relationship. In this context, it is part of a call for emancipation from both families. Europe and nations within Europe seek 'emancipation from the Cold War'.

Despite the new intimacy, a 'pacifist tendency' remains within the peace movement, since some 'separate' that which Charter is attempting to constitute as 'indivisible'. In the process of separating, a hierarchy is re-established which sets questions of peace apart from democracy. The latter is often degraded and placed in a subordinate position, with some peace activists going so far as to 'applaud openly undemocratic speeches'. This is counterproductive because the only way to get out of 'the blind alley of a policy of military might is to unite precisely that which many peace activists separate: opposition to nuclear madness within a democratic coalition'. The division between peace and freedom is among the 'internal divisions' between European peoples which 'provide the basis for the geopolitical division'. The geography of division is first and foremost political. It is only possible to overcome this political division by constituting peace and democracy as indivisible. The internal structure of the state and respect for the rights of individuals cannot be separated from military policies towards others. The author argues that 'those who deny the dignity of individual human beings and freedom of opinion, are bound to seek to resolve national and international problems by means of violence'.

The Charter text names the political nature of the division of Europe. The Dutch IKV also names the political as opposed to the military nature of the deployments in Western Europe.[26] The deployments reinforce the cohesion of the NATO family and subsequently keep European political

25   Charter 77 Document No. 13/84, *PPB*, 25 (1984).

structures 'intact'. If politics underlies the arms race, then politics has to be the place of change. In fact, the status quo no longer exists, however. While people talk in terms of amorphous and immobile blocs, of cohesion and of maintaining the status quo, what exists in fact is a 'high degree of interdependence', as well as 'people and nations with their own culture, history and identity'. Europe is not two blocs; it is diverse in every respect, yet underlying this diversity is the unity of a 'common history and destiny'. While NATO names a common history and destiny between Western Europe and the United States, the peace movement, and some Eastern European dissidents, revive the notion of a single Europe with a single history and culture, recognising both the positive and negative aspects of this history. The model for this Europe of unity and diversity is provided by the Helsinki Final Act.

Place Five: opening the closed

In 1984 Mient Jan Faber of the Dutch IKV addressed a letter to the Polish dissident, Janusz Onyszkiewicz.[27] He was responding to Polish concerns regarding the inseparability of peace and freedom, given the threat posed to world peace by the Soviet Union.[28] Faber structures his text around a dichotomy of open and closed:

> It is my conviction that more *openness* is a preconditon for overcoming the East–West conflict. I am asking, I realise, that the *closed* systems pay a heavy price for the solution of the conflict. But this price is for such a 'moral good' that we may ask for it, or even better, should ask for it. To make this possible I ask the *open* socities to exercise restraint in the field of armament; and to extend cooperation on economic and other levels with countries of Eastern Europe. This should all happen with the acknowledgement that cooperation is not a thing as such and that it should be more than a personal interest: it should be a contribution to the *'opening'* of a *closed* society. Of course, this implies support for those groups striving for *openness* within their society.

Themes of being closed and opening reappear in comments from the Soviet Peace Committee to another text prepared by Faber in the same year.[29] Faber has allegedly made an assertion – which the Peace Committee 'cannot pass over in silence' – that 'disarmament seems contradictory to the

---

26 'Letter from B. ter Veer and M. J. Faber, IKV, and J. van der Meer and J. ter Laak, Pax Christi, to J. Kuron, Poland, January 1985', IKV Archives, no. 338, ISG, Amsterdam.

27 'Letter from M. J. Faber, IKV, to Janusz Onyszkiewicz, Poland, 14 September 1984', IKV Archives, no. 338, ISG, Amsterdam.

28 See, for instance, 'Letter from KOS to END', *END Journal*, 11 (1984).

29 'Comments on M. J. Faber's Draft for the Athens Conference by the Soviet Peace Committee, 10–12 December 1984', IKV Archives, no. 508, ISG, Amsterdam.

continuation of the socialist system itself'. They state 'bluntly' that 'the very presentation of the question according to which disarmament and détente are impossible' without an 'evolution of the socialist system' shows a presence of spirit of Reagan's malicious fables about the "empire of evil'. It is from Reagan that the Soviets hear 'month after month that we "must change" or else there will be war and we shall be "thrown out onto the dustheap of history"'. If Faber is also suggesting that the Eastern bloc must change, this must mean he is in the same camp as Reagan.

There were still only two possible voices in the Cold War. In another document from the same meeting,[30] the Soviet Peace Committee says: 'We shall never agree with the arguments of those who assert that for the sake of peace, détente and disarmament it is necessary for us to change, to acquire more "likeness" with some foreign "example".' The Peace Committee emphasises that détente means 'one must forget such a thing as interference in each other's domestic affairs' or upsetting the post-war territorial arrangement agreed to at Yalta. 'Mr. Reagan now also loudly declares that he too does not recognise the "artificial" division of Europe.' Reagan's adoption of the language of independent initiatives was a further sign of their complicity.

Place Six: the participation problem revisited

The Danish peace movement, Nei til Atomvaben, invited Charter 77 to participate in the 1986 Copenhagen Peace Congress, which would include the World Peace Council, the global representative of Soviet peace policies.[31] As in past discussions with the officials, the topic of who should participate was central.

Charter's participation would make it possible to 'publicise' its views, which should be known more widely since 'the Danish public does not sufficiently understand that "peace" does not concern only weapons, nor must the necessary détente between East and West be allowed to cement the division of Europe.'

The problem for Charter 77 was that the concept of participation as a 'European citizen' was in conflict with Czech citizenship. Attending the meeting could mean being 'deprived of one's nationality and prevented from returning home'.[32] According to law, the Ministry of the Interior can deprive a person of citizenship if, while travelling abroad, they commit any activity that 'can undermine the interests of the state'. The underlying assumption

---

30 Soviet Peace Committee, 'Dialogue I, 10–12 December 1984', IKV Archives, no. 508, ISG, Amsterdam.

31 'Letter from the Danish Peace Movement to Charter 77, 15 March 1986', *PPB*, 27 (1986).

32 'Letter from Charter 77 to the Danish Peace Movement, 25 March 1986', *PPB*, 27 (1986).

was that engaging in dialogue with Western peace movements 'undermines the interests of the Czech state'. If the peace movement was really interested in Charter's participation, it could intervene by asking for a repeal of the law, or by asking the authorities to 'publicly guarantee' that they would not apply this legal provision to independent participants in the Congress.

Charter was unable to participate directly and sent a letter to be read at the Congress.[33] In this letter Charter analysed the meaning of peace, this awkward concept in the Eastern European context. Peace in a whole Europe cannot be based on distinctions between individuals and states, or between peace and human rights. Twice in this century threats to peace have come from countries where 'the citizens lost control over the militarist forces of their own state'. Because citizens lost control, the state was able to undertake aggressive policies: 'aggression had first to disperse the institutions of democratic control and imprison citizens with differing opinions in gulags and concentration camps'. Making war requires silencing critical voices, the construction of the state as a cohesive unit, projecting its power outward. For this reason, human rights and democracy, which create a space for critical voices to be heard, are inseparable from disarmament.

The conference itself became an expression of tensions regarding the division of Europe and the divisibility of peace. Charter's participation problem arose precisely because official Eastern bloc committees wanted to act as the single voice on questions of peace in the Eastern bloc. According to Charter 77, such acts were contrary to peace since 'peace in Europe can only be secured through the contributions of all social forces, including governments and official peace committees'. It could only be secured through a process of dialogue. While officials 'exclude' critical voices, Charter emphasised the 'inclusion' of all social forces.

Official reflections on the meeting reinforced elements of the traditional discourse but also indicated a shift. One participant stated that his impression of the Congress was 'very bad'.[34] The Western peace movements, and especially the Danish, 'did not bring something constructive' since 'the sole thing they had done was to make it possible for "the East European émigré" to speak'. The future cannot be considered bright if it means that 'Western preconditions to talk with semi-official Eastern European organisations [are] a recognition of so-called independents as equal'. In 1986, the two were still not considered capable of occupying the same space, speaking with distinct voices. Another official presented a quite different view, however.[35] He

---

33 Charter 77 Document No. 28/86, *PPB*, 28–9 (1987).
34 Letter from Jozef Halbersztadt, Poland, 8 November 1986, to M. F. Faber, the Netherlands, IKV Archive, no. 470, ISG, Amsterdam.
35 Letter from Yuri Zhukov, President, Soviet Peace Committee, regarding the World Peace Congress in Copenhagen, 18 November 1986, IKV Archive, no. 473, ISG, Amsterdam.

suggested that the single voice of the Eastern family had begun to proliferate into more voices. In his words, the Congress was 'genuinely open', providing all of its participants complete freedom of speech, amounting to a 'full scale dialogue among the people, many of whom not infrequently assume differing ideological stances'. The sharp political focus of the discussion was defined by the timing of the meeting just two days after the superpower summit in Reykjavik, a 'coincidence that no one could have foreseen'.

The larger space: superpower dialogue

In 1986, after years of talking through the differences between East and West and a two year process of working out the details, independent initiatives in the two parts of Europe published a common statement entitled *Giving Real Life to the Helsinki Accords*.[36] The themes of the document were not new, but represented a new consensus among the signers about the direction in which Europe should be moving.[37] In contrast to the security of a bipolar world, the continent should 'liberate itself' from the constraints of the 'bipolar straitjacket'. The possibility would depend on the ability of Europeans in both East and West to 'articulate their own interests vis-à-vis the superpowers and political and social change within the superpowers themselves'. In contrast to a Europe of confrontation, or exclusion of the US and Soviet Union, Europe must be made in a 'common effort of all CSCE countries', based on 'viable compromises with both leading powers'. In contrast to relations involving only states, which 'are incapable of creating mutual trust on their own', trust must be 'built up between citizens' as well. The Helsinki principles mean not only the mobilisation of public opinion to put pressure on governments, but also thinking about 'what they can do themselves to further develop détente from below and to build bridges across the rift dividing our continent'. In contrast to the view that Helsinki 'confirms the status quo', the meaning of Helsinki can be renamed. The Accords 'do not cement the bipolar structure of the power blocs, but leave open the door for peaceful and gradual change towards a pluralistic Europe'.

36 *Giving Real Life to the Helsinki Accords: A Memorandum, November 1986* (Berlin: European Network for East–West Dialogue, 1987).
37 The goals of this initiative were similar to that of the END appeal of 1980 calling for a dissolution of the two blocs. This initiative was organised by the European Network for East–West Dialogue and signed by over 400 people, including a range of political and cultural personalities in both blocs. It also included a lengthy list from Czechoslovakia, the German Democratic Republic, Hungary, Poland and Yugoslavia, as well as Austria, Belgium, Canada, Denmark, the Federal Republic of Germany, France, Italy, the Netherlands, Norway, Sweden, Switzerland and the United States. The only signatory in the Soviet Union was 'The Group for the Establishment of Trust between the United States and Soviet Union' in Moscow.

The categories of this reinterpretation of Helsinki were similar to those articulated by Gorbachev the same year.[38] For Gorbachev, liberation from nuclear weapons involved a process of common security. Confrontation would be overcome through dialogue. The structural act of 'building' a new pluralistic Europe in the independent document is given a more concrete spatial form with the notion of a Common European House. This house is also meant to be pluralistic and fluid, in that 'there can be no monopoly on the interpretation and practical implementation of democracy and freedom'. These concepts are not static, but can have multiple meanings. Security involves liberation, overcoming confrontation, breaking through barriers, listening. Dialogue and contacts with the end of establishing trust are the means to overcome the confrontative structures of the Cold War. The dialogue does not only involve governments, however, since 'New Thinking means an ability to listen to the voice of the European and world public and not to separate one's own security from the security of a neighbour in our interconnected world'. A superpower renames the relationship to the other and shifts into the position of 'listener', away from that of one who 'answers' with weapons, in a dialogue of mutual security.

The division breaks down

The world of mutually exclusive households and that of citizens in a whole Europe were embedded in different spatial fields. They also involved distinct ways of speaking and acting. These different fields of action were superimposed and came into conflict within Europe during the last ten years of the Cold War. The contrasting action fields belonging to each are as follows:

HOUSEHOLDS	CITIZENS
secure/insecure	secure/set free
negotiate	dialogue
construct obstacles	break down barriers
inside/outside	indivisible
two mutually exclusive voices	multiple voices

In the renaming process, the bloc, the household, became a space from which one had to be emancipated in order to engage with 'other' citizens from a starting point of difference. These actions took place within a larger

---

38 'Soviet Diplomacy Turns to Europe', *CDSP*, 38: 29 (1986); M. Gorbachev, 'Gorbachev's Plan to Scrap all Nuclear Arms', *CDSP*, 38: 3 (1986); 'Gorbachev Extends Test Ban Until January 1', *CDSP*, 38: 33 (1986); 'Shevardnadze Asks for Cooperation in Europe', *CDSP*, 38: 45 (1986); M. Gorbachev, 'Gorbachev Talks to Moscow Peace Forum', *CDSP*, 39: 7 (1987).

field of relationships in which the inside/outside distinction, domestic and international, became indivisible.

In the second half of the decade, the language games of Reagan and Gorbachev began to converge with those of the independent initiatives. In 1984 and 1985, after the introduction of SDI, the breakdown of barriers to citizen exchange between the two blocs, and dialogue, based on a shared humanity and the recognition of difference, took a prominent place in Reagan's speeches.[39] Gorbachev wanted to humanise international relations.[40] This was the period of the first face-to-face meetings between the two leaders. One witness at the Geneva and Reykjavik Summits recorded the importance of these meetings in very human terms. He described two superpowers momentarily allowing the boundaries of their distinct positions as negotiators to fall away so that they might face the gravity of the problems they shared in common. The following quotes from each side are revealing. As stated by US diplomat, Charles Hill:

> [In the past] you knew you were talking to someone who wasn't a real human being: You were talking to a programmed mind of someone doing something for some reason other than what an individual human being would do on his own hook. And suddenly somebody at the top said, 'It is okay to be a human being again.' And their officials from top to bottom changed. Their personalities changed, their approach changed. Their scathing wit changed. ... Suddenly the lid was off and you could be yourself to a certain extent. (Oberdorfer, 1992: 192–3)

And from the Soviet side:

> For all the backbiting and backsliding, something fundamental had changed in the Soviet perception of Reagan. 'Some initial feelings came that it's possible to talk with him, possible to convince him of something,' said Gorbachev's close adviser, Aleksandr Yakovlev ... 'In Rekyjavik I first saw [Reagan's] human hesitation about what decision to make, and it seemed to me he wasn't acting. I saw his internal hesitation, his batting back and forth in his mind what to do. On the one hand, as it seemed to me, he was interested in the idea of universal nuclear disarmament, on the other hand sticking to

39 'Nothing can justify the continuing and permanent division of the European continent. Walls of partition and distrust must give way to greater communication for an open world.' R. Reagan, 'Life and the Preservation of Freedom', *VSD*, 53: 3 (1985); 'My mission ... is to engage the new Soviet leader in what I hope will be a dialogue for peace that endures beyond my presidency. It is to sit down across from Mr. Gorbachev and try to map out together, a basis for peaceful discourse even though our disagreements remain fundamental.' R. Reagan, 'A Mission for Peace', *CP*, 765 (1985).

40 'At present, international relations have been rendered soulless by the cult of force and the militarisation of consciousness. Hence, the task of humanising international relations.' Gorbachev, 'Gorbachev Talks to Moscow Peace Forum.'

the idea of such a funny toy as SDI ... In this man I saw that his professional ability to put on an act somehow wavered. He could be seen from a different angle as a human being and as a politician. (Oberdorfer, 1992: 208–9).

In the first case, Hill speaks of someone above giving permission to be human. In the second, Yakovlev points to a human side of Reagan, of being open to persuasion, of being capable of hesitation as well as acting, of wavering. Both Reagan and Gorbachev frequently said that they were learning to talk to each other rather than about each other.

The language of 'becoming human' does not fit well with any notion of causality, being hit by some external force, like a rock propelled by a boulder. Soviet leaders were undoubtedly aware of the dialogue from below process, given the participation of official peace councils and the exaggerated response of state authorities in the Eastern bloc, but the idea that this dialogue 'caused' the dialogue above seems inappropriate. 'Becoming human' is part of a language game of dialogue, as opposed to negotiation. The emphasis is less the formal contract than the stakes of one's relations to other people. Dialogue does not fit with the means–end logic of being forced to do what one otherwise would not do. Gorbachev or Reagan may have been 'moved' but, if this was the case, it was probably more the result of 'radiation', to use Havel's (1991: 320–1) metaphor, 'that even something as apparently ephemeral as the truth spoken aloud, as an openly expressed concern for the humanity of man, carries a power within itself and that even a word is capable of a certain radiation, of leaving a mark on the "hidden conscious-ness" of a community'.

Adam Michnik suggested that Gorbachev appropriated the discourse of Solidarity in his *perestroika* programme.[41] A former executive committee member of the official World Peace Council said in 1988 that Gorbachev was moved by the peace movement and saw an opportunity.[42] The parallel between the words of Gorbachev and the texts of Charter 77 is often striking. But the specific source of radiation or the internal motives of either leader for acting as they did, are less important than the contrast between the two worlds and the transition of the superpowers from the one world of fixed positions into a second meeting place where they were able to find some common ground as different human beings.

Without attempting to address 'why' the two leaders began playing a new game, or whether they were sincerely acting as 'humans' concerned about the stakes of the relationship, as opposed to 'politicians' driven by their own survival, the central point is that the superpowers began to

41 A. Michnik, 'Gorbachev's Counter-Reformation', *END Journal*, 28–29 (1987).
42 T. Tairov, 'The World Peace Council Must Change', *END Journal*, 36 (1988–89). See also Gorbachev (1987: 154–6).

engage in the language games of this alternative world and, as the quotes above illustrate, others within their ranks did as well. The transition was marked by a sense of surprise for those watching, surprise that the other, assumed to be pure politician or purely programmed, could begin playing as a 'human'. If the Cold War was, as the dissidents claimed, a form of barbed wire running through human hearts as well as continents, a form of social division as well as geographical, then it should come as no surprise that the healing would commence on all levels, that other citizens in the Eastern bloc might find themselves suddenly 'speaking a different language', with the old suddenly losing its power. As more and more people began to play the alternative game, the 'normal language games began to lose their point' (Wittgenstein, 1958: para. 142).

The disappearance of the division of Europe almost overnight, accompanied by Velvet Revolutions throughout the Eastern bloc, took place as people *en masse* began to speak a different language and to act on the basis of a different set of rules. The rules of the old game sustained the Cold War as long as people continued to articulate them publicly. When they stopped, the whole structure of relationships began to collapse, like a house of cards. All the endings, from the INF agreement to the dismantling of the Berlin Wall, to the collapse of the Soviet Union were interrelated in the transition between two different games of security.

PART III

Changing strategies

9

Victory

> Our mistake is to look for an explanation where we ought to look at what happens as a 'proto-phenomenon.' That is, where we ought to have said: *this language-game is played.* (Wittgenstein, 1958: par. 654)

PART II ADDRESSED the question of how an alternative to the Cold War became possible. States, which had been entangled in the rules of the Cold War, were empowered to move towards alternatives as a new game began to take hold in a broader sphere of public opinion. The final section of this book will examine the implications of this investigation for understanding the end of the Cold War and the evolving practices of NATO and Russia, the former superpower, in its aftermath.

The first implication is that the analysis raises questions about the conventional wisdom that the end of the Cold War was a case of the West 'winning'. The 'winning' argument has several manifestations. NATO's consistent policy of deterrence caused the Soviets to back down. Reagan's threat to outspend the Soviet Union caused a policy reversal on the part of the Soviet leadership. The Soviet Union collapsed because of the spread of Western ideas, and their attractiveness, to the former Eastern bloc.[1] The claim to a zero-sum victory by the West is problematic. If moves are situated in the larger grammars of the Cold War, we see states in both blocs engaged in a range of 'maintenance' acts, from maintaining a structure to maintaining the cohesion of their respective alliances. Critical movements in both blocs were attempting to change the game by dismantling and breaking down the structures of the Cold War. The outcome was a collapse, whether the object was the Berlin Wall, the deterrence relationship between the superpowers or the Soviet Union.

To use a more traditional scientific language, there is a negative correlation between acts of maintenance and collapse. There is a positive correlation

---

1 An extensive list of realist explanations is provided in Chapter One. The most famous example of an explanation that emphasises the spread of Western ideas is Fukuyama (1992). Analyses that emphasise the role of ideas and learning in general include Checkel (1993), Blum (1993), Goldstein and Keohane (1993) and Risse-Kappen (in Lebow and Risse-Kappen, 1995).

between dismantling or breakdown and collapse. The point about correlation is not to suggest that we have identified causal relationships in an objective reality; rather, the *meaning* of these changes was constituted in a grammar. We cannot get behind this grammar to compare it with the world. The Cold War was a structure that collapsed. The collapse of the Soviet Union has to be embedded within a whole series of collapses.

The argument that the end of the Cold War represents a victory by the West is an *explanation* of the change. It identifies a causal link between acts by the West and subsequent acts by the Soviet Union. In this explanation, the end of the Cold War is synonymous with the demise of the Soviet Union. By contrast, the argument that the Cold War collapsed provides a *description* of the change based on the shared grammars of the participants whose acts and interactions constituted the transformation. The explanation points, after the fact, to a 'truth' in a world beyond human meaning; the grammatical investigation, by contrast, begins with the language games of the actors themselves.

The explanation postulates a zero-sum outcome in which one side won. The description, by contrast, reveals a contest between the zero-sum game of the Cold War and an alternative positive-sum game. The collapse was generated in the tension and conflict between these two games. Maintenance of the zero-sum game was dependent on the assumption that it is the only possible game in a world of anarchy. The foundations began to crumble as more and more people, and eventually the superpowers, began to 'act as if' an alternative was possible.

A grammatical investigation seeks not the cause of a change but its meaning.[2] What type of context was this? How did the change become possible? Answering these questions requires situating the actors in a broader social and political space within which they interacted with one another over time. Part II addressed a question about how a change on the part of the superpowers became possible. One might also ask how the critical movements became possible. Peace movements in the West and reform movements in the East arose at different points throughout the Cold War. Why, at this historical juncture, would these challenges have opened up spaces when at earlier points in time they may have reified the division of Europe?

First, the relationship between processes in East and West is crucial. The Soviet Union's field of manoeuvre was shaped by the coincidence of campaigns in both East and West. Gorbachev's domestic policy changes were closely tied to disarmament initiatives in the larger international

---

2 As Wittgenstein (1958: 225) stated, 'For this reason the word "methodology" has a double meaning. Not only a physical investigation, but also a conceptual one, can be called "methodological investigation".'

context, which made it possible to introduce the former without 'losing face'. This is not to say that Gorbachev or the reformulation of Soviet foreign policy *were not* influenced by an assessment that the Soviet economy could not handle another stage of the arms race.[3] Likewise, Reagan's motive may have been to bring the Soviet Union down by initiating a new round in the arms race. But in what type of context could Reagan introduce SDI as a palatable political option? This is not an argument about the *motives* of either side in introducing policy changes; it is about the type of *political* context in which these changes could be meaningfully introduced and, therefore, embraced. By situating both within an ongoing game involving more players, a broader view of the rationale and the ability to realise these moves at *a particular point* in history emerges.

As Lebow and Stein (in Lebow and Risse-Kappen, 1995) have argued, previous Soviet leaders were unable to make the types of move that Gorbachev made with any kind of success. The context did not *determine* Gorbachev's or Reagan's behaviour. Different leaders might have responded differently. The context did make it possible for both to make moves within a new game, however. Both acted against the backdrop of a growing number of voices which were calling into question not only the assumptions underlying deterrence but the Cold War relationship itself. The challenge was fundamentally a moral challenge to the practices of states within the Cold War, both domestically and internationally.

Second, not only state leaders but the citizens' initiatives were embedded in a historical context. Movements in both blocs were acting upon the earlier promise of the Helsinki Final Act, that is, the promise of reduced tensions between East and West, promises by Eastern leaders in the area of human rights, and the promise of greater openness between the blocs. Their critical actions were a reaction to a renewed arms race, violations of human rights norms by the Eastern bloc and a hardening of the division of Europe. The prior articulation of principles in the Helsinki Accords provided the backdrop for citizens' initiatives to hold states accountable for their words. These critical activities correspondingly opened up spaces of opportunity for realising the Helsinki principles in practice. The relationship is not causal; it is rather *constitutive*. States formulated principles and then failed to realise them. Citizens' initiatives held this discrepancy up to the public light. States then had an incentive to act in such a way that the principles would be realised. This grammatical investigation uncovered the structure of the change in the language of the various actors, but this does not mean that it represents merely an analysis of language. Human actors

---

3 Explanations that emphasise economic factors in the changing decisions of Soviet leaders include MccGwire (1991), Bunce (1985), Blacker (1993) and Meyer (1988).

are continuously having to make sense of their material, social and political environment to act at all. This 'sense' is not made in a vacuum. Actors are always already embedded in a context of historical meanings that constrains definitions of the possible. In a context of contestation, the room for manoeuvre may be enlarged as actors begin to transform the game.

NATO's victory?

By situating NATO in this larger context, its victory over the Soviet Union acquires a different meaning. NATO constructed a series of victories *vis-à-vis* the Soviet Union as they competed in the public realm.[4] NATO's victory in the Cold War is now most often understood to be synonymous with victory over the Soviet Union. Glancing backward in time, based on NATO's own accounts, one sees NATO engaged in a battle for public opinion which relates fundamentally to the meaning of security. After the decision in 1979 to deploy a new round of nuclear missiles in five Western European countries, NATO was faced with the development of a mass peace movement, which was calling into question its foundations in deterrence, and in particular challenging a conception of security that relied on the idea of MAD.

After a prolonged domestic battle, NATO went ahead with the deployments in 1983. The deployment decision did not represent a clear victory, however; it did not bring an end to the battle for public opinion. Despite the decision to proceed with the deployments, by 1985 and 1986 NATO was, more than ever, faced with the effect of the deployment decision on public opinion.[5] In 1986, NATO was preoccupied with a growing division and 'estrangement' between the Atlantic partners. The estrangement was attributed to differences over Reagan's SDI,[6] on the one hand, and to growing anti-Americanism in Europe and increasing isolationism in the United

---

4 As Wohlforth (1994–95: 127) argues in his 'realist' account of the end of the Cold War, 'material capabilities had little to do with what happened in world politics after 1987'. While he claims that the real issue was how capabilities were assessed by actors, I look at these assessments as part of a shared language directed towards public opinion.

5 'NATO is a defensive alliance and when there is no consensus about what it is defending against, we are in trouble ... At the core of the erosion of consensus is the fact that there is no common perception of the nature and objectives of Soviet foreign policy, in other words, the Soviet threat.' E. H. van der Beugel, 'The Atlantic Family – Managing its Problems', *NR*, 34: 1 (1986).

6 '[The Soviet strategy] is aimed at Western Europe where, on the whole, scepticism about SDI has been more widespread both among the critics of nuclear deterrence and the proponents of flexible response.' K. Kaiser, 'The NATO Strategy Debate After Reykjavik', *NR*, 34: 6 (1986).

States, on the other hand.[7] Young people in Europe were expressing resentment about European dependence on the United States and named the two
superpowers to be moral equivalents.[8] Against this background, NATO began
to emphasise the importance of defining a more distinct European identity.[9]

The 1986 meeting between Reagan and Gorbachev in Reykjavik was
initially a source of concern for the allies. First, they were not consulted in
advance.[10] Second, a potential disarmament agreement was seen to have a
potential effect on Western security.[11] Third, there was increasing pressure
from the public for such an agreement.[12] Finally, the United States was
demanding that Europe shoulder more of its own defence burden.[13] Once an
agreement was signed, NATO claimed it as a vindication of its policy all

7 'Diverging perceptions among the publics on the two sides of the Atlantic were at the
   centre of a vigorous debate in the Civilian Affairs Committee ... [A report to the
   Committee] emphasised the growing anti-American tendencies in Europe and anti-
   Europeanism in the United States.' J. Cross, 'North Atlantic Assembly Legislators Debate
   Key Challenges Facing the Alliance', *NR*, 35: 1 (1987).

8 'In many countries of the Northern tier of Europe, the strongest foreign policy sentiment
   today is increasingly deep-seated exasperation and resentment over Europe's dependence
   on two great powers who are coming to be seen by many as equally to blame for the
   continuation of their confrontation.' J. Dean, 'Can NATO Survive (Relative) Success?', *NR*,
   34: 6 (1986).

9 'The need arises once again to identify more accurately a European identity and structure,
   better suited to express certain specific continental needs, while increasing the political
   and negotiating credibility of the Alliance as a whole, thus helping to allay any erroneous
   perceptions concerning Western cohesion.' G. Andreotti, 'The Alliance's Political
   Dimension: Time for a Renewed Commitment', *NR*, 34: 2 (1986).

10 'The Europeans found it difficult to accept that they had not been consulted [about the
   Reykjavik proposals], and they appeared to be shocked by the speed at which agreement
   was (almost) reached. Like any dependent, Europe sets great store by formalities, which in
   principle act as checks on the whims of the leading nation of the Alliance.' P. Moreau-
   Defarges, 'Anti-American Feeling in Europe: Between Fear of War and Obsession with
   Abandonment', *NR*, 35: 2 (1987).

11 'On the question of zero option, many parliamentarians expressed concern about the
   'decoupling' implications for Europe and the increased vulnerability to the threat posed by
   Soviet shorter range nuclear forces if such an agreement [eliminating all longer range
   INF] were concluded.' Cross, 'North Atlantic Assembly.'

12 'In Reykjavik, the Soviet Union made grand and generous offers in principle thus inducing
   the opposing side, which is under public pressure to achieve progress on arms control, to
   make concrete concessions.' Kaiser, 'The NATO Strategy Debate.'

13 'There is, within the Alliance, an increasing perception that the Europeans should take a
   larger share of the collective responsibility. Of course the issue is not new. Like a volcano it
   smoulders continuously. But the pressure is rising again because of the growing budget
   deficit in the United States and the perception that so much American money has to go to
   defend increasingly rich allies who might reasonably be expected to do more to help
   themselves.' Lord Carrington, 'East–West Relations: A Time of Far-Reaching Change', *NR*,
   36: 3 (1988).

along,[14] including its success in maintaining internal cohesion.[15] In place of earlier concerns about estrangement between the two partners, some emphasised the impossibility of divorce.[16] 'Unilateralists', 'pacifists' and 'neutralists' were spoken of in condescending terms and NATO congratulated itself for not following their advice.[17]

NATO did claim to be a 'victim' of its own success since, among other problems, the INF agreement increased demands from the public to reduce defence budgets.[18] A reduction in defence spending would make it difficult for NATO to carry out its plans; shouldering more of the defence burden, placing less emphasis on nuclear weapons and reducing the defence budget were incompatible. In addition, the success of the INF treaty was as likely to be attributed to Gorbachev's skill in charming Western public opinion as the alliance's own 'coherent' stand.[19]

NATO, at this point, was already engaged in two competing language games in naming these changes. On the one hand, security was embedded in a realist game about the success of military pressure in securing particular ends, and the role of a cohesive unitary identity in putting forth a credible threat. In this conception, security was inseparable from military foundations. On the other hand, NATO spokespersons were clear about the basis of

14 'There are now for the first time real prospects of agreements which would result in sizeable reductions in nuclear weapons. That would be an historic achievement. The progress made so far totally vindicates NATO's policy of maintaining strong defences while seeking negotiated reductions.' G. Howe, 'The Atlantic Alliance and the Security of Europe', *NR*, 35: 2 (1987).

15 'Each time we fail to stress the point that NATO's cohesion in the face of high political odds was the major factor in the successful outcome of the INF negotiations, we make it easier for Mr. Gorbachev to be given credit for the zero–zero option.' P. Beatty, 'Gaining Public Support for Greater Defence Efforts – A Herculean Task', *NR*, 36: 2 (1988).

16 'The U.S.–European couple cannot be divorced. For the US, such a divorce would mean surrendering the role of a superpower; for Europe it would mean a reexamination of everything which it has been since 1945.' Moreau-Defarges, 'AntiAmerican Feelings.'

17 'It means that NATO's strategy and perseverance since 1979, in the face of the hysteria of the peace movements and the equivocations of the Soviet Union, have been totally vindicated ... Had NATO followed the unilateralists' advice, we would today face a greatly increased threat from Soviet missiles with no countervailing forces on our side.' D. Mellor, 'The INF Agreement: Is it a Good Deal for the West?', *NR*, 35: 6 (1987).

18 'We are victims of our own success because the progress in East–West relations, and its impact on public opinion, has made support for defence spending harder to win.' Carrington, 'East–West Relations.'

19 'In many quarters, Gorbachev is perceived as a man of goodwill and initiative, and NATO as an increasingly outdated and grudging obstacle to better East–West relations. Some argue that, with Gorbachev in charge, the Soviet Union no longer represents a threat to the West. The Gorbachev effect has made it harder for the Alliance to promote its own agenda and to persuade Western publics of its continued relevance.' M. Alexander, 'The Political Challenge from the East', *NR*, 36: 3 (1988).

state power and action in public opinion. A threat could not be credibly communicated nor tax dollars raised in the absence of a consensus at this level. The latter also evoked the success of Gorbachev in winning domestic support in the West and NATO's own vulnerability in the face of a declining threat. Gorbachev argued that the context of security relations had changed. The new situation, he said, 'marks a break with traditions, a way of thinking and a way of acting formed over the centuries, even millennia'.[20] Security had to be conceived more in political than military terms.

As the consensus further dissolved in the aftermath of the cruise and Pershing debates, NATO was less concerned about the peace movements *per se* than the fact that many of their language games had seeped into public opinion and, subsequently, into its own ranks, including claims about over-dependence on the United States, the need for a more independent European identity and the responsibility of both superpowers in maintaining the Cold War conflict. The Cold War itself – and the inability to reach an arms control agreement – became the central problem rather than the Soviet threat. On the one hand, NATO claimed the INF agreement as a victory. On the other hand, it expressed concern about the threat these public games would pose to its own future.

As a second 'ending' approached, with the collapse of Eastern Europe, NATO constructed its victory once again in the tension between these two games. NATO had said all along that its guiding principles were defined in the Harmel Report, which included the two pillars of deterrence and détente.[21] Deterrence related to the nuclear equation and the necessity of providing a credible threat. Détente referred primarily to state-level interactions, and specifically arms control, for the purpose of improving communication[22] – but not for overcoming the spatial division of Europe. This communication took the form of negotiations between the two superpowers. Eastern Europe was all but invisible and the NATO allies were consulted, or were supposed to be consulted, in the course of negotiations.

Dialogue was occasionally used in reference to East–West relations, but arms control negotiations were the central forum of interaction.[23] Dialogue

20 'Gorbachev Proposes to U.S. a Ban on Space Strike Arms', *CDSP*, 37: 40 (1985).
21 'The primary function of the Alliance is "to maintain adequate military strength and political solidarity to deter aggression" ... [The other element of security policy] embodied in the Harmel Report [is] the aim of complementing the military pillar by political means, primarily by détente.' P. Corterier, 'Modernization of Theatre Nuclear Forces and Arms Control', *NR*, 29: 4 (1981).
22 'Détente is neither more nor less than the recognition that our relationship with the Soviet Union *cannot* realistically aim at a common view of a new world order.' Beugel, 'The Atlantic Family.'
23 References to dialogue with the East are framed in terms of something that needs to be pursued or promoted rather than something that exists, for instance: 'I believe that the

was a goal of East–West relations but, in the second half of the 1980s, was primarily a phenomenon within the domestic context, either within individual societies or within the transatlantic alliance, necessitated by the public's 'misunderstanding' of Western security policy.[24]

Détente, and state-level contacts, had largely crumbled in the period of intensified superpower conflict, except at the level of superpower negotiations, which suffered periods of disruption after the re-emergence of heightened tension and disagreement. Throughout this period a dialogue was developing between portions of the Western European peace movement and different independent human rights initiatives within Eastern Europe. Dialogue and overcoming the division of Europe, replacing it with a Europe free and whole, were language games structuring the interactions between social movements in the two blocs throughout the entire decade. The dialogue was an implementation of the promise of détente and the Helsinki Final Act, given the failure of states in this area.

In the second half of the decade, the language games of Reagan and Gorbachev began to converge with those of the independent initiatives. As already mentioned, NATO at this time was concerned primarily with 'dialogue' within the Western space, a dialogue necessitated by divisions within Western societies and within the alliance. In 1988, in light of processes opening up in Eastern Europe, the definition of the two pillars of the Harmel Policy in terms of deterrence and détente were increasingly articulated in the language of defence and dialogue,[25] as well as the possibility of greater contact with Eastern Europe at the state level.[26] In 1989, the year the Berlin Wall collapsed, overcoming the division of Europe became a centrepiece of NATO

Soviet Union, pursuing its own advantages, will come to realise that dialogue, not cold war, is in its best interests. But until it is established that the Soviet Union is taking a constructive attitude in the newly begun American–Soviet disarmament negotiations, as well as in the Vienna and Stockholm talks, our optimism must be guarded, and we must accept the fact that vigilance is the price of freedom.' A. Mertes, 'East–West Relations: The Political Dimension', *NR*, 33: 1 (1985).

24 'The ... unfocused national or transatlantic dialogue ultimately creates an image of NATO as an alliance beset with inescapable strategic contradictions, grown irrelevant in a changing world and caving in on itself as the waves of the domestic debate loom ever larger and crash down with greater frequency.' P. Corterier, 'The ATA and a New Approach to NATO Information', *NR*, 34: 2 (1986).

25 'On the basis of its twin pillars of defence and dialogue, we have moved with firmness on the one hand and flexibility on the other towards a more peaceful and stable world order.' M. Wörner, 'NATO in the Post-INF Era: More Opportunities than Risks', *NR*, 36: 4 (1988).

26 'New commitments have been undertaken to facilitate contacts across the East–West divide and to improve the flow of ideas and information; a breakthrough has been achieved in institutionalising the human dimension as a full and integral part of the East–West dialogue.' M. Wörner, 'Building a New East–West Relationship: A Demanding Task', *NR*, 37: 1 (1989).

policy,[27] along with constructing a Europe free and whole.[28] Once again, some claimed this 'ending' to be the result of NATO policy.[29]

On 3 December 1989, Bush and Gorbachev, meeting in Malta, declared an 'end' to the 'epoch of the Cold War'. Gorbachev was still in power. The Soviet Union was still standing. NATO argued the need for its continuing existence on the basis of predictions that the Soviet Union would remain a major power on the European continent.[30] The possibility of a victory by Gorbachev still hung in the air. While the victory of the West was constituted as a victory 'over' communism, Gorbachev had 'won' the trust of Western public opinion after refusing to act in the predictable way of using force against the Velvet Revolutions in Eastern Europe.[31]

At each ending, NATO claimed credit for changes it had resisted until the last moment. While the possibility of dialogue had been implied by NATO's Harmel principles, the realisation of a dialogue, and its potential for overcoming the division of Europe, has to be understood against the background of a dialogue between citizens and a competition between the superpowers for public opinion. It was not that dialogue, overcoming the division of Europe or constructing a whole Europe, including the East, had *never* been articulated by the alliance. Rather, these were sporadic articulations pointing towards what should happen in the future, as well as being inconsistent with what NATO was actually doing.

27 '[The centrepiece of the Declaration] is the Alliance's effort to overcome the division of Europe and to offer the Eastern countries a wide-ranging scheme of cooperation.' H. Wegener, 'The Management of NATO's Anniversary Summit', *NR*, 37: 3 (1989).

28 'Indeed terms like "East–West relations" have now disappeared from the Declaration and are replaced by formulations that stress the wholeness of the continent.' H. Wegener, 'The Transformed Alliance', *NR*, 38: 4 (1990).

29 'There was much continuity in a deeper sense. Not only had the Alliance unceasingly sought to overcome the division of Europe and Germany, but it had, already in 1967, endowed itself with the two-pronged Harmel strategy of credible defence on the one hand, and détente and political dialogue and cooperation on the other.' Wegener, 'The Transformed Alliance.'

30 'The Soviet Union, however much it may be weakened by economic disaster, however sincere in abandoning the tenets of Marxist-Leninism, however genuine its desire for admission to the global community of nations, will remain (barring its total disintegration) a superpower with a formidable arsenal of nuclear weapons and an equally formidable conventional capability. The Cold War may be over, but power politics will continue.' M. Howard, 'Military Grammar and Political Logic: Can NATO Survive if the Cold War is Won?', *NR*, 37: 6 (1990).

31 '[Gorbachev] has won the trust of the West by not using force when his predecessors would have done so, perhaps at some risk – but if his long-range aim was to influence the mixture of anti-Americanism, anti-nuclear feeling and semi-neutralism in part of Western Europe so as to influence NATO governments in his direction, then Gorbachev has done remarkably well.' R. McGeehan, 'The U.S. and NATO after the Cold War', *NR*, 38: 1 (1990).

Prior to 1989, NATO acted on the basis of predictions that the Soviet Union and the Soviet bloc were lasting phenomena. The serious possibility of a different kind of East–West relationship or an undivided Europe was not among the state-level forecasts as late as 1988.[32] In 1989, the possibility of dialogue in a whole Europe moved to centre stage, shaping the practices of NATO. The adoption of this language game was a rhetorical move, not only to claim credit but to claim credit for a reason: to garner public support for its continuing relevance and survival.

Truth and meaning

Given the backdrop of the Helsinki Final Act, and based on this grammatical investigation, the end of the Cold War looks more like a victory of the CSCE than a victory of NATO. So what? The game has continued and NATO is now the victor. The Soviet Union collapsed in 1991. NATO has survived and is expanding eastward. States in the former Eastern bloc are lining up to enter NATO's door.

In the first part of this chapter I emphasised a distinction between an explanation of the end of the Cold War as a victory and the meaning of practices situated in a context of change. The purpose was to question the 'correctness' of the explanation. But the explanation also establishes the meaning of the context. The choice is not between two explanations of the change, but rather two meanings. The one was expressed in the practices of the actors as the change was unfolding; the other was imposed after the fact and has been partially constitutive of the possibilities of the post-Cold War world, including, as I shall argue in the next chapter, NATO's survival. In so far as we accept the victory explanation as 'true', it affects a closure on our thinking about the future and the lessons to be drawn from it. The end of the Cold War becomes a static picture of a war that has been won by the West. When we 'look and see' the contestation between language games, we open up a space for rethinking the past, the present and the future. In the first case, the Cold War had a definite ending point in 1991 and a single cause. In the second, the beginnings and ending are not so clear cut. The change is understood to be generated through the dialectical tension between competing games, rather than a single unilinear cause. Subsequently, the

32 See, for instance, 'East–West relations are not going to improve magically overnight whatever we or the Russians do: it will be a long slow haul before the climate of mutual distrust begins to change fundamentally. All the while we have to remain *vigilant* for our own security. Whatever we think of Gorbachev, the Soviet Union's size and location, coupled with its expansionist history and ideology and a military capability far in excess of that required for defence, mean we cannot afford to relax our guard now or in the foreseeable future.' Alexander, 'The Political Challenge.'

end point may not yet have arrived. The 'victories' of the West can be understood as a series of moves within a context that continues to unfold.

Explanation goes in search of the truest picture. A messy reality is neatly packaged. When the package is compared with the grammatical investigation there is a dissonance. There is a difference between the packaged meaning and the meaning in an unfolding context. But this is not first and foremost a claim that the 'victory of NATO' package is wrong and instead we should adopt a 'victory of the CSCE' package, which is more true. The point is to *describe* the language games by which the meaning of the change was constituted. The CSCE principles were more generative of the collapse of the Cold War, but NATO's victory, even if imposed, has played a role in constituting the possibilities of the post-Cold War world. The notion of a packaged 'truth' requires that we isolate a point of time, a beginning and an ending, an independent and dependent variable, and hold this in place. By contrast, a critical investigation traces the contours of a changing context over time.

It is not that either 'package' contains the truer account of this change. Each set of meanings represents a particular type of game. The NATO victory represents a zero-sum game. The CSCE victory represents a positive-sum game based on the principles agreed to by both sides in 1975. The change was, and continues to be, generated through the tension between these two types. The purpose of the chapters in this final section is to analyse how post-Cold War relations between NATO and Russia have been constituted out of this tension. Before moving on to those chapters, it is useful to recap the broad contours of the zero- and positive-sum games.

Cold War game

In Part I, I 'established the context' of the end of the Cold War as the collapse of a structure. As Paul Chilton (1996) argues in his book on security metaphors, 'structure' has been an important metaphor for conceptualising security. Structures have clear insides and outsides, distinguishing the secured within from the threat outside. The structure of deterrence kept the Eastern enemy out. As the Cold War was ending, a competition emerged between Gorbachev's Common House and NATO's blueprints for a European architecture.

The Common House would have enclosed the Soviet Union within Europe and, based as it was on the CSCE model, would also have included the United States and Canada. Nonetheless, it was viewed by the West as an extension of the traditional Soviet objective of decoupling Europe from the United States, leaving it alone on the European continent with the dominant military presence of the Soviet Union. NATO's concept of an architecture shifted the centre of gravity towards Western Europe. While originally a 'blueprint', the architecture is now being 'built'.[33] It has 'foundations' resting on the transatlantic relationship and is held up by a number of 'pillars'.[34] The architecture is composed of a range of interlocking institutions, including NATO, the European Union, Western European Union (WEU) and OSCE (Organisation for Security and Cooperation in Europe – formerly the CSCE), but is identified as NATO's concept and NATO is at the centre.

NATO's architecture contains particular identities, that is, members of a club. Being a member relates to an act of joining.[35] Being a member makes one eligible for security benefits.[36] Membership is also attached to conditions. To become 'normal' a potential member has to demonstrate that they hold, and will act upon, a set of values, growing out of a common European heritage and attached to the Judeo-Christian and Enlightenment tradition, which is said to be the opposite of nationalism.[37] Identity as a club member is distinguished from the identity of those who are waiting at the door to get in and those who will not become members.

Language games relating to the architecture and its club occupants have a historical relationship to the Cold War. As explored in earlier chapters, structural maintenance and preservation were the central tasks of the two Cold War alliances. For NATO, deterrence, the foundation of the alliance and Western security, had to be maintained. The Soviet Union was preserving a framework that rested on the foundations of socialist production, Marxism-Leninism and the unity of socialist countries. Both

33 'Thus the need arose to build a framework of interlocking institutions defining a new European security architecture.' E. Colombo, 'European Security at a Time of Radical Change', 40: 3 (1992).

34 'NATO needs firm foundations on both sides of the Atlantic.' V. Ruhe, 'Adapting the Alliance in the Face of Great Challenges', *NR*, 41: 6 (1993); 'This European security is based on three mutually reinforcing pillars, which have been consolidated to provide the support for structured links and a process of effective, consistent cooperation in which NATO, in particular, the linchpin of the entire system, will interact with the other institutions involved – first and foremost with the Western European Union and with the CSCE.' Colombo, 'European Security'.

35 'Our main guidelines in achieving this aim are to: join the *club* of recognised democratic states with market economies, on a basis of equality.' A. Kozyrev, 'The New Russia and the Atlantic Alliance', *NR*, 41: 1 (1993).

36 'There is an important new mission: to help the emerging democracies to the East share in the benefits we have gained from this Alliance.' W. Christopher, 'Towards a NATO Summit', *NR*, 41: 4 (1993).

37 'The sharing of common values – that community of values which has come down to us from Judaeo-Christian antiquity, medieval Christianity and the philosophy of the Enlightenment – is, in a way, suspended as long as a population is prey to forms of domination rooted in opposite principles. Today, Poland, Hungary and Czechoslovakia are once again free to join us, though it is clear that in economic terms they are not ready for EC membership. What we have to do is devise transitional processes by which these nations can become *normal* members of the EC'. J. Rovan, 'A Unified Germany in a United Europe', *NR*, 38: 6 (1990).

structures enclosed 'families'. While both clubs and families provide security, the club is a less intimate form of relationship, where protection is a form of insurance.[38] Also, while one can, with some difficulty, 'join' a family, joining or bringing in new members is a regular practice of clubs. One can move from the 'outside' to the 'inside' of a club. The issue of who will potentially belong and where the boundaries of Europe will be drawn has been central to the debate over accession to the NATO club.

There is a temporal relationship between the historically related but distinct language games. The transition from maintenance to collapse of the Cold War to building a new security structure, containing a club rather than families, did not happen in one fell swoop but rather involved a longer-term process. This book has mapped changes in the structures of security, and the identities contained within, over time. Adding these post-Cold War changes to the earlier grammars, below is a simplified representation of the relationship.

The coherence provided by the grammars makes it possible to identify the contestation in historically specific contexts. In the first half of the 1980s, the contest was between maintaining and dismantling the structures of the Cold War. Later, NATO's blueprint for an architecture emerged against the background of Gorbachev's Common House.

Even though the architecture would not by definition exclude Russia, the traditional association of security with stable foundations, as well as NATO's position at the centre, has made it easy to conflate this notion with boundaries distinguishing an inside and an outside. Russia has clearly put the movement of NATO's 'infrastructure' eastward within this framework, emphasising the exclusion of Russia.[39] The conceptualisation of Central European countries 'waiting at the door' to get in, suggests a wall with an opening through which one enters[40] and control of that opening by an agent, that is, NATO, within. In addition, one of the central benefits of joining is the Article Five guarantee that NATO will come to the aid of any

---

38 'NATO is still the principal life insurance for its members based on collective commitments and rights.' J. J. Holst, 'Pursuing a Durable Peace in the Aftermath of the Cold War', *NR*, 40: 4 (1992).

39 For instance, as Aleksi Arbatov, Vice-Chairman of the State Duma's Defence Committee, stated: 'The main problem is that instead of the "common European home" that Gorbachev, Mitterand and Brandt dreamed of, the intention now is to replace the balance of forces between the two cold-war-era military blocs with the expansion of one of the alliances to all of Europe, but excluding Russia and ignoring its objections. Yet if it hadn't been for Moscow, the cold war would not have ended, communism in Eastern Europe would not have collapsed, and the newly acquired unprecedented security of Western Europe would not exist.' 'Military Alliances', *CDPSP*, 68: 52 (1996).

40 'Seeking to earn closer ties with NATO, many partners took early steps to affirm their future democratic orientation. None of this would have happened so speedily without the

	Structure	Self	Other
	COLD WAR		
Acts	Cold War	family	criminal
Attributes	maintaining	protecting	negotiations
	foundation	hierarchical	liar
	END OF COLD WAR		
Acts	dismantling	emancipation	renaming crime
Outcome	collapse	equal partnership	disarmament
		in NATO	human rights
			dialogue
	POST-COLD WAR		
	architecture	club	neighbours
Acts	building	joining	dialogue
Attributes	foundations	insurance	reliable
	pillars	benefits	

of these countries if an outside power crosses over the line distinguishing its insides and outsides. Structures provide stability by projecting control over a space. 'Projecting stability' to the former Eastern Europe is the main objective of NATO's expansion strategy.

End of the Cold War game

Critical initiatives in East and West began to 'act as if' the Cold War was over by engaging in a dialogue across the division of Europe. Observers of the interactions between Gorbachev and Reagan reacted with surprise that the two, for the first time, were engaging in a dialogue as human beings. Dialogue in partnership, as a language game involving a range of moves, represents a very different form of life and conception of identity and security than the more traditional structural model. While structures have clear insides and outsides, dialogue emphasises avoiding processes of exclusion.[41]

firm commitment of the allies to open the door to new members.' J. Solana, 'Preparing for the Madrid Summit', *NR*, 45: 2 (1997).

41 'By not excluding any of the Cooperation Partners, we make it clear that this partnership is not designed against anyone.' M. Wörner, 'Shaping the Alliance for the Future', *NR*, 42: 1 (1994).

While structures separate selves and others, dialogue constructs 'webs' and 'networks' that 'bind together' partners whose security is 'indivisible'.[42] Dialogue as a form of security emerged as the Cold War was ending. It began as an exchange of independent citizens' initiatives in both East and West, which, throughout the 1980s, were attempting to break down the division of Europe. Gorbachev also began to 'act as if' an alternative to the traditional games of security were possible. By refusing to 'hit back' and making concili-atory gestures of disarmament, he generated trust among the Western public and created a climate for engaging his counterpart, Reagan, in a dialogue.

While structures provide a spatial orientation to security, dialogue is security in process. The conventional use of the term 'dialogue' can be distinguished from other forms of communication. Alliance partners, for instance, do not normally engage in dialogue, but rather 'consult' with one another within an existing institutional framework. Although the two are sometimes used interchangeably, dialogue can also be distinguished from more formal 'negotiations' that involve bargaining towards an explicit agreement. Negotiations belong to the structural model, where the self attempts to realise its own ends *vis-à-vis* another. Dialogue is a more open and fluid process of communication, where the participants adapt their own understandings and grow as a result of the interaction. Dialogue is a reciprocal exchange through which both parties grow and change. It involves a moral element, an attempt to resolve conflicts in a way that 'heals tears in the fabric of relationships' (Pitkin, 1972: 150–2).

One of the stated intents of the East–West dialogue between NATO and its partners has been to 'heal the division of Europe'.[43] The main forum of this dialogue was first the North Atlantic Cooperation Council (NACC) and later the Partnership for Peace. Within the Partnership, the goal was less to extend NATO to the East than to 'extend the hand of friendship' to 'neigh-bours', whose security was inseparably linked.[44] While Cold War military structures closed off spaces and depended on secrets to maintain security, dialogue emphasises greater 'openness' and 'transparency' as the key to

---

42 'The NACC is becoming a central element in the growing web of security ties that bind us together.' Christopher, 'Towards a NATO Summit'; 'European security is indivisible, although not everybody realises this or is ready to accept this obvious fact.' P. Koloziejczyk, 'Poland – A Future NATO Ally', *NR*, 42: 5 (1994).

43 'The NACC was conceived as a means for NATO to contribute to healing the division of Europe. It aims to foster political dialogue, practical cooperation, transparency in military affairs, and the peaceful integration of the new democracies into the transatlantic community.' Christopher, 'Towards a NATO Summit.'

44 'The hand of friendship and partnership has been extended to the nations of Central and Eastern Europe.' G. Von Moltke, 'NATO Takes Up Its New Agenda', *NR*, 40: 1 (1992); '[The NACC] is tangible proof that the security of NATO members is inseparably linked to that of all other states in Europe.' Christopher, 'Towards a NATO Summit.'

stability.[45] While enemy others were separated by enmity and distrust, dialogue involves building 'trust' with others.[46] In the traditional foundational game, security is first and foremost self-regarding. In the game of dialogue, one's own security is dependent on other-regarding behaviour, on taking into account the concerns and interests of others.

These two games of security are in tension, yet both are interwoven in the emerging strategies of the two players in different ways. NATO conceptualises the two as complementary, arguing that it is possible to expand its military framework eastward, excluding Russia, while maintaining a partnership including Russia. For Russia, dialogue is less compatible with an architecture centring around NATO. Russia has had two responses to NATO's plans for expansion. First, it has accused the West of trying to re-create the Cold War[47] by constructing a new division of Europe. NATO should avoid moving its 'infrastructure' closer to Russia's borders.[48] Second, it has called for a pan-European security structure, based on the model of the CSCE, or for the transformation of NATO into a political organisation, within which NATO's Article Five guarantee would fade in importance and be replaced by common efforts at peacekeeping and crisis management.

I refer to these two post-Cold War conceptions of security as games in so far as there is a coherence to each. Each relies on a different constitution of identity, a different range of moves and different objectives in playing. The next step is to situate moves belonging to each of these games in the context of an unfolding strategy employed by each side as they reconstituted their identities in the post-Cold War world.

45 'Steps have been or will be taken to promote transparency ... and to ensure the democratic control of defence forces.' G. Von Moltke, 'Building a Partnership for Peace', *NR*, 42: 3 (1994).
46 'Through [the Partnership for Peace] we seek to build the habits of consultation, trust and cooperation which the Allies have developed among themselves for decades.' W. Claes, 'NATO and the Evolving Euro-Atlantic Security Architecture', *NR*, 42: 6 (1994–95).
47 'Eastward expansion of NATO's zone of responsibility would result in a situation similar to the cold-war period, when opposing groupings were deployed against each other and maintained in a high state of combat readiness.' I. Rodionov, 'Russia and NATO after Bergen', *CDPSP*, 68: 39 (1996).
48 'The main objective of Russian diplomacy is to block the idea of moving NATO's military infrastructure in Central and East European countries.' D. Gornostayev, 'Russia won't Bargain with NATO', *CDPSP*, 69: 9 (1997).

10

Survival

The fundamental fact here is that we lay down rules, a technique, for a game, and that then when we follow rules, things do not turn out as we had assumed. That we are therefore as it were entangled in our own rules. This entanglement in our rules is what we want to understand (i.e. get a clear view of). (Wittgenstein, 1958: para. 125)

STRATEGY, SINCE CLAUSWITZ, has been thought about as the achievement of political ends by military means. With the demise of the East–West conflict, a rethinking of strategy by NATO and Russia was needed. Both NATO and Russia admit that there is no explicit threat from an enemy at the moment. The post-Cold War development of strategy by the two sides has military consequences for the future, but the struggle, up to this point, has been political in nature. Strategic issues have been inseparable from questions about the shape of the post-Cold War system of security in Europe. During the time frame explored in the next two chapters, from 1991 to 1997, both sides have been engaged in a process of reconceptualising their identities and interests, against the background of a battle over the definition of the new European order. A central issue in this battle has been whether the new structure would be primarily military or political in orientation.

While strategies usually relate to specific games, I argued in Chapter One that games at the international level are not incommensurable in the way that, for instance, a game of monopoly and chess are incommensurable. They overlap and intersect; new possibilities are constituted as players interact with one another. In the chapters that follow, the two games of security, as discussed in the previous chapter, are constitutive of distinct and unfolding strategies employed by NATO and Russia.

Both NATO and Russia have had a hard time 'finding their place' in the post-Cold War world. Both have had to redefine their identities and interests in order to survive. Within the Cold War two relatively equal superpowers were involved in a 'maintenance' game. In the post-Cold War world, both players have switched to a more 'activist' strategy. They are no longer engaged in maintenance activities but have become agents of change. Both sides now express concern that the other remains trapped in the old Cold

War game, which involves 'spheres of influence' and re-creating the 'division'. Both claim to be more interested in dialogue, cooperation and overcoming the division of Europe. It is the tension between these two possibilities that drives their interactions.

The focus of this chapter is the evolution of NATO's post-Cold War strategy of survival. In what follows, I look at the relationship between NATO's language of manoeuvre and its eventual entanglement in this language. Language of manoeuvre suggests the strategic use of language. However, as Hollis and Smith (1991: 167) argue, this language both constrains and enables actors. A policy will fail, regardless of one's purpose in pursuing it, if it cannot be presented as legitimate and plausible. Their focus is on individuals within a bureaucratic forum where collective decisions are taken. My point is that the scope of this legitimating language is much wider in so far as whatever decisions are taken 'behind closed doors' these must also be legitimate and plausible to a wider public.

It should be clarified that the relationship between a language of manoeuvre and entanglement is different from the distinction made, for instance, by Habermas (1972, 1987), between the strategic and communicative use of language. While Habermas's ideas about communicative action are derived from Wittgenstein, his distinction represents a divergence (Smith, 1997). For Habermas the strategic use of language is instrumental. It is a means–end relationship by which the strategic actor causally exerts an influence, through threats and rewards, on others to act in accordance with the strategic actor's goal. By contrast, the communicative use of language is oriented towards reaching understanding and consensus through a dialogical process. What is lost in this construction of strategic use as a monological relationship is the Wittgensteinian point that all meaning, whether strategic or everyday, relies on a form of intersubjective understanding. As Nicholas Smith (1997: 115) notes: 'In order for the manipulation of meanings to be possible, there must first be meanings to manipulate, there must be something to be used as a means to an end. But if meaning is itself not something that can be strategically decided upon then the strategic use of language cannot be originary.'

Rather than one type of communication being monological and the other dialogical, both are intersubjective. Language of manoeuvre and entanglement do not in fact represent a distinction, but rather a relationship. A language of manoeuvre must be meaningful to have strategic effects; for precisely this reason, actors become entangled in their language. Even if the intention is to achieve pre-determined ends, once an act, for instance a promise or threat, is undertaken publicly, the actor may also be constrained or enabled in making further moves, whatever their personal aims (Hollis and Smith, 1991: 167).

Remaining relevant after forty

In the previous chapter I argued that the end of the Cold War was less an objective victory by NATO than constituted, in its aftermath, as a victory. NATO reacted in each case, from the INF agreement to the collapse of the Berlin Wall, presenting itself as the source and inspiration of change. When the Soviet Union collapsed, NATO announced another victory. One school of realist thought attributes the end of the Cold War to the success of NATO's containment policy (Kissinger, 1994). In NATO discourse, claims to victory were often coupled with arguments regarding NATO's continuing relevance, such as the following:

> NATO has emerged triumphant from the Cold War. The combination of sufficient strength, steadfastness and a willingness to engage in dialogue and negotiation has paid off. Its imminent demise has frequently been announced by all those pundits who saw the Alliance as a waning institution haunted by a succession of debilitating crises. But it refused to die, its internal discussions and adjustments were a sign of vitality and relevance rather than indications of atrophy.[1]

NATO's victory was due both to its military strength and its willingness to engage in dialogue. NATO was the sole survivor of the Cold War and the 'most successful alliance in history'.[2]

Despite this success, the end of the Cold War raised doubts about the need for NATO. The visible signs of division were gone. The alliance no longer had an enemy. Subsequently, many were questioning why NATO, as an organisation created primarily to counter the Soviet threat, should continue. Its death was portended by many.[3] The central problem was the reluctance of publics and parliaments on both sides of the Atlantic to direct resources to the organisation in the absence of any apparent threat.

A new strategy was needed in light of the changed geostrategic environment. But NATO's survival was also on the line. It was not physical survival against predators that was at issue, as in traditional realist discourse. Survival, the first priority of states in a situation of anarchy, has traditionally been conceived of in terms of military survival. Most agreed in the post-Cold War world that this was not the central concern: the alliance was

---

1 J. J. Holst, 'Pursuing a Durable Peace in the Aftermath of the Cold War', *NR*, 40: 4 (1992).
2 'NATO is perhaps the most successful alliance in human history.' Holst, 'Pursuing a Durable Peace.'
3 For a discussion of why the alliance survived, in contrast to arguments that it would die with the end of the Cold War, see McCalla (1996: 471). See also 'Failure to come up with an answer to [the questions of how policies can be brought in line with current and future, rather than past realities] would condemn the Alliance to death by irrelevance.' B. George, 'The Alliance at the Flashpoint of a New Era', *NR*, 41: 5 (1993).

faced with new 'risks' rather than 'threats' from a clear enemy. The real threat to survival related to a more public process of defending the continuing relevance of the alliance before a public and parliaments on both sides of the Atlantic, at a time of shrinking budgets.[4] NATO had to compete for scarce resources in the public realm. Survival was not primarily related to manoeuvres on the battlefield, but rather to a language of manoeuvre by which it argued its continued relevance.

Prior to the collapse of the Soviet Union, NATO retained its classic function of organising security *vis-à-vis* the Soviet Union, although deterrence had been superseded by a more cooperative relationship in light of Moscow's 'new thinking'. In 1991, NATO approved a new Strategic Concept that would adapt its military forces to the realities of the post-Cold War period. The strategy would no longer rely on the relatively static and heavy concentration of forces around the Central region, as in the Cold War, but would rather emphasise a reduced, more complex and multi-directional defence posture. In the post-Cold War world, NATO needed a more flexible and mobile system, capable of responding to a diverse array of threats.

In addition to the adaptation of NATO's military apparatus, the alliance had a new political mission: to assist the former Eastern bloc countries in their transition to democracy. NATO's success was attributed to a set of shared values which had benefited Western Europe in the post-World War II period and could now benefit the East in its reconstruction effort.[5] In adapting to Western values, the former Warsaw Pact countries would become civilised like the West.[6]

NATO's new mission implied a political expansion into Central and Eastern Europe, but the alliance was initially reluctant at best to consider *military* expansion. However, through a process of interacting with others over time, NATO became entangled in its own language games. It tried to lay down a set of rules, but then things did not turn out as had been assumed.

---

4 'In democracies, armed forces and alliances depend on public support. It is not necessary for every opinion poll to reflect this acceptability but, in the long run, no successful security policy can be pursued without public support for its fundamental elements.' E. Lubkemeier, 'The Political Upheaval in Europe and the Reform of NATO Strategy', *NR*, 30: 3 (1991); 'The new shape of their respective military forces should also take account of the reductions in defence budgets made in the context of overall cuts in public spending in this period of widespread economic crisis.' S. Ando, 'Preparing the Ground for an Alliance Peacekeeping Role', *NR*, 41: 2 (1993).

5 'The Communist dictatorships in Eastern and Central Europe have been replaced by new states based on core values which, three years ago, could only have been described as Western – democracy, respect for human rights and the rule of law.' U. Elleman-Jensen, 'The New Europe – A Danish View', *NR*, 40: 1 (1992).

6 'The renewal of Russia and its transition to a civilised condition is no easy task.' A. Kozyrev, 'The New Russia and the Atlantic Alliance', *NR*, 41: 1 (1993).

Stage One: avoiding expansion

Neither NATO nor the countries of Central and Eastern Europe assumed from the beginning that NATO would militarily expand to the East. Initially, after the collapse of the Berlin Wall and prior to the collapse of the Soviet Union, many of the former dissidents in Central Europe, who had become heads of state, advocated a new European security structure centred around the CSCE. This vision was consistent with the 'dialogue from below' in the 1980s, which had been framed in terms of a new Helsinki. The sentiment was most clearly articulated by the Czechs. Vaclev Havel, then President of Czechoslovakia, said the following in his April 1991 address to the NATO Council:

> At the time when the totalitarian systems in Central and Eastern Europe fell and democracy prevailed there and when, as a result of that, the Iron Curtain, that used to cut Europe in half, broke down ... everything appeared to us to be clear and simple: The Warsaw Treaty Organisation, a relic of the Cold War and a formal expression of our satellite position ... would peacefully dismantle itself while the North Atlantic Alliance would proceed speedily to transform itself, so as to eventually merge in an entirely new security structure that would cover the whole of Europe and link it with the North American continent on the one hand and with what the Soviet Union would turn into on the other.
>
> It appeared to us that the best suited political framework for the creation of such a security structure could be provided within the CSCE [...] We in Czechoslovakia were not alone in thinking along these lines – thoughts of a number of other European politicians and of a considerable part of the public went in similar directions.[7]

The CSCE would provide the framework for a pan-European security system and what had formerly been NATO would be embedded within it. The Paris Summit of the CSCE in November 1990 gave the organisation more of an institutional underpinning and put it on a more permanent footing.

Initially, many assumed that the CSCE would be the core of a new pan-European structure of security. However, faced with political and economic instability, the new leaders in Central and Eastern Europe approached the West for help. While initially these requests were more economic and political than military, historical fears of the Soviet Union were generated by the failed coup in 1991 that sought to depose Gorbachev. The attempted coup gave rise to concern that the former communists would return to power.[8]

By 1991, prior to the collapse of the Soviet Union, all of the former Warsaw Pact countries had expressed an informal interest in becoming

7 'President Havel's Address to the NATO Council', *NR*, 39: 2 (1991).
8 T. Taylor, 'NATO and Central Europe', *NR*, 39: 5 (1991).

associated with NATO.[9] But NATO was not interested. Through 1992, NATO expressed clear opposition to military expansion eastward, at least 'for the foreseeable future'.[10] Arguments for avoiding expansion ranged from concerns about Russia's response to fears that it would weaken the alliance or be a source of division in both East and West.[11] At this point, extending military protection to the East was conceived of in opposition to extending stability. As the Norwegian Minister of Defence, Johan Jurgen Holst put it:

> Sometimes, it is argued that NATO should extend protection to others by now opening up to new members, but in the current phase of political developments, such an extension could weaken the process of reconciliation. To some countries it might convey the message that the victorious coalition is pushing its border eastward, that a new confrontation is in the making. The result could be xenophobic and nationalistic reactions further east enveloping Europe in a tragic cycle of self-fulfilling prophecies. Rather NATO is seeking to extend stability by creating new frameworks for association with former adversaries, by raising the threshold against aggression and repression through networks of cooperation and commitments to certain basic standards or codes of conduct. The process of association and cooperation provides for implicit protection. As Europe grows together, the distinction between explicit and implicit protection may lose its saliency. The integrity of NATO must be preserved as the anchor of security in Europe.[12]

Rather than extending protection to new members, NATO should extend stability through frameworks of political association. One of NATO's central concerns in 1992 was that expansion would exacerbate nationalist tensions in Central and Eastern Europe. A 'hot war', motivated by ethnic divisions, had begun in the Balkans, the first hot war in Europe for over forty years. Violent nationalism was rearing its head in Nagorno-Karabakh, Georgia and Moldova.

In contrast to the conflicts emerging in the former Eastern bloc, NATO was a symbol of the potential for an integration transcending nationalist divisions. NATO's song of self-praise in 1992 emphasised its role in internationalising

---

9 'All the former Warsaw Treaty Organisation countries have expressed some informal interest in becoming associated with NATO.' Taylor, 'NATO and Central Europe.'

10 'The Alliance has made it clear that it cannot for the foreseeable future invite these countries to become members nor offer them security guarantees.' M. Wörner, 'NATO Transformed: The Significance of the Rome Summit', *NR*, 39: 6 (1991).

11 'First, extending NATO eastward could cause future governments of Russia to fear that the West sought domination over them ... Second, admitting Central European states as NATO members would be very disruptive of the Alliance's arrangement and machinery [...] Third, NATO countries lack the resources to extend their defence commitments ... Fourth, a serious debate about membership could well split the alliance.' Taylor, 'NATO and Central Europe.'

12 Holst, 'Pursuing a Durable Peace.'

defence policy and its future political function of preventing a renationalisation of defence establishments in NATO.[13] While expansion would potentially exacerbate nationalist tensions to the East, NATO survival was essential to avoid the re-emergence of conflict between Western European states.

NATO was necessary to maintain the 'habit' of internationalised security policy in the West; by revising its mission, NATO could also be a force for projecting stability to the Eastern bloc. Peacekeeping and crisis management, in cooperation with the CSCE, would play a role in dampening the disintegrative tendencies of nationalism in the territory of the former enemy.

While no military guarantees would be provided to Central and Eastern Europe in the foreseeable future, the security of states in East and West would be 'inseparably linked' through political ties. This political consultation and cooperation was expressed through the NACC, which was inaugurated in December 1991. The new organisation was not to be an alternative to a strengthened CSCE process, but rather a complement to it. It was not NATO's military infrastructure but its information programmes that would be expanded to Central and Eastern Europe.[14] The NACC embodied an end of the Cold War game, constituting a 'framework for dismantling the remnants of the confrontation of the Cold War, both physical and mental relics'.[15] The NACC was a forum for political dialogue and cooperation with former Eastern bloc countries which would prevent the formation of competing alliances in Central and Eastern Europe by addressing their security concerns.[16]

NATO's discussion of military strategy continued to focus primarily on the relationship between the United States and Europe. Many were concerned about a possible withdrawal of the US from Europe.[17] At the core, NATO was still primarily a military alliance designed to protect the security of its member states.[18] The Article Five guarantee was the expression of the

13 'The inescapable habit of denationalised security policy is embodied in [NATO's] policy and procedure.' W. H. Taft, IV, 'The NATO Role in Europe and the US Role in NATO', *NR*, 40: 4 (1992).

14 'The workplan [to be drawn up by the end of February] will contain important new initiatives such as an expansion of NATO's information programmes in Central and Eastern Europe.' G. G. Von Moltke, 'NATO Takes Up its New Agenda', *NR*, 40: 1 (1992).

15 Holst, 'Pursuing a Durable Peace.'

16 M. Wörner, 'A Vigorous Alliance – A Motor for Peaceful Change in Europe', *NR*, 40: 6 (1992).

17 'NATO keeps the US and Canada engaged in Europe at a time when the change in the geostrategic situation and the pull of domestic affairs might make many North Americans advocate withdrawal.' Wörner, 'A Vigorous Alliance.'

18 'At its core, NATO constitutes a military alliance designed to protect the security of its member states. Hence, its ability to perform the protective functions under novel conditions will be the principal test of its continued relevance.' Holst, 'Pursuing a Durable Peace.'

European commitment to a common European defence and security policy, as well as the transatlantic commitment to an alliance security policy. NATO remained relevant, it was argued, as the only organisation that could guarantee the security of member states against all military threats. But the geopolitical context that had originally led to its birth had changed. As a result, NATO was broadening its security agenda and creating flexible forces capable of responding to diverse security risks.

Stage Two: justifying the expansion

In 1993 the expansion issue became an object of contestation within the alliance. Germany, which was providing the lion's share of aid to the former Soviet Union and absorbing most of the refugees from the former Eastern bloc, led the call for an opening of the European integration process towards the East, in both economic and security matters. The larger discussion had shifted from no enlargement in 'the foreseeable future' to the choice for enlargement 'at an appropriate time'.[19] Enlargement was becoming more thinkable but the focus continued to be the expansion of the NACC as a vehicle for 'healing the division of Europe', fostering political dialogue and encouraging transparency in the militaries of Central and Eastern Europe.[20]

Western avoidance of the expansion issue was increasingly arousing suspicions among the Central and Eastern countries that Western Europe was trying to isolate itself behind a new *cordon sanitaire* from the problems of post-Cold War Europe.[21] The Cold War victor, which had challenged Eastern bloc leaders to tear down the walls that had kept Eastern Europeans in, was now constructing barriers to keep them out. While enthusiastic about cooperation within the NACC, Poland took the lead in articulating the hope of the Visegrad countries that this discussion would result, over time, in an increasing commitment by NATO that would eventually lead to integration in the alliance.[22]

19 'At an appropriate time, we may choose to enlarge NATO membership. But that is not now on the agenda.' W. Christopher, 'Towards a NATO Summit', *NR*, 41: 4 (1993).

20 'What is most important is that we intensify and expand the work programme for the NACC and broaden its mandate. The NACC was conceived as a means for NATO to contribute to healing the division of Europe.' Christopher, 'Towards a NATO Summit.'

21 'It is dangerously naive to expect that Western Europe can isolate itself by a *cordon sanitaire* from the problems that have arisen since the fall of communism. The sooner this new post Cold War isolationism disappears the better for all of us, the better for Europe and the world.' H. Suchocka, 'Poland's European Perspective', *NR*, 41: 3 (1993).

22 '[Poland expects] that the passage of time will bring about further and increasingly substantial commitments of NATO to the Czech Republic, Slovakia, Hungary and Poland, commitments which will eventually lead to integration with the Atlantic security system.' Suchocka, 'Poland's European Perspective.'

One argument against expansion was that it would arouse fears in Russia that the West sought domination over the former enemy, exacerbating xenophobic sentiments and a reluctance to proceed with cuts in defence spending.[23] This concern was eased somewhat on 25 August 1993, when Russian President Yeltsin, in signing the Russian–Polish declaration, granted Poland leave to join the alliance. Yeltsin's act was received hopefully as a sign that the 'old perception of enemies that derived from the Cold War, and its paralysing taboos, are fading away'.[24] For the Central and Eastern Europeans, joining the alliance, and other Western institutions, would enhance their ability to behave like partners in a positive-sum game, by which they could better realise their national interests.[25] Yeltsin's move was not received in Russia in the same way. Instead, 'non-democratic forces' interpreted the possibility of NATO expansion as a move to re-establish the Cold War and isolate Russia. The Russian response will be explored in more depth in the next chapter.

The strong Russian reaction created some nervousness in the West, which was reflected in NATO's Brussels Summit in January 1994.[26] Faced with pressure from Eastern and Central European countries to join the alliance, and with the prospect that a decision to expand would mobilise nationalist forces in Russia, the January Summit mapped a middle course. While agreeing in principle to open the alliance to new members, the alliance had, the previous autumn, reached a consensus that there should be 'no immediate enlargement'.[27] The consensus was based on a belief that such a move would risk 'new divisions in Europe, which ultimately would harm rather than aid the security of the Central and Eastern European states and of Europe as a whole'.[28] In place of a decision regarding enlargement, a new institution was created to expand cooperation and dialogue with the East: the Partnership for Peace. As US Congressman Les Aspin stated:

> The Partnership for Peace avoids drawing new security lines across the map of Europe that are liable to be destabilising. Critics who wanted immediate NATO expansion have been allowed to ignore the issue of which countries should be admitted and in what sequence. It's not trivial. What would it have said about countries that were excluded if others were taken in right now? Would it signal to the hardliners in Russia that it was OK to bully countries that were left out? Instead of drawing new lines that would divide nations, the Partnership will establish new lines that connect nations.[29]

23 Taylor, 'NATO and Central Europe'; Holst, 'Pursuing a Durable Peace.'
24 T. Melescanu, 'Security in Central Europe: A Positive-Sum Game', *NR*, 41: 5 (1993).
25 Melescanu, 'Security in Central Europe.'
26 A. Pushkov, 'Russia and the West: An Endangered Relationship', *NR*, 42: 1 (1994).
27 M. Wörner, 'Shaping the Alliance for the Future', *NR*, 42: 1 (1994).
28 Wörner, 'Shaping the Alliance.'
29 L. Aspin, 'New Europe, New NATO', *NR*, 42: 1 (1994).

The Partnership for Peace would potentially include all cooperation partners and would, therefore, make it clear that it was not designed against anyone. The Partnership would make it possible to delay the decision about expansion, but at the same time would allow Central and Eastern European countries to prepare for such an eventuality. The logic of the Partnership was one of 'self-selection'. Rather than placing the alliance in a position of having to choose, for the time being, who would become a member, countries could, through their own efforts and according to their level of participation, signify their desire to 'draw closer to NATO'.[30]

Stage Three: preparing for expansion

The decision to create the Partnership for Peace took place against the background of the emergence of an ultra-nationalist voice in Russia. NATO expansion had become more thinkable; the result was an exacerbation of nationalist conflicts to the East, as had been feared by some. Two corresponding shifts in language that accompanied the Partnership suggest its role in ameliorating Russian concerns. The first was a shift away from the language of architecture to that of dialogue.[31] The second was a shift from NATO as the core of a future European security structure to the CSCE.

The shift away from the architecture, centred in NATO, to a dialogue with the CSCE at the core is not incidental. On the one hand, it represented a concession to Russian hopes for a security structure revolving around the CSCE, going back to Gorbachev; on the other hand, given NATO's role as the central pillar of the architecture and the traditional meaning of security provided by foundations that include and exclude, the latter was more likely to exacerbate Russian fears. Russian Foreign Minister, Andrei Kozyrev emphasised that the Partnership, as well as cooperation within the CSCE and NACC framework, would make the Eastern expansion of NATO less pressing and avoid confining military and political cooperation to a geographically limited area, creating new barriers in Europe and a sense of isolation among Europeans.[32]

With the emergence of the Partnership, the CSCE recaptured its position at the core of the dialogue. In 1994, Kozyrev claimed that the 'CSCE has won the Cold War'. According to Manfred Wörner, then Secretary General

---

30 Wörner, 'Shaping the Alliance.'
31 While the language of architecture is a recurring feature of NATO texts since the concept emerged, it largely disappears in the first half of 1994.
32 A. Kozyrev, 'Russia and NATO: A Partnership for a United and Peaceful Europe', *NR*, 42: 4 (1994).

of NATO, 'By contributing to the further building of confidence among all European states, the Alliance hopes that [the Partnership for Peace] and the efforts that continue to be undertaken through the NACC will aid in bringing about the conditions under which the CSCE can become the core of an effective pan-European security system.'[33] The Partnership was constructed by both as a partnership between NATO, on the one hand, and the countries of Central and Eastern Europe, including Russia, on the other, but the broader context, unlike previous discussions of the architecture, was provided by the CSCE rather than NATO.

The Partnership temporarily delayed NATO expansion, shifting attention to the dialogue with the East. However, given the dual purpose of the Partnership, it also lent momentum to the expansion effort. While the West initially sought to mollify public opinion in Russia through the Partnership, the former Central and Eastern European countries, concerned about the same development, emphasised the promise of the Partnership to prepare candidates for future NATO membership. Later that year, the Polish Minister of Defence Kolodziejczyk stated: 'We expect and would welcome NATO expansion that would reach to democratic states to our East.' Poland undertook the Partnership as 'the best route towards its goal of full integration in the Alliance'. Kolodziejczyk took US President Clinton's June speech in Warsaw, during which he said that it was no longer a question of whether the alliance would expand but when and how, as an indication 'that most of the doubts about the necessity of that step have disappeared'.[34] The Partnership relied on a language of manoeuvre to mollify two conflicting tendencies, represented by Russia and the Central and Eastern Europeans. It became entangled in this language, however, as the latter drew on the promise of the Partnership to further their goal of eventual membership.

Within the Partnership, the political goal of dialogue with the former enemy – an end of the Cold War game – took on a clearer military dimension.[35] The dialogue revolved around NATO members which were attempting to draw the former Eastern European countries and Russia closer. The dialogue

---

33 Wörner, 'Shaping the Alliance.'
34 P. Kolodziejczyk, 'Poland – A Future NATO Ally', *NR*, 42: 5 (1994).
35 'The Partnership for Peace is an invitation to these countries to deepen and intensify their ties with the Alliance through practical cooperation. Most of this will be in the military sphere, and will concentrate on fostering the ability to work together in such fields as peacekeeping and humanitarian assistance. In addition, the Partnership has a wider, more political dimension to it, which is the promotion of, and commitment to, democratic principles, thereby increasing stability and diminishing threats to peace.' G. Von Moltke, 'Building a Partnership for Peace', *NR*, 42: 3 (1994).

related to military strategy and defence.[36] The end was to incorporate the East into the practices of NATO. The Partnership was about building trust between military personnel and establishments. The dialogue of the Partnership was an attempt to move beyond the traditional secrecy of the military; but it was a lop-sided dialogue which would school the East in the ways of the West.

At the beginning of 1994, NATO said there would be no immediate enlargement. By mid 1994, after Clinton's speech in Warsaw, the momentum had shifted towards enlargement. At the end of 1993, the Clinton administration policy appeared to be tilting away from its partnership with Western Europe towards Asia. The increasing gulf between the Europeans and Americans[37] was exacerbated by questions within the American Congress and public opinion about why they should continue to invest in the alliance, given the failure to take any effective action in Bosnia.[38] At the same time, alliance countries were faced with major cuts in defence spending and renewed questions about the relevance and need for NATO in the absence of a Soviet threat.[39] Expansion was the answer to these problems. The desire of the Eastern Europeans to join the alliance became proof of its continuing relevance and mission.[40]

36 'In just one year of Partnership for Peace, we have made great strides in opening up the dialogue with the militaries of the new democracies to the East, many of whom were our former adversaries.' General G. A. Joulwan, ' NATO's Military Contribution to Partnership for Peace: The Progress and the Challenge', *NR*, 43: 2 (1995).

37 'Late in 1993, during preparations for the NATO Summit, statements by Clinton Administration officials appeared to tilt US policy away from the traditional closer partnership with Western Europe. This policy shift created the impression that the Administration was taking a 'zero-sum' approach to relations with Asia and Europe, requiring that US policy move its focus away from Europe in order to construct a more profitable relationship with Asia.' S. Sloan, 'Transatlantic Relations in the Wake of the Brussels Summit', *NR*, 42: 2 (1994).

38 'For the moment, many members of Congress appear ready to judge NATO according to what the Allies can do about Bosnia. Against this difficult measure, members of Congress may find little reason to support continued US investment in the Alliance.' Sloan, 'Transatlantic Relations.'

39 'We must not run the risk of losing the support of the public in Alliance member nations, part of whom question the need for maintaining even reduced levels of defence expenditure or contributing to peacekeeping operations in areas remote from national interests.' E. Bruce, 'NATO's Information Activities at a Time of Increasing Demands and Dwindling Resources', *NR*, 42: 4 (1994).

40 'Some have criticised NATO for not responding to new threats such as Bosnia more quickly. Others have questioned whether NATO is even necessary with the Soviet threat gone – a strange question to ask about an organisation whose most burning question is how to cope with the desire of numerous additional nations to join.' Aspin, 'New Europe, New NATO.'

181

Stage Four: inevitable expansion

At the December 1994 Brussels meeting of NATO Foreign Ministers a decision was made to proceed with the expansion. The enlargement of NATO was placed in the context of building a European security architecture which would extend to countries throughout the whole of Europe.[41] The decision would be followed by an extensive study of how NATO would enlarge. Two concerns predominated. The first was ensuring that a larger NATO would remain a strong defensive military alliance. The second was to outline the rights and duties of prospective members within the alliance.[42]

The enlargement was to be one element of a three-part strategy. Since the enlargement would progress slowly, inviting a few candidates at a time, the Partnership continued to be an important vehicle for providing security to other future candidates, who would not be covered by the Article Five guarantee. Countries desiring to become allies would have to pass through a period of transition within the Partnership before becoming 'producers as well as consumers of security'.[43]

The other part of the strategy was a new NATO–Russia relationship. The Russian engagement in Chechnya had fed the anxiety of the Central Europeans, encouraging them in their bid to become fully fledged members; it had also reinforced the necessity to deal with Russia in a way that would avoid provoking an extreme response.[44] Building an enlarged alliance and building a unique relationship to Russia were conceptualised as two sides of the same coin. A strategy of insurance for the Central and Eastern European countries and assurance for Russia was needed. On the same day that the expansion decision was made, Russian Foreign Minister Kozyrev met with the North Atlantic Council in the first 16+1[45] format to discuss the development of an enhanced NATO–Russian relationship beyond the Partnership for Peace. Russia had joined the Partnership the previous June; the new consultations were an indication of NATO's intent to develop a relationship with Russia that would go further. While not wanting Russia to influence its decisions on enlargement, NATO recognised it had a strong interest in reassuring Russia that it did not pose a threat and that its efforts in Central Europe would enhance the common security of all.[46]

Enlargement was initially avoided out of fear that it would re-create the division of Europe. Expansion was now proceeding; dialogue and coopera-

41 Claes, 'NATO and the Evolving Euro-Atlantic Security Architecture', *NR*, 42: 6/1 (1994–95).
42 R. E. Hunter, 'Enlargement: Part of a Strategy for Projecting Stability into Europe', *NR*, 43: 4 (1995).
43 Hunter, 'Enlargement.'
44 G. L. Williams, 'NATO's Expansion: The Big Debate', *NR*, 43: 4 (1995).
45 16+1 refers to the member states of NATO plus Russia.
46 Hunter, 'Enlargement.'

tion with countries which did not join would be the central vehicle for avoiding a new division of Europe.[47] The OSCE, as the most inclusive European security organisation, remained the key to transcending these divisions.[48] At the same time, the indispensable role of the alliance, *vis-à-vis* the OSCE, as the organisation most capable of confronting the military challenge of post-Cold War Europe was recognised.[49] Avoiding the weakening of NATO, and particularly its Article Five guarantee, was crucial to the success of the expansion effort.[50] This implied the possible stationing of foreign forces and nuclear deployments on the territory of future members.[51]

If the goal of expansion in 1995 was to avoid new dividing lines, by 1996 it was said to have rendered the idea of dividing lines in Europe 'obsolete'.[52] Any distinctions between countries resulting from expansion would be 'contours' indicating 'degrees of difference' rather than dividing lines. By developing a 'true partnership' with Russia[53] and making a conceptual linkage between the enlargement of the European Union and NATO, the expansion was to communicate 'the parallelism of integration and cooperation: the integration of new members and the deepening of cooperation with those nations who are not, or not yet, ready or willing to join'.[54] The

47 '[The three part strategy] can help provide a deep sense of security for European countries which do not join NATO as well as for those which do – in the process avoiding a new division of the continent.' Hunter, 'Enlargement.'

48 'As the most inclusive institution in the European security architecture, the OSCE has a key role to play in maintaining security and transcending divisions in Europe.' Chapter Two, 'Study of NATO Enlargement' (September 1995), http//www.nato.int (Basic Documents), Web.

49 'As was stated, "the OSCE has neither the resources nor the authority to take the place of NATO or the WEU, but may act to settle differences, if possible by preventing them or failing that, to propose a settlement." This is not the time either to weaken alliances or relax our efforts to promote dialogue and consultation in the European continent as a whole.' R. Bussiere, 'A Europe of Security and Defence', NR, 43: 5 (1995).

50 'Enlargement, when it occurs, must preserve the assurances provided by the Washington Treaty – notably through Article Five – in both the military and the political fields.' J. M. D. Barroso, 'The Transatlantic Partnership in the New European Security Context', NR, 43: 5 (1995).

51 'If NATO is to retain its current high level of credibility as an effective military alliance it is clear that the Visegrad Four must accept the stationing of foreign forces and nuclear deployments which we know will be sensitive in terms of public opinion.' Williams, 'NATO's Expansion.'

52 'Extending the Alliance will not be an isolated event. It must be seen in a broader context. It is only one – but an important – element of a broad European security architecture that transcends and renders obsolete the idea of "dividing lines" in Europe.' G. Von Moltke, 'NATO Moves Toward Enlargement', NR, 44: 1 (1996).

53 'Highlights of NATO Secretary General's Address to the Russian Council on Foreign and Security Policy', NR, 44: 3 (1996).

54 K. Voigt, 'NATO Enlargement: Sustaining the Momentum', NR, 44: 2 (1996).

integration of the former enemy would ensure that the 'old game' of competing spheres of influence would not return.[55]

But the Central and Eastern Europeans were not convinced. They had consistently viewed expansion and integration as a positive-sum game in which there would be no winners and losers.[56] No one wanted to be seen to be involved in a Cold War game. The Poles viewed Russian opposition to expansion in these terms. As Prime Minister Cimoszewicz stated:

> The Russian government openly and steadfastly opposes the expansion of NATO eastward and this view, it should be noted, is shared by the leaders of major opposition parties. According to this line of reasoning, the enlargement of the Alliance would be no more than another Cold War arrangement. The admission of new members in Central and Eastern Europe would only mean that the dividing line would be drawn closer to Russia ... Such objections to NATO enlargement, it seems, are really based on the logic of the past epoch; they fail to recognise the changes which have taken place in Europe.[57]

The expansion discussion had been fuelled by the Central and Eastern European countries, along with Germany in the West.[58] The problem, which had emerged early on, was the differential treatment of countries in this region. NATO claimed to have an equal opportunities policy.[59] The former Central and Eastern European countries would demonstrate, through their own efforts, their readiness to join the alliance. But early on there had been suspicions that this policy was based more on a cultural litmus test than democratic credentials. The Romanian Minister of Foreign Affairs expressed this concern:

---

55 'Left alone, the countries of Central and Eastern Europe could fall victim yet again to the rivalries and tensions that have plagued the region from time immemorial; only through integration can we ensure that the "old game" of competing spheres of influence does not return. A wait and see attitude could invite the very instabilities that membership of NATO could alleviate.' Voigt, 'NATO Enlargement.'

56 'By behaving like partners in a positive-sum game, these countries can better accomplish their own interests.' Kolodziejczyk, 'Poland.'

57 W. Cimoszewicz, 'Building Poland's Security: Membership of NATO a Key Objective', *NR*, 44: 3 (1996).

58 'The flames of enthusiasm for enlargement were fanned by a lobby which has strong links with Central European countries, particularly Poland. Indeed, these arguments are not based on security policy alone, but more on emotional factors. The strong preference in Germany for countries to join as soon as possible is based on considerations of security policy. Germany wants to extend the zone of stability as far east as possible.' F. Bolkestein, 'NATO: Deepening and Broadening?', *NR*, 44: 4 (1996).

59 'The Partnership is and will remain an equal opportunity for all, while allowing each partner to develop progressively closer relations with the Alliance on the basis of its own interest and actual performance.' Von Moltke, 'Building a Partnership.'

The taxonomists in question insist on a cultural-religious kinship test. As a result, one learns that only the so-called northern tier of former Eastern Europe would 'fit in' with Western standards and projects, while 'the rest' which, not being part of Western Christianity, would inevitably be 'undemocratic' and 'unable to democratise' deserve a different destiny.[60]

The first wave of expansion was likely to incorporate members of the Visegrad Four, which were in the 'Northern tier' of Europe. While enthusiastically embraced by these countries, those outside, in the 'grey zone' between West and East, feared that this piecemeal approach would create a division of Central and Eastern Europe into two groups of states, those securely embedded in Western institutions and those outside; those protected by the Article Five guarantee and those left unprotected in a 'buffer zone' between great powers. These countries, fearing the development of a 'security vacuum' and of new spheres of influence, began, against the background of preparations for accession of the Visegrad countries, to hold the West accountable for its words. In an argument regarding the importance of including the Baltic states, Ambassador Stankevicius of Lithuania pointed to statements of American leaders that they would avoid the construction of new spheres of influence:

> On this score, I would refer to President Clinton's letter of 27 November 1994 to Estonia's President Lennart Meri, in which Clinton wrote that the goal of the US was to expand across all of Europe the area of democracy, stability and welfare that had been achieved in Western Europe after the Second World War. The US President emphasised that he believed in a 'New Europe' united by common values, where there is no room for '*spheres of influence*'.
>
> This position was confirmed by US Secretary of State Warren Christopher in Prague on 20 March 1996, when he said that '*No nation in Europe should ever again be consigned to a buffer zone between great powers or relegated to another nation's 'sphere of influence.'* Any exclusion of the Baltic States from the process of accession to NATO would not conform to these principles.[61]

NATO had once again become entangled in its words. The argument that NATO expansion would render the division of Europe obsolete, that it would end the Cold War game based on a politics of 'spheres of influence', was being used by states outside the initial wave of expansion; they too should be included under NATO's security guarantee. Russia, already opposed to the inclusion of the Visegrad group, was clear that it would not

---

60 Melescanu, 'Security in Central Europe.'
61 C. V. Stankevicius, 'NATO Enlargement and the Indivisibility of Security in Europe: A View from Lithuania', *NR*, 44: 5 (1996). See also, I. Golob, 'Preparing for Membership: Slovenia's Expanding Ties to NATO', *NR*, 44: 6 (1996).

tolerate an expansion up to its borders. NATO's 'true partnership' with Russia, based on a promise to take its concerns into account, was in conflict with the demand for unlimited expansion. Critics in the West had begun to make their voice heard. Even those who supported the expansion were concerned that the alliance would be weakened by giving guarantees that it would not or could not fulfil.[62] As a result, some had begun to question the meaning of collective defence, arguing that it no longer had the same interpretation or the same requirements. Karsten Voigt, the President of the North Atlantic Council, articulated the concern:

> It goes without saying that the new Alliance members will benefit from the mutual defence commitment contained in Article Five of the North Atlantic Treaty. But the principal issue is what means are necessary to support this commitment in today's security environment ... present Alliance defence needs have changed fundamentally and collective defence no longer has the same interpretation nor the same requirements. The most striking example of this is provided by the fact that the requirement for NATO to station forces and nuclear weapons on the territory of certain member states has lost its importance; there is no need, therefore, for NATO to deploy such conventional forces on the territory of new members ... The NATO study should have been more explicit on these points, particularly as it would provide an important signal to Russia regarding the non-threatening nature of enlargements.[63]

To expand eastward and, at the same time, to signal to Russia that it was not a threat, NATO would have to rethink the nature of its commitment to collective defence. Stationing forces and nuclear weapons in Central Europe, once thought to be necessary, was no longer as important. Central and Eastern European demands for enlargement had to be handled in such a way that would neither weaken the alliance nor upset Russia. Sustaining the momentum of expansion had become essential to the continuing relevance of the alliance.[64] The question remained whether all three would be possible. Russia's eventual strategy towards the West by 1997, when the Founding Act was signed, relied on the premise that expansion could not but weaken NATO, which would serve Russia's long-term interest in a pan-European security organisation.

62 'If NATO countries invite an interested state to join the Alliance without seriously addressing the question of whether they are prepared to defend this new member, this could lead to an erosion of the Alliance.' Bolkestein, 'NATO: Deepening and Broadening?'
63 Voigt, 'NATO Enlargement.'
64 'Sustaining the momentum of the enlargement process is essential to the future role and relevance of the Alliance.' Voigt, 'NATO Enlargement.'

Conclusion

Realists have traditionally distinguished the public language of states from their real interests. This relies on an instrumental notion that language is rationally employed to realise ends that may be distinct from those expressed in public justifications. I have tried to show that the relationship between a language of manoeuvre and the underlying interests of states is more complex. Actors are always already embedded in a context of meanings that constrains their room for manoeuvre. The boundaries of manoeuvre can change. During the Cold War, NATO was the maintainer of the status quo. In post-Cold War Europe it has adopted an activist strategy, based on an end of the Cold War game, within which it is now the agent of change.

This end of the Cold War game might be understood as a language of manoeuvre, which can be distinguished from NATO's real interests. With the end of the Cold War, NATO became the organiser of dialogue. Like the social movements earlier, NATO is attempting to heal the division of Europe. The dialogue was, however, lop-sided. It also did not look like a dialogue as conventionally understood. The purpose was to draw the former enemy countries closer to NATO, incorporating them into its practices. It became a dialogue regarding military practices. In this respect, NATO's dialogue might be understood as part of a language of manoeuvre, which would facilitate the construction of a new structure and new rules which it controlled.

However, while NATO tried to lay down the rules of a new game, it was also increasingly constrained by these rules. Over time emphasis shifted from the military dimension of the relationship to the political, and from a focus on NATO to a more equal dialogue within a positive-sum game. In the months preceding the signing of the NATO–Russia Founding Act, in July 1997, NATO was claiming that its partnership with Central and Eastern Europe was 'no longer a question of the one-way traffic of ideas and expertise',[65] particularly with Russia and Ukraine. Within this more genuine dialogue, the importance of taking into account the needs of those not acceding to membership was key.[66] Expansion was proceeding, but by 1997 NATO was emphasising the political over the military nature of expansion. The Article Five guarantee to collective defence was receding into the

---

65 J. Solana, 'Preparing for the Madrid Summit', *NR*, 45: 2 (1997).

66 'In order to ensure that the opening of NATO increases security and stability for all of Europe, not just those who join the Alliance, we will have to take into account the needs of those who do not join or who may join later.' J. Solana, 'The New NATO and the European Security Architecture', Speech, Vienna, 16 January 1997, natodata@cc1.kuleuven.ac.be, Web.

background.[67] As Western critics of the expansion decision emerged,[68] this shift towards the political became essential to NATO survival. As the German journalist, Christoph Bertram noted:

> Just imagine for a moment that, as Western critics of enlargement postulate, NATO remained as it emerged from the Cold War, a military-political organisation, limiting itself to deterring an attack on its members and perhaps a few out-of-area interventions of the Bosnian kind. It would soon be exposed as obsolete. There is no enemy on the horizon capable of launching such an attack, and while such an eventuality cannot be excluded forever, this purposely speculative possibility will not suffice to convince citizens, voters and politicians in NATO countries of the need to make sacrifices for the sake of solidarity, least of all the citizens, voters and politicians in the US.[69]

By maintaining the primacy of its deterrent function, NATO would become obsolete. Enlargement was presented less in terms of collective defence than of healing the division and of a more equal dialogue.[70] Earlier, the need for the deployment of troops and nuclear weapons in Eastern Europe had been a strong possibility. Now, NATO promised to avoid such deployments. Earlier, NATO had been the only organisation capable of coordinating collective defence; now, it was the only organisation capable of coordinating crisis management and peacekeeping. NATO had redefined its role from that of the West's protector to that of Europe's anchor of stability. This role was essential to its survival.[71]

NATO needed to expand in order to survive. But the logic of expansion was embedded in a positive-sum game, in which there would be no winners

---

67 'Indeed NATO has changed beyond recognition. Instead of being focused on a single mission – collective defence – NATO has turned into a motor of European security cooperation and a catalyst for political change. It has adopted a new approach to security based on the principle of cooperation with non-member countries and other institutions.' Solana, 'The New NATO.'

68 'The prospect of a larger NATO has generated a lively debate in the press.' Solana, 'Preparing for the Madrid Summit.'

69 C. Bertram, 'Why NATO Must Enlarge', *NR*, 45: 2 (1997).

70 'NATO has helped bring within our grasp the most elusive dream of this century: an undivided Europe, at peace, in which every nation is free and every free nation is a partner.' M. Albright, 'Statement to North Atlantic Council Special Ministerial Meeting, Brussels, 18 February 1997,' natodata@cc1.kuleuven.ac.be, Web.

71 'The only such common purpose is for NATO to carry on with its reforms undertaken over the past few years, in order to redefine its role from that of the West's protector to that of Europe's anchor of stability. That is the role that history and political logic have bestowed on it; it is also the one which, more than any other of its functions, can assure its survival. NATO enlargement is essential for Europe; it is also existential for NATO itself.' Bertram, 'Why NATO Must Enlarge.'

or losers.[72] While these moves might simply belong to a language of manoeuvre, the promise of partnership and dialogue, of avoiding a new division of Europe, provides a basis for the public and those not included in the initial expansion to hold NATO accountable for its words. NATO may once again become entangled in its promises. The form at present is NATO expansion; in substance, the need to avoid feelings of exclusion or a reconstruction of the division is contributing to a deepening partnership with those outside the boundaries of NATO's military infrastructure.

NATO has been engaged in a set of delicate manoeuvres. The driving concern has been its own survival. Traditionally, this survival would have been facilitated by the creation of a new enemy. In this context, in the absence of overtly aggressive acts by Russia, any act that diverges too far from the claim to a cooperative partnership would expose NATO to be an agent of aggression rather than the catalyst of change. Its relevance is bound to its role as an anchor of stability that will dampen rather than contribute to new conflicts.

A tension between the military and political dimensions of NATO's new strategy remains, however. NATO expansion has a double paradox at its core. First, NATO has to expand in order to survive; yet expansion will lead to a weakening of the traditional core function of the alliance. Second, each wave of expansion will lead to new demands for inclusion, which is in conflict with NATO's 'true partnership' with Russia. The logic of the situation is such that, at the next juncture, the choice may be between a new round of accessions that will exacerbate tensions with Russia or a trans-formation of NATO into a truly pan-European security organisation. These contradictions at the heart of the expansion process are central to under-standing the Russian response, which will be explored in the next chapter.

---

72 'The process of enlargement began three years ago at the NATO summit here in Brussels. It will not end in Madrid. Nor will it end with a division between winners and loser, for ultimately all who are interested in a peaceful and democratic Europe whether they are in NATO or partners of it – will win.' Albright, 'Brussels Statement.'

11

Besting

For the princessa, who is always fighting a come-from-behind war, besting is the only way to win because it means winning with a losing hand. Anyone can win with a winning hand. Only the princessa can win with less. (Rubin, 1997: 90)

THE PREVIOUS CHAPTER ended with a claim that a contradiction inherent in NATO's expansion strategy is at the heart of the Russian response. Many are likely to view the signing of the NATO–Russia Founding Act as a defeat or concession on the part of Russia. The former superpower had no choice but to agree, given its weak economic and military position. This final empirical chapter is an attempt to rethink the Russian response to NATO expansion, a response that came as a surprise to many. The conclusion represents an alternative to both the claim that the Western decision to expand will re-create the division of Europe (Brown, 1995; Mandelbaum, 1996) and a more realist argument that the response of Russia is a concession or defeat. Within the context of a 'guy game', as discussed in Chapter Six, the latter is a logical conclusion; however, the potential of this move looks very different if situated in the contest between a 'guy game' and a 'girl game'.[1] As one Russian, commenting on the expansion, stated in 1995: 'by accepting the rules of the (Western) game, which are being forced on her, ... Russia will lose.'[2] I argue that Russia's strategy of 'besting' the West was an attempt to transform the game in such a way

---

1 It may seem counter-intuitive to think of a large state engaged in a 'girl' game, the paradigm of which, in the Chapter Six discussion, was provided by nonviolent movements. Yet many of the moves made by Gorbachev in the 1980s provide a precedent for thinking in these terms. MccGwire (1991: 215) refers to Gorbachev 'besting' Reagan at his own game, that is, manoeuvring the US administration into accepting what it had previously condemned. Krasner (1985) also makes an argument that weak states try to change the rules of the game. There are obvious differences between the application of these tactics by a nonviolent resistance movement and by a state such as Russia, which has a history of acting oppressively. My main point is to distinguish a game of maintaining the rules from one that emphasises changing them. Actors in a position of weakness, whether states, women or nonviolent campaigners, have a greater interest in the latter.

2 V. Velichkin, 'NATO as Seen Through the Eyes of the Russian Press', *NR*, 43: 2 (1995).

that its interests might, over the long term, be realised.

Russia, following the collapse of the Soviet Union, was incapable of playing a 'guy' game from a position of strength. It was economically shattered, politically unstable and militarily weakened. There were also questions about whether a strong Russia would be a desirable outcome, that is, whether anyone wanted the former superpower to succeed. This material state of affairs was given meaning and expressed in the feminisation of Russia. Subsequently, the range of moves available to Russia, if 'she' wanted to realise her interests, was different from those of a 'strong' guy player.[3]

While Russia, following the collapse of the Soviet Union, maintained aspects of the 'new thinking', including the emphasis on dialogue and partnership, the context had changed. Confronted with an identity crisis, Russia's new relationship to the West developed in three stages, as she worked through a range of possibilities. During the first, in the immediate aftermath of the collapse, Russia, lacking any clear strategy or voice of her own, was servile to, and dependent on, the West. In the second, she overcompensated for this weakness by becoming 'tough', which only increased her isolation. In the third, she reasserted an identity that assumed greatness, that stood firm while weak. During this stage she – perhaps a bit too late – began to 'best' the West, to act rather than react in an attempt to change the game so that her own interests would be taken into account against the background of NATO's expansion eastward.

Russia, the weak partner

There is a logic to situating Russian action in the context of a 'girl' strategy. In the aftermath of the Soviet collapse, Russia's identity was constructed as the feminine counterpart of a masculine West. The feminisation of Russia is evident in the use of adjectives characteristic of cultural representations of the feminine (which usually presume a masculine opposite), such as weak, unpredictable, vulnerable, docile, shy, lacking an identity, obedient, having an inferiority complex, emotional and hysterical.[4] In the aftermath of the

---

3 I consistently, throughout this chapter, attach feminine pronouns to Russia. This is a convention which, in this case, reinforces the gendering of Russia's identity.

4 The following is a sampling from the Russian press: 'Never before have we [Russia] been so weak.' 'Yelstin Speaks at UN, Meets with Bush', *CDPSP*, 64: 5 (1992); 'The December elections ... reminded the Americans that unpredictable Russia is still potentially ... a threat to world security.' 'A "Chill" in Russia–US Ties?, Kozyrev Opposed', *CDPSP*, 56: 10 (1994); 'Russia ... finds itself far more alone and vulnerable in the world arena than the Soviet Union was.' 'Kozyrev Under Fire from Right and Left,' *CDPSP*, 66: 50 (1994); 'Kozyrev is still viewed in the West as thoroughly docile.' 'Kozyrev Under Fire from Right and Left'; '[Russia has] been "shy" about openly declaring to the world what our strategic interests

collapse, Russia was weak and ailing, and dependent on the West to transform herself. She desperately wanted a partnership which, hopefully, would turn into an alliance.[5] While making declarations of support and 'assuring' Russia,[6] the West did not respond in the way that she would have liked. Russia had a romantic view of the relationship,[7] but her love was unrequited,[8] a theme that is reinforced in another analysis of the Russian press, which included the following:[9]

> The end of a love affair?
> Kozyrev doubts the sincerity of his Western partners
> Russia is not happy with double standards
> Russia and NATO: engagement broken off
> NATO does not need Russia
> The Russian fiasco makes journalists probe into the reasons for the failure of the NATO–Russia 'love affair'
> Why, they ask, isn't Russia's opinion taken into account?
> Ignoring Russia's claim to the role of equal partner with NATO member countries led to a crisis in relations between Russia and the Alliance

The Russian press presents Russia as the weak counterpart of NATO, potentially isolated, capable of greatness yet not taken seriously; the victim of unrequited love who is trying to change but is still held at arm's length and not treated as the equal partner she deserves to be.

are.' 'Rodionov Proposes Changes in Military Doctrine', *CDPSP*, 68: 50 (1996); 'The question of who "we" are is not completely clear. Russia?' 'Coordinated CIS Arms-Control Stand Asked', *CDPSP*, 64: 9 (1992); 'Yeltsin has obediently followed the Western powers on the majority of international issues.' 'A Russian Foreign Policy Conflict with the US?', *CDPSP*, 65: 4 (1993); 'In foreign policy [the Russian position] is semi-confrontational with respect to the West and semi-ingratiating toward it, a position that gives the country an inferiority complex.' 'Kozyrev Offers Draft Foreign Policy Guidelines', *CDPSP*, 64: 48 (1992); 'The NATO Secretary General said that Russia's objections [to expanding the alliance] are based on "emotions rather than facts".' 'Russia Resists US Push for NATO Expansion', *CDPSP*, 68: 12 (1996); ' [Russia] shouldn't make the mistake of reacting hysterically or taking military countermeasures.' 'Military Alliances', *CDPSP*, 68: 41 (1996).

5 'We [Russians] sometimes overstep the bounds of reason in our desire for alliance.' 'Russian Foreign Policy Under Fire', *CDPSP*, 64: 8 (1992). As stated by Kozyrev, 'One shouldn't think that partnership relations rule out the possibility of any kind of tiffs, or that we can move from confrontation to utopia. These are normal partnership relations. I would call it a mature partnership.' 'A Russian Foreign Policy Conflict?'

6 'European and American diplomats assured [Russia] that they understood [her] concerns.' 'Military Alliances', *CDPSP*, 65: 49 (1993).

7 'A "Chill" in Russia–US Ties?' Other related uses include: '[The US has] not yet yielded to the euphoria of romanticism.' 'Russian Foreign Policy Under Fire.'

8 'It would behoove us to avoid succumbing solely to unrequited love and to consider the extent to which our interests coincide with those of the U.S.' 'Russian Foreign Policy Under Fire.'

9 Velichkin, 'NATO as Seen.'

Russia wanted a special relationship. She felt 'humiliated' by the prospect of being just one among many potential partners forming a line outside NATO's door.[10] Even worse, Russia suspected that she was being isolated.[11] The alliance did not bother to take her opinion into account in making decisions.[12]

NATO's deliberations over the possibility of expanding eastward made her feel deceived and betrayed, as well as violated. Vladimir Lukin, Chairman of the Duma's Committee on International Affairs, used a rape metaphor, comparing the 'proposition that Russia join the Partnership for Peace program to the propositions made by a rapist who has cornered a girl: she can either resist or submit, but the result will be the same'.[13] Russia was confused and in pain, feeling a loss of dignity.[14]

The feelings of betrayal related to promises made several years earlier, as Germany was reunifying, that the West would not expand its infrastructure eastward towards Russia's borders.[15] While the West emphasised the unpredictability of Russia because of present weakness, Russia identified her predicament with the broken promises of her potential partner.

Part of the problem of the first period, when Kozyrev was leading the Foreign Ministry, was that Russia was trying to emulate the West.[16] After several years of trying to learn to play by the rules of the Western game,[17]

10 Lukin stated that 'the proposal that [Russia] stand in a row and push others in the line is humiliating to us.' 'Russia Decides to Join NATO Partnership for Peace', *CDPSP*, 64: 11 (1994).

11 'Russia's reward for destroying the totalitarian Soviet empire is not a return to civilisation as a respected and equal partner, but the isolation and serious weakening of the country.' 'Kozyrev under Fire.'

12 'At a time when the countries of Central and Eastern Europe and the Baltics, together with NATO, are preparing demonstrations ... of their combat unity right under Russia's nose, we have a right to ask whether NATO intends to consider Moscow's opinion.' 'Prospect of NATO Expansion Worries Moscow', *CDPSP*, 66: 8 (1994).

13 'Russia Decides to Join NATO Partnership for Peace.' There are also references to US 'penetration' into Russia. 'Foreign Ministry Aid Defends Russia's Record', *CDPSP*, 64: 30 (1992).

14 'Like a person lying prone on the ground, Russia does not have a face of its own, or if it does it is one on which an expression of confusion and pain, not dignity, predominates.' 'Kozyrev Offers Draft Foreign Policy Guidelines.'

15 'Russia Resists US Push for NATO Expansion.'

16 'Many Russian parliamentarians accused the Ministry of Foreign Affairs of blindly emulating the West.' 'Parliament, Ministry Clash over Foreign Policy', *CDPSP*, 64: 30 (1992).

17 'The interests of a democratic Russia do not seriously conflict in strategic terms with American interests, and as long as we follow the civilised world's accepted rules as we pursue these interests, the U.S. will take a fully understanding view of this.' 'Russian Envoy Critiques Foreign Policy', *CDPSP*, 64: 36 (1992); 'It would seem that Washington ought to behave in the international arena in accordance with the rules that it is tirelessly trying to teach Russia.' 'Kozyrev Under Attack: Two Sides of the Case', *CDPSP*, 64: 35 (1992).

Russia realised she could not win because these rules were not her own and no one seemed to want her to succeed. Russia had to change the game. Her eventual strategy for doing so was less the Machiavellian strategy of trying to manipulate and control the other than a Machiavella strategy of modifying her own behaviour, of acting rather than reacting, so that the West would find itself playing by her rules.

Stage One: strategic partnership

In 1993, Russia articulated its Partnership Strategy, which drew on the historical analogy to the Marshall Plan. Kozyrev presented the rationale for this strategy as follows:

> The essential question is one of a new partnership strategy. In its political energy, financial, organisational and material provisions, this strategy should be translated into action no less farsighted than the Marshall Plan and the West's strategy of deterrence. The nations of the West found the strength and resolve in the different post-war years to deal with the challenge of Communism; the same effort is required today to meet the problems of post-Communist Europe, in order not to miss the opportunities which are now available and to win the democratic peace, just as the Cold War was won. The new strategy must be a joint one, and it will require efforts by both sides. The West has to make the transition from offering political solidarity, humanitarian aid and uncoordinated credits, however vital these may be, to providing stable financial, technical and organisational support for the economic reforms in Russia, including the encouragement of investment for our process of conversion.[18]

The partnership Kozyrev appeals for is one in which the West aids a weak and ailing Russia in becoming a 'civilised' country modelled on the developed nations of the West. The West, through an infusion of aid, should rebuild Russia, just as the United States helped to rebuild Western Europe after World War II. As suggested earlier, the Western response to this appeal was mixed, vascillating between 'providing reassurance' and taking a 'wait and see' attitude with regard to the durability of economic and political reforms in Russia. There were concerns about the consequence of a strong Russia, as there were concerns about a weak Russia.

Kozyrev quickly came under attack for 'blindly emulating the West' and for his excessive obedience and servility,[19] at the expense of former allies. In

---

18 A. Kozyrev, 'The New Russia and the Atlantic Alliance', *NR*, 41: 1 (1993).

19 'This year will be a period ... of transition from blindly following the West to defining the parameters and limits of constructive cooperation and competition.' 'Experts Critique Russian Foreign Policy', *CDPSP*, 65: 1 (1993); 'Kozyrev has acquired a reputation as "Mr. Yes" for his servile behaviour.' 'Kozyrev's "Phony" Hard-Line Talk Causes Stir', *CDPSP*, 64: 50 (1992).

particular, the administration was accused of demonstrating solidarity with the West against Iraq by sending ships to the Persian Gulf and of failing to embrace the cause of the Serbs in the former Yugoslavia. After the United States, followed by its French and British allies, carried out bombing and missile strikes against Iraq, Russia's posture vis-à-vis its potential partner began to change. The US was accused of having a 'tendency to dictate terms instead of engaging in dialogue' and of failing to realise the changing nature of international relations.[20] It persisted in believing that complex international problems could be solved with brute force and that it, 'acting virtually alone and at its own discretion', could function as global police-man. Judging from Yeltsin's statements, if not the Foreign Ministry's, Russia was beginning to 'test its own voice' and speak in a 'tougher tone' in the hope of getting 'Clinton to pay attention to Russia'.[21] At the same time, Moscow made initial attempts to construct a 'dialogue' with both Iraq and the countries in the Association of South-East Asian Nations forum, where it, along with China, was viewed as a 'debutante'.[22]

In 1993, the expansion of NATO eastward was little more than an idea. It was placed on the table as a possibility at one of the first meetings of the NACC,[23] but NATO remained divided about the wisdom of expansion.[24] Russia had openly articulated her opposition, but then made a surprise move. In August, in Warsaw, Yeltsin and Walesa signed a Russian–Polish Declaration that granted Poland leave to join NATO. The official response to this apparent contradiction was that there was no contradiction, that the Foreign Ministry 'feels that rushing to join NATO is an anachronism, but if some country wants to take this anachronistic path, that it is ultimately its own business and Russia does not intend to prevent it from doing so'.[25] The desire of the Eastern Europeans to join NATO was situated in the context of an obsolete Cold War game, 'smelling of mothballs'.[26] The Eastern Europeans remained trapped in this game, but Moscow had moved beyond it to a view of European security as 'indivisible'.[27]

20 'A Russian Foreign Policy Conflict?'
21 'A Russian Foreign Policy Conflict?'
22 'Far East: Asia Has Finally Realised How Much it Needs Russia', *CDPSP*, 65: 29 (1993).
23 'Military Alliances', *CDPSP*, 64: 3 (1992).
24 M. Wörner, 'Shaping the Alliance for the Future', *NR*, 42: 1 (1994); L. Aspin, 'New Europe, New NATO', *NR*, 42: 1 (1994).
25 'Military Alliances', *CDPSP*, 65: 36 (1993).
26 'Poland: Russia Gives Poland Leave to Join NATO', *CDPSP*, 65: 34 (1993).
27 'Military Alliances', *CDPSP*, 65: 37 (1993).

Stage Two: getting tough

The expansion idea was not taken so lightly by some political forces in Russia. A series of events in 1994 was linked to a more explicit naming of the possibilities of a new Cold War.[28] In December 1993, the ultra-nationalist Zhironovsky and the former communists, represented by Zyuganov, did surprisingly well in the parliamentary elections. In the immediate aftermath, NATO made an explicit decision not to expand eastward for the time being, but created the Partnership for Peace as a way of quieting both the Eastern Europeans and Russian public opinion. The Partnership idea was initially claimed by Russia as her own.[29] As NATO's idea, in new packaging, potential membership came to be seen as a further sign of servility to the West. When Russia finally joined it was viewed as an 'act of capitulation' or 'treachery', equivalent to succumbing to Hitler.[30] A two-level game became visible. The Eastern Europeans were campaigning for NATO expansion, a possibility that the press constructed as a move in a Cold War game; Zhironovsky and the communists were eager to play this game. Yeltsin and the Foreign Ministry had to manoeuvre in relation to both.

Russia experienced an initial victory with the delay of the expansion decision, in part because the West realised that this would hand a major trump card to the ultra-nationalists.[31] But Kozyrev's offensive against the latter went too far. In response to claims about his docile attitude towards the West, Kozyrev flipped to the other extreme, trying to beat Zhironovsky at his own game.[32] In 1994, he got tough. As Aleksei Pushkov of *Moskovskiye novosti*, put it:

> Kozyrev's entire policy in 1994 was aimed at putting proof of Russia's greatness on Yeltsin's desk, in some cases by pointedly challenging the Americans. This ... explains his theatrical appearance at the meeting of the

28 'The spectre of a new Cold War already looms in Russian–American relations.' 'A "Chill" in Russia–U.S. Ties?'; 'Military Alliances', *CDPSP*, 66: 16 (1994).

29 'To look back into recent history, the foundation of the [Partnership for Peace] concept was laid by Russia in [Yeltsin's] message to the NATO Council meeting in December 1991, in which he spoke of an intention to establish full-scale cooperation with the bloc in specific areas, not to join the bloc. Later, when a number of East European countries ... put forward the idea of recklessly joining NATO immediately, the Americans proposed this concept – in new wrapping, it's true.' 'Military Alliances', *CDPSP*, 65: 49 (1993).

30 'Military Alliances', *CDPSP*, 66: 25 (1994); 'World Politics', *CDPSP*, 66: 26 (1994).

31 'Russia Issues a Warning on NATO Expansion', *CDPSP*, 65: 47 (1993); 'Military Alliances', *CDPSP*, 66: 2 (1994).

32 'A little more than a year ago, after his deliberate shift toward a policy of asserting Russia's status as a great power, I expressed doubt that Kozyrev would be able to beat Zhironovsky at his own game. But now I have to admit it: He's done it. As of today, the zealous crusader against the red-browns and champion of human rights on a global scale, the man who loves to talk about morality and ethics in world politics, has in practice outdone Zhironovsky by signing on as an activist in the "war party".' 'Kozyrev Under Fire.'

NATO Council of Foreign Ministers in Brussels, where, it turned out, he had showed up only to declare that he was not pleased with the text of the meeting's final communique and therefore would not sign the programme of cooperation with the bloc [...] Kozyrev openly put Yeltsin in an awkward position at the Budapest summit of the [CSCE] in getting him to make a tough speech that reminded the New York Times of speeches by Soviet leaders in the cold war era. Kozyrev probably convinced Yeltsin that such toughness would bring positive results and influence the stance taken by Western Europe, which has certain doubts about NATO expansion. But the results were quite the opposite: Russia found itself virtually isolated in Budapest, and its opponents gained a compelling argument in favour of strengthening the bloc – the argument that Moscow was obviously backsliding toward its traditional confrontation with the West.[33]

In 1994 proclamations that Russia was 'doomed to be a great power' were thrown about.[34] Russia began to take a more aggressive attitude towards countries in the 'near abroad'. She invaded Chechnya and took a more pro-Serbian line in Bosnia. The consequence of this 'tough' line and the resort to 'brute force' was to find herself more isolated and alone, while lending momentum to Eastern European demands for NATO protection, based on Moscow's unpredictability.

In June of 1994 President Clinton went to Warsaw, where he declared that it was not a question of 'whether' NATO would expand but 'when and how',[35] after which the movement acquired an air of inevitability. One year after the December 1993 Brussels meeting, which put expansion on the back burner, NATO, again in Brussels, made a decision to proceed. While the emergence of 'imperial' tendencies on the part of Russia reinforced Eastern European demands, NATO had its own interest in playing the expansion card by this time. Its failure to undertake any effective action in Bosnia was raising questions about the continuing relevance of the alliance.[36] The persistent desire of the Eastern Europeans to join 'the most successful alliance in history' provided proof that it still had an important function. Russia, in the meantime, took pause to think about her foreign policy direction and the reason for all her problems.[37]

33 'Kozyrev Under Fire.'
34 'The Russian Federation is doomed to be a great power. Under Communists or nationalists, an aggressive and menacing power; under democrats, a peaceful and prosperous power. But a great power!' 'A "Chill" in Russia–US Ties?'
35 President W. Clinton, 'Address to the Polish Parliament, 7 July 1994', *U.S. Policy Information and Texts 67 (8* July 1994).
36 M. Walker, 'Bill's Dream Offer Hides a Nuclear Nightmare', *The Observer* (23 March 1997).
37 Against the background of Russia's failure to play the 'masculine' game, some began to recognise that a rethinking of Russian 'moves' was necessary: 'the "cold shower" of Brussels and Budapest should work to our advantage. Russian foreign policy needs to take a pause. ... This pause should be used to reformulate Russia's priorities.' 'Kozyrev Under Fire.'

In 1995, the expansion issue was less prominent than the Bosnia débâcle. Russia shaped an indispensable place for herself in this conflict, playing an important mediating role in relation to the Serbs. NATO and the UN stumbled to the point of collapse, in light of two hostage takings by the Serbs of UN peacekeepers and the ethnic cleansing of Srebrenica. NATO finally, after a series of blunders and after removing a large proportion of its peacekeepers, managed to implement its bombing campaign against the Serbs, after which a negotiated settlement was quickly reached.

Stage Three: a Machiavella strategy

Further changes in Russia's strategy towards expansion became evident in 1996. After Primakov's appointment to the post of Foreign Minister in January, there was an increasing characterisation of acts by Russian officials as moves within a game.[38] This new game shared a family resemblance with a Gorbachev game.[39] The Russian leadership began playing by a 'girl' strategy of a different kind than the 'docile' approach of Kozyrev. It was a strategy characterised by surprise moves, acting as if one's dignity were assumed, even though weak,[40] moving away from a zero-sum game[41] and

38 'Yelstin Names Primakov New Foreign Minister', *CDPSP*, 68: 2 (1996); 'Russia and NATO: "Special Relationship" Proposed', *CDPSP*, 68: 8 (1996); 'Russia Resists US Push'; 'Primakov: No Softened Stance on NATO Expansion', *CDPSP*, 68: 23 (1996); 'Military Alliances', *CDPSP*, 68: 45 (1996).

39 Given that Primakov was an official in the Gorbachev administration, this is not surprising. Direct comparisons between Gorbachev or Shevardnadze and Kozyrev were actually more common. Kozyrev was accused, like Gorbachev, of selling out to the West, and, at the same time, compared unfavourably with the strength and independence of Shevardnadze. 'Kozyrev Under Attack.' Primakov, who headed Russia's Foreign Intelligence Service under Kozyrev, was said to follow a noticeably different course than the Foreign Ministry during the 'early Kozyrev' period. Under Primakov's leadership, 'intelligence offices [in the FIS] mastered a new way of interacting with public opinion'. 'Yeltsin Names Primakov New Foreign Minister.'

40 As stated by political scientist Dmitry Yevstafyev: 'Russia's task for the immediate future is to avoid the possibility of a version of a "new Cold War", a scenario that is being worked out by Washington's inexhaustible strategists just in case. Let's be frank – in such a situation Russia would be doomed to defeat. We cannot give the U.S. any pretext for switching to confrontation; it is necessary to take a calm attitude, even toward possible provocations and unfriendly actions by the U.S. At the same time, we should take a position of dignity and self-sufficiency in relations with the West and, most importantly, never strive for "eternal friendship" with the U.S. at any price, much less beg the West to take us into the [Partnership for Peace].' 'Prospect of NATO Expansion Worries Moscow', *CDPSP*, 66: 8 (1994).

41 'The sides' positions [towards eastward expansion] have not changed in any fundamental way, but they have developed nuances that would make it possible, given certain conditions, to get out of the previous "zero-sum game" in which victory for one means defeat for the other.' 'Russia and NATO: "Special Relationship" Proposed.'

engaging in battle with the West by maintaining a tension between opposites. Combining opposites in order to manage the tension in a situation is a central feature of a Machiavella strategy:

> *A skilled princessa acts in order to build tension.* She acts to assume mastery not of other people but over the tension among them ... The use of tension disarms opponents; more important, it makes them react to you. Use contradictions. Find the prevailing sentiment or law in any situation and act as if it were cast not in stone but in sand. When a princessa appreciates how she herself is a combination of opposite characteristics – ferocity and tenderness, openness and determination – and doesn't struggle for consistency, she will find it easier to address the opposing tensions in a confrontation.[42]

In the context of a divided administration, Primakov managed the tension between two opposing tendencies. The one reverted back to a 'Cold War' game, threatening a counterreaction by Russia to NATO expansion. The other was simply to 'surrender' and accept the West's plans. In managing the tension between a hard and a soft, a masculine and a feminine response, Russia transformed the battlefield, increasingly putting her interests rather than NATO's plans in the spotlight.

While earlier, in Poland, the Russian policy elite was not overtly concerned about the residues of Cold War thinking in Eastern Europe and among some in the West, the context had by now changed. In 1993, Russia did not believe the West would find it in its interest to expand, in part because this move would substantially 'weaken' NATO.[43] Pushed into a corner by its own and Russia's bungling moves, expansion had come to be seen as 'inevitable'. By 1996, the game was defined by whether expansion would or would not re-create the Cold War conflict. But there were also questions about the necessity of framing the issue in these terms. Yes, there were a number of 'unbridled cold war knights' in the West, and a 'glut of experts from the Cold War era' who had nothing better to do than 'harp on old themes', but these were dying out.[44] By acting on the basis of more long-term possibilities, Russia might change the game, even against the background of NATO expansion, in such a way that her interests might eventually be realised.[45]

Russia now consistently articulated a position independent of the West. This new strategy maintained a tension between opposites. Primakov

---

42 Rubin (1997: 69–70).
43 'The U.S. doesn't want an expansion of NATO, for the reason, among others, that this could weaken it as an instrument of American policy.' 'Military Alliances', *CDPSP*, 66: 2 (1994).
44 'Military Alliances', *CDPSP*, 68: 41 (1996).
45 'Don't be deterred by small upsets. Define the battle in terms of a long-range war, not isolated skirmishes. No one episode is a defeat if you define your goal as large.' Rubin (1997: 119).

exhibited both 'firmness and flexibility',[46] both softness and toughness,[47] unlike his predecessor who had either bent to the whims of the West or 'pounded his fist on the table' in a manner reminiscent of the Cold War. Primakov managed the tension between an international requirement that Russia not appear too tough, thereby encouraging the momentum for expansion, and domestic demands that it not hand over the ball to the West.

One way Russia did this was by making 'surprise' moves that threw the West off balance and required them to react to Russia. While the Russian elite was seen to be divided in its response to NATO expansion, this division might be understood as part of a strategy of surprise. For instance, while Primakov and the Foreign Ministry maintained a consistent position against expansion, other high-level officials made unexpected moves. First, Security Council Secretary Rybkin said that Russia should become integrated into NATO's political structures, a statement that 'dumbfounded' Western diplomats.[48] As Rubin (1997: 103) points out, one tactic of surprise in a Machiavella strategy is to adopt the enemy's position:

> Adopting his position shocks the enemy. What you gain from doing so is much more effective than anything you ever accomplish by holding firm to your position. This tactic is valuable when you face an entrenched enemy who just appears to be getting stronger, no matter what you do. A quick change, a shock to everybody's system, is in order.

The remark about joining NATO could have been an impulse or a sign of ignorance, but its underlying strategic value was recognised: offering to join the alliance was an act that put the West in a position of having to respond.[49] As one commentator noted:

> If Moscow now asks for NATO membership but entirely different countries are invited to join the alliance, a long-term confrontation will ... be inevitable. Those who oppose any kind of cooperation with NATO will then have direct evidence that the alliance's expansion has an anti-Russian thrust. It is quite possible that Rybkin's statement was more carefully considered than may seem at first glance.[50]

The statement placed NATO in a position of having either to embrace

---

46 'Military Alliances', *CDPSP*, 68: 41 (1996).
47 'Yeltsin Names Primakov New Foreign Minister'; 'Russia Resists US Push for NATO Expansion.'
48 'Military Alliances', *CDPSP*, 68: 46 (1996).
49 As Rybkin stated, 'Let the people in NATO rack their brains now over how to respond.' 'Military Alliances', *CDPSP*, 68: 46 (1996).
50 'Military Alliances', *CDPSP*, 68: 46 (1996).

Russia or to show its underlying antagonism towards her.[51] What seemed on the surface to be an expression of division between the different ministries looked suspiciously calculating.

A second surprise in 1996 showed Moscow playing with the tension between a soft and an extremely hard line towards the expansion. On the one hand, Defence Minister Rodionov made the 'sensational' statement that he had become convinced that NATO 'does not pose a threat to Russia but millions of people, especially Russians, need to be convinced of this'.[52] A high-ranking official in the Ministry of Defence had never said anything so conciliatory about NATO expansion. This move also represented a reverse of the traditional tendency, going back to Shevardnadze and Kozyrev. In the past, the Ministry of Foreign Affairs had taken the softer line while the military represented a harder line. In this case the military was basically saying there was no need to overdramatise NATO expansion, while Foreign Affairs was making definitive statements against expansion. On the same day, Oleg Grinevsky, Russia's ambassador to Sweden, articulated a more extreme hard-line position, 'that NATO expansion increases the risk of nuclear war', while reminding Western listeners that Russia had enough missiles to destroy both the United States and Europe.[53] The articulation of these extremes on the same day 'confused' the West, raising questions about what Moscow's policy towards expansion really was. However, the tension between the two generated support for the Foreign Ministry's intermediary position at a time when critics of expansion in the West were becoming increasingly vocal.[54] Primakov's consistent position began with an objection to NATO expansion but called for the formation of a 'special relationship'. In this formulation, both NATO and Russia would maintain their independence but form a contractual relationship of cooperation.

On the one hand, Russia, at this point, was no more able, officially, to back away from opposition to expansion than NATO was able to cancel its

---

51 Lukin also noted that a negative response would begin to work in favour of Russia's image. 'NATO expansion in defiance of the interests and position of a Russia that is proposing a formula of political cooperation would be virtually impossible.' 'Military Alliances', *CDPSP*, 68: 45 (1996).

52 'Military Alliances', *CDPSP*, 68: 47 (1996).

53 'Military Alliances', *CDPSP*, 68: 47 (1996).

54 'At the very time that defeatists have come to life in our country and are doing everything they can to show that Russia should agree to NATO expansion ... people in the West itself are starting to give serious thought to the possible consequences of expansion and are drawing some rather gloomy conclusions.' 'Russia vs. NATO Expansion: The Latest Round', *CDPSP*, 68: 51 (1996).

plans.[55] She could not do so because such a move would seal 'once and for all [Russia's] reputation as a country that doesn't respect its own word and from which one can demand and get anything'.[56] On the other hand, the issue, for the Foreign Ministry, was not the adoption of either position, but rather 'delicate manoeuvring' between them. A 'yes' to expansion would hand a trump card to the nationalists and communists, as Yeltsin did after signing the Russian–Polish Declaration in 1993. At the same time, too tough a position could lend further momentum to Eastern European demands. Managing the tension between the two, against the background of a 'divided leadership' and the spectre of a change in public opinion, might increase the likelihood that NATO would make concessions[57] and that it would see the wisdom of a 'special relationship' with Moscow. The game would then have begun to change, and Moscow could seize the initiative by articulating the parameters of a new security system in which it maintained an independent position.[58] Once a 'special relationship' was formed, it 'would lead to the emergence of a new European system' in which 'the question of NATO expansion would become peripheral. It would appear in a different light'.[59] In any case, despite the divisions, the Foreign Ministry's line clearly prevailed.[60]

And the game had begun to change. Notice the difference between the categories constituting Russia's identity and relationship to the West when Kozyrev was Foreign Minister and those, by 1996, during Primakov's tenure as Foreign Minister:

55 Given the momentum that had developed behind expansion, an about face would have damaged the legitimacy of both the Alliance and the political elites in Central Europe who were trying to get in. See Allin (1995: 62).
56 'Military Alliances', *CDPSP*, 68: 41 (1996).
57 'Could it be that Moscow's tough position toward NATO is a means of getting its partners to make concessions on other questions?' 'OSCE Summit: Evaluating Russia's Gains, Losses', *CDPSP*, 68: 49 (1996).
58 'The changes on Smolensk Square [i.e. in the Ministry of Foreign Affairs] allow one to hope for an adjustment in Russia's foreign policy line in the sense that Russia's prestige and greatness and the independence of its policy will consist not in constantly saying "no" to the West but in its ability to influence the international situation. That might give both sides greater freedom to manoeuvre on such questions as interaction between NATO and Russia [...] Russia would be best suited by a "special relationship" codified in a treaty that combines the ideas of mutual security and strategic partnership. 'Russia and NATO: "Special Relationship" Proposed.'
59 'Russia and NATO: "Special Relationship" Proposed.'
60 In what was referred to as the 'well-known pastime called "find ten differences", the foreign ministry line clearly prevailed. "[Russia] is against expansion and that's that!".' 'OSCE Summit: Evaluating Russia's Gains, Losses.' The author, Georgy Bort, *Kommersant-Daily*, refers to these as 'games that will now have to be left behind'.

LOSING IN WESTERN GAME	CHANGING GAME
weak and unpredictable	weak, but standing firm
unrequited love	West realises it needs Russia
servile and obedient	independent
romantic desire for alliance	special relationship
concerns ignored	concerns taken into account, NATO fears losing partner
violation of integrity	possible consummation[61]

The expansion of NATO had become an unchangeable reality but, rather than ignoring Russia's interests, NATO was now stating its desire for a 'genuine partnership' that would 'cement a relation of trust' between them.[62] In December of 1996, NATO, at its pre-Christmas Brussels meeting, agreed to enter into a dialogue with Russia that would lead to the signing of a charter between the two. Western public opinion had begun to ask serious questions about the political costs of expansion. The alliance was being held to account for the seriousness of its intentions towards Russia and its claim that expansion would remove the division of Europe once and for all. NATO was seen to be involved in a typical diplomatic game, 'following the same rules used in bargaining at a bazaar: trying to get the most at the lowest price',[63] but there were indications that it was willing to make concessions. NATO had already said that nuclear weapons would not be deployed in the East.

As the new year began, Russia was not interested in compromise or bargaining, however. In March, Primakov, in a series of talks in Brussels,

---

61 'While you're weak, stand firm.' 'Military Alliances', 68: 41 (1996); 'Solana's endeavour to persuade Moscow to agree to expansion stems ... from the West's need to include Russia in some sort of system of relations with NATO.' 'Russia vs. NATO Expansion'; 'The "special relationship" would allow Russia and NATO to remain independent entities with their own interests.' 'Russia and NATO: "Special Relationship" Proposed.'; 'We proceed from the premise that the main indication that our partners' intentions are serious will be ... first and foremost, NATO's willingness to take our concerns into account.' 'Primakov: Setting a New, Tougher Foreign Policy?', *CDPSP*, 69: 2 (1997); 'If [the] North Atlantic Alliance rejects Moscow's Proposals, it could lose Moscow as a partner.' 'Military Alliances', *CDPSP*, 69: 9 (1997); 'Moscow is confident that [for it and its Western partners] "consummations are possible, we have no doubt about that".' 'Russia Resists US Push for NATO Expansion'.

62 'The NATO which offers Russia a genuine Partnership is a NATO which has fundamentally transformed itself over the last several years [...] We should develop a political framework which will cement a relationship of trust between us.' 'Highlights of NATO Secretary General's Address to the Russian Council on Foreign and Security Policy, in Moscow, on 20 March.' *NR*, 44: 3 (1996).

63 'Russia vs. NATO Expansion.'

Oslo, Copenhagen and London, made it clear that Moscow was not bargaining with the West or attempting to exact a price for expansion of the alliance.[64] Russia's core concern was a dialogue that focused on building a new relationship to NATO. Primakov shifted the definition of the game away from Russia's *reaction* to NATO expansion to what she wanted, to her own concerns and interests. By acting, rather than reacting, Primakov put the ball 'in NATO's court'.[65]

In the first few months of 1997, prior to the signing of the Founding Act with NATO, the Foreign Ministry allowed the tension between opposites to build. On the one hand, Primakov began the new year in a very active and tough mood.[66] The identification of NATO expansion with a Cold War game that would 'create new dividing lines in Europe' was repeated.[67] Prime Minister Chernomyrdin assured the Russian public, after inspecting the combat potential of the Strategic Missile Forces at the Central Command Post near Odintsovo, that Russian missiles were still capable of 'destroying the US in less than an hour after receiving an order to do so'.[68] But Russia also softened her tone, emphasising that these concerns could be eliminated or eased by a document defining the relationship between Moscow and NATO. The real task of Russian diplomacy was not to try to intimidate the West with a new Cold War, but to compel the US to 'recognise the need to reckon with Russia and to take action to satisfy Moscow's legitimate demands.'[69]

At the Helsinki Summit in late March, Clinton brought five draft agreements, which Yeltsin signed. NATO was seen to be making concessions. The response in Russia to the signing ranged from a 'big win' for Yeltsin, to a positive compromise that would 'weaken the negative consequences of this process', to comparable to the 'humiliating peace terms imposed on a defeated Germany' in Versailles in 1919.[70] The actual result of the meeting was an agreement that NATO's nuclear weapons would not be moved eastward, nor would there be an advance of NATO combat forces. Clinton and Yeltsin agreed that a fully fledged document, of a firm and binding nature,

---

64 'Russia won't bargain with NATO ... Perhaps the most important result of the Russian Foreign Minister's talks in Brussels, Oslo, Copenhagen and London is that Moscow clearly stated that its dialogue with the alliance is focused on issues involved in building new relations with NATO, and not at all on the problem of NATO expansion. Primakov stressed repeatedly that Moscow is not bargaining with the West or attempting to exact a price for expansion of the alliance, but, on the contrary, has constantly voiced its negative attitude toward this process.' 'Military Alliances', *CDPSP*, 69: 9 (1997).
65 'Military Alliances', *CDPSP*, 69: 9 (1997).
66 'Military Alliances', *CDPSP*, 69: 2 (1997).
67 'Military Alliances', *CDPSP*, 69: 4 (1997).
68 'Western Hemisphere', *CDPSP*, 69: 8 (1997).
69 'Clinton, Yeltsin Meet in Helsinki.'
70 'Clinton, Yeltsin Meet in Helsinki.'

defining relations between Russia and the North Atlantic alliance would be signed. Finally, accord was reached on the issue of missile defence and reductions in strategic offensive arms. Clinton also promised that the US government would increase its support for American investment in Russia. In the US, Yeltsin's acceptance of the five agreements was viewed as a stunning 'victory'. The *Washington Post* tried to persuade Clinton 'to keep the rejoicing in check and to emphasise instead a tie game in which friendship triumphed, so as not to upset Yeltsin and make life hard for him at home'.[71]

On 27 May the 'sacred ritual' took place in the Elysée Palace in Paris as NATO and Russia layed the foundations for an 'equitable and stable partnership'.[72] Yeltsin referred to the signing of the Founding Act as a 'commitment' to draw up a charter of European security. The document, while lacking any formal juridical status, imposed a range of commitments based on 'firm obligation'.

A long-term strategy

The choices offered by Machiavelli's game are to win or lose as a man. Russia's more successful strategy over the long term relies on the rules of Machiavella. Russia's 'Machiavella' strategy involved a complex set of moves. On the one hand, she was firm in stating her objections to expansion, placing NATO expansion in the context of a Cold War game that would potentially reconstruct the division of Europe. In part these objections were necessary to play to portions of public opinion waiting to pounce on the administration for being too 'soft'. On the other hand, the objection was stated more in principle than as a threat. Moscow could 'have angrily knit our brows and banged our shoe on the table, as was done in the cold war years',[73] but this would have been an empty gesture that would only have contributed to the further isolation of the country. It wouldn't have been politically effective *vis-à-vis* the West because it only gave them an excuse to ignore Russia and proceed unhindered. By 'toughly' stating its objections and 'softly' acting as if cooperation were possible, Moscow managed the tension between two opposing games. By acting rather than reacting, Russia put the West in a position of having to respond in kind or risk being exposed as the agent in creating a new division of Europe.

NATO had advocated dialogue rather than antagonism with its former

71 'Western Hemisphere', *CDPSP*, 69: 13 (1997).
72 'Founding Act on Mutual Relations, Cooperation and Security between NATO and the Russian Federation', Paris, 27 May 1997, NATO Basic Texts, http://www.nato.int (Basic Texts), Web.
73 'Clinton, Yeltsin Meet in Helsinki.'

enemies. In practice, the dialogue has been lop-sided in so far as it has involved drawing its liaison partners to the East closer to NATO for the purpose of incorporating them into *its* practices. Russia, while initially hoping for alliance, increasingly demanded to be treated more as an equal and as an independent entity. She wanted a dialogue of equals within a special relationship. As public opinion in the West became more vocal in expressing its fears that expansion would create a new Cold War, NATO was under pressure to take Russian fears into account. Russia encouraged this moderation by avoiding a 'hysterical' reaction[74] to the expansion and by presenting herself as a great power, of prestige and dignity, with whom the West should engage in dialogue. For NATO to press ahead, oblivious to Russian concerns, would present NATO as an expansionary power in the traditional sense, rather than the peaceful and restrained anchor of stability.

The expansion is proceeding. Western assurances and promises have not been codified in legally binding form. The Founding Act contains no commitment to limit expansion to the Visegrad group. But this only represents a defeat if one thinks in zero-sum terms. Russian moves have to be placed in the context of a larger ongoing game. She has moved in five years from 'unrequited love' to signing a contract for a special relationship within which her legitimate concerns are acknowledged and within which the West has made important concessions. Russia has succeeded in weaving a middle course between virulent strains, both inside and outside, who want to re-create the Cold War, and the 'soft' Atlanticists in Russia who want the integration of Russia in NATO. Instead, she has refused to engage in the Cold War game, but extended the hand of cooperation on her own terms.

By now 'acting as if' cooperation were possible in a broader European security system, she is contributing to the construction of that reality even while the framework continues to be monopolised by NATO. One of the demands that Russia had hoped to have codified in the NATO–Russia Founding Act was the transformation of NATO from a military to a political alliance, focused on peacekeeping.[75] The main distinction between the two is the continuing importance of the Article Five guarantee. Russia realises that this aspect of the alliance will be weakened by its expansion plans. As Konstantin Eggert, from *Izvestia*, stated:

> Paradoxically, it seems that the most farsighted members of the Russian military elite have been the first to realise the futility of opposing NATO expansion. They can't help but be aware of the debate this process is

---

74 'Military Alliances', *CDPSP*, 68: 41 (1996).
75 Moscow stated its desire to see the alliance gradually transformed into a purely political organisation with primary emphasis on peacekeeping functions. 'Clinton, Yeltsin Meet in Helsinki.'

prompting among those who are concerned about the purely military aspect of the matter. After all, the inclusion of Hungary, Poland and the Czech Republic will most likely weaken the alliance's infrastructure.

'All told, NATO can count on only a couple of combat-ready brigades from the future new members ... ,' a top official of the British Ministry of Defence said quite frankly on this subject. 'But the territory that the alliance will have to defend in the unlikely event of a military conflict in Europe will be far larger than it is now'.[76]

If the Western Europeans have in the past been concerned that Americans would not trade New York for Paris, Eastern Europeans are even less likely to feel certain that it would trade New York for Budapest. This is the paradox of NATO's decision to expand. On the one hand, expansion provided an argument for NATO survival at a time when its relevance was being called into question. On the other hand, the inclusion of more countries will further weaken the commitment to collective defence that has been at the core of the alliance.

The decision is also paradoxical from the Russian side. Russia has an interest in a stable European security system, within which it is included and recognised as a major player. As a result, it has to be opposed to the expansion of NATO as a military organisation. However, if the traditional function of NATO is weakened as a result of this move, NATO functions are likely to evolve towards the more political role desired by Russia. The prince, operating with a zero-sum strategy, would have responded with a counterreaction to NATO expansion, in an attempt to regain control of the game. The princessa, viewing her ends through the prism of the long term, recognises that her acts of cooperation will only further the weakening of NATO's defences against her. In acting, rather than reacting, she disarms the alliance. If NATO does not simply treat the Founding Act as a rubberstamp for a military buildup, but responds to this gesture with further gestures of cooperation, there will be movement in practice towards a larger European infrastructure. So long as Russia continues to 'act as if' cooperation is possible, there should be no reason to invoke the threat and, as Sergei Karaganov, Deputy Director of the Institute of Europe, said in a 1996 article: 'in ten years or so, perhaps NATO will change, and with it our own approaches. And perhaps [Russia] will be able to turn the situation around. The important thing is to prevent the situation from deteriorating in the next few years while we are weak.'[77]

---

76 'Military Alliances', *CDPSP*, 68: 48 (1996). Vladimir Lukin made a similar point at an Oxford seminar on 28 May, the day following the signing of the Founding Act.
77 'Military Alliances', *CDPSP*, 68: 41 (1996). See also 'OSCE Summit: Evaluating Russia's Gains, Losses.'

The current administration in Russia will not be in office for ever. There is no way to predict the outcome of this match. As Leonid Kuchma, the President of Ukraine, stated immediately following the agreement, 'not even the computer which won against Kasparov' could predict whether the relatively liberal Russia of Boris Yeltsin or the aggressive and nationalistic one of Zhironovsky will in the end dictate Russia's moves. This is not an argument about where this state of affairs will end. This analysis stops in May 1997, with the signing of the NATO–Russia Founding Act, but the game continues. If, by the time this is published, events have taken a further turn towards increased hostility, a historical opportunity will have been lost.

It may be that a new 'Cold War' is less likely in this context than an older form of balance of power. In the months prior to the signing of the Founding Act, both sides had begun to 'flirt' with others outside the special relationship, which is a language that harks back to the 'wooing' characteristic of the classical European balance of power. In early 1997 US Secretary of State Warren Christopher 'charmed' a 'receptive' Ukraine by saying that relations with it were becoming strategic for the United States. The US and Czech Republic were engaged in 'mutual flirting aimed directly at Russia'.[78] Russia formed special relationships with Belarus and China on the eve of the signing of the Founding Act. In the document signed with China, parties went to great lengths to emphasise that these agreements do not represent the formation of bloc alliances, but are for the purpose of dialogue and cooperation.[79] Forming a special relationship with China to the East is not inconsistent with Russia's desire to become a 'bridge between East and West'.[80] However, should NATO's flirtations with the Baltic states turn into an invitation to join the alliance, the partnership in dialogue with China would provide a foundation for a more formal alliance. A weak Russia's interests are better served by these partnership arrangements than by the creation of new antagonisms; nonetheless, these moves were undoubtedly intended as a sign for NATO to think twice before proceeding with further expansion.

78 'Primakov: Setting a New, Tougher Foreign Policy?'
79 'In connection with the opinion, expressed by a number of analysts, that the stepped-up activity of Russian foreign policy on the Asian front is a kind of counteraction to NATO's plans for eastward expansion, Sergei Yastrzhembsky said that "the very notion of creating opposing blocs is reprehensible and counterproductive". The basic feature of Russian–Chinese relations is the two sides' unanimous position that "the time of blocs is over", the Press Secretary emphasised [...] The Russian Federation and the People's Republic of China [are] proceeding from the development of equal partnership relations based on trust and aimed at strategic cooperation in the 21st century.' 'Yelstin, China's Jiang Call for "Multipolar World",' *CDPSP*, 69: 17 (1997).
80 'Military Alliances', *CDPSP*, 66: 16 (1994).

If NATO follows a strategy consistent with the needs of post-Cold War cooperation, buttressed by the development of common practices between the former superpowers, and if Russia continues on her present course, momentum may build for a transformation of NATO into a broader European security structure that is primarily political in its orientation. As Vladimir Lukin remarked in a seminar at Oxford, immediately following the signing of the Founding Act, if Russia were to join NATO, NATO would have to change its name since it would no longer be an organisation focused on the North Atlantic. At that point it would be a wider European security organisation and Russia's interests would have been served. But if this outcome were to unfold, it is less the case that Russia will have won. Rather she will have won over the West. That would be a victory for all, first, because a new dividing line in Europe, and a new conflict with a more aggressive Russia, would have been avoided; second, because the two could then join together in tackling the problems of security in Europe.

On the eve of the fiftieth anniversary of the Marshall Plan, NATO expansion was presented in the framework of a new Marshall Plan for Eastern Europe. Most commentators recognise that this will not take the form of massive economic aid to the former Eastern bloc, as it did in Western Europe after World War II. The original Marshall Plan was in part an effort to dampen enthusiasm for the communist alternative by strengthening the war-torn economies of Western Europe. But the Marshall Plan was also an attempt to avoid the mistake of the post-World War I Versailles Treaty, which gave rise to an economically weakened Germany, with a desperate population that was ready to listen to the promises of Nazi leaders. Commentators in both East and West have drawn on the historical precedent of Versailles to present the potential consequences of excluding Russia from a new European structure.[81] It is the former communists and ultra-nationalists in Russia who are likely to want a reversion back to the Cold War rules of the game. The Russian population may not be as understanding as the current leadership in interpreting future moves by the West. Consequently, there is every reason to look beyond the rhetorical value of the Marshall Plan analogy to the historical lessons it provides in this context. NATO has a historical opportunity for a winning strategy based on Machiavella's game. Let's hope 'she' will see it and act accordingly.

81 See reference to Rodric Braithwaite, a former ambassador of Great Britain to Moscow, in 'Russia vs. NATO Expansion: The Latest Round'; and reference to Zyuganov in 'Clinton, Yeltsin Meet in Helsinki.'

12

Language is power

> The aspects of things that are most important for us are hidden because of their simplicity and familiarity (One is unable to notice something – because it is always before one's eyes) ... we fail to be struck by what, once seen, is most striking and most powerful. (Wittgenstein, 1958: para. 129)

THIS BOOK BEGAN with a methodological argument about the importance, in a context of change, of moving away from the formulation of abstract theory towards the practices of political actors. The issue is not whether language is important, but rather whose language should provide the point of departure: the analyst's or the subjects of study?

I have argued that the methodology developed here provides the basis for a 'better' description of changing security relations over the last twenty years. The description is 'better' in so far as it situates the moves of any one actor within a context of relationships to others which unfolded over time. Gorbachev, for instance, did not introduce changes in a vacuum; his moves make more sense when embedded in a larger international context. This approach was distinguished from three others within the discipline. In the first, the categories of a particular theory do the work in determining, prior to the analysis, which actors are most relevant. The second makes the individual the point of departure for change. The third rests on a claim that multiple narratives are always possible. I have moved away from the categories of an abstract theory towards those of the actors themselves, constructing a multi-layered narrative, based on their interactions over time, thereby situating the moves of individual actors within a larger framework.

The contours of transformation were systematically analysed on the basis of a range of metaphors and grammars shared by the actors. Actors were entangled in, or constrained by, a shared language by which their actions were given meaning. Each of the grammars explored in this book was employed by all of the different state and non-state actors included in the analysis. These grammars were discovered in the course of the analysis[1]

---

1 Many would argue that it is impossible to undertake research without some kind of theory, including assumptions about the most relevant actors. I did begin with the assumption that it was important to look beyond the narrow focus on states; however, I did not approach

as the archive of documents was expanded. When put together, the various layers of the description demonstrate the correlation between structures containing families existing in a relationship of antagonism with criminal neighbours; the efforts of social movements to dismantle the structures, emancipate the families and rename the crime as the Cold War itself; and the various endings, including the collapse of various parts of the Cold War structure, the transition from families to a club and the move towards dialogue in a whole Europe. There is a coherence underlying these changes that was discovered in the context itself.

The coherence provided by the shared grammar is contrasted with the contestation between the language games of actors occupying different positions. In Chapter Three I made a distinction between grammars and language games. Grammars express the possibilities belonging to an object or language area; language games, by contrast, are language use in action within a particular context and weave together acts with language, for instance, threatening, with other types of action involving material objects, such as deploying nuclear weapons. States and social movements shared a range of grammars belonging to structures and relationships, but they made moves within distinct language games that were in conflict. States were attempting to maintain a dominant game and social movements were attempting to transform it.

Language and power

There may be a temptation to argue that this description is 'merely' at the level of language and ignores the more real power relationships in this context. The purpose of this chapter is to explore more directly the relationship between language and power. Language use, I argue, is fundamentally intersubjective and constitutive of the power to act politically.

In describing contesting language games, I have put a new twist on the realist argument regarding the distinction between appearance and reality. First, the key issue is less one of appearance and reality than the contest between language games that provide conflicting frameworks for reasoning and action in the world. Second, the subjects of analysis do often point to a distinction between words and practice. The articulation of this distinction is part of a language game itself, which became an important element of the political conflict between state leaders and social movements.

The difference between these two claims is not easy to grasp. The

the analysis with a set group of actors or these particular grammars in mind. Both the method and the specific grammars have emerged over time. See the preface for more background on these issues.

211

Western case is somewhat more straightforward. NATO situated the logic of the INF deployments in a different language game than the peace movements. For the former, cruise and Pershing II would enhance nuclear deterrence; for the latter, the deployments represented a move beyond deterrence towards a strategy for fighting a limited nuclear war. One can argue endlessly about who was right – and they did – but the point is that the peace movement argument rested on a contradiction between the justification for deterrence, that is, it would prevent any kind of war, and a practice, that is, deployment of a new generation of missiles which, given their greater accuracy and speed, would increase the likelihood of nuclear war.

In the Eastern bloc, the relationship is more complex. From a Western perspective, or from that of the 'dissidents' in Eastern Europe, there was an unmistakable contradiction between the signing of the human rights provision of the Helsinki Final Act by Eastern European governments and practices that violated human rights. However, the Eastern governments may not have recognised the problem because they attached a different meaning to the words 'human rights'. As John Vincent (1991: 61) notes, the meaning of 'human rights' in the socialist countries was such that:

> equality is opposed to liberty, group rights to individuals, economic and social rights to civil and political rights. In practice, the East claims superiority in the actual provision of such rights as that to work, and to an adequate standard of living for all, while the West claims to do better on individual freedom, civil liberties, freedom of information and the other values associated with an 'open society'.

The Eastern European governments were more likely to view Western criticisms related to human rights as an 'act of interference in their internal affairs' and, therefore, a violation of Helsinki.[2] Likewise, groups such as Charter 77 were said to be concerned only with the 'rights of individual renegades who have broken the law of the country' (Golubnichy, 1978). In the view of the authorities, these 'dissidents' were engaged in criminal acts and deserved punishment.

States and social movements situated the logic of the Cold War within distinct language games. The Western peace movements, as well as the citizens' initiatives in the East, claimed there was a distinction between the language and practices of state actors. They engaged in acts of immanent critique to expose the contradictions in this context. At the heart of the conflict was a battle over the meaning of nuclear deterrence, of human rights and of the boundaries of Europe.

2 *For Peace, Security, Cooperation and Social Progress in Europe: On the Results of the Conference of the Communist and Workers' Parties of Europe, Berlin, June 29–30, 1976* (Moscow: Novosti Press Agency Publishing House, 1976).

The purpose of the analysis was not to uncover the greater truth of one position or the other; the main concern was the dynamics of the conflict itself. This raises a third issue about 'truth' in relation to my claim to a 'better' description. If there is no way to evaluate the truth of arguments by either side, am I merely describing their 'talk' as opposed to providing a description of what 'happened'? The question assumes a distinction between language and events in the world. There is talking, on the one hand, and the real stuff of international relations, on the other. But how can the real stuff of international relations be divorced from human practice? Wittgenstein provides a point of departure for thinking about language use as a form of action in itself, which also cannot be separated neatly from other types of action. The focus of the analysis was not on events *per se* (in so far as we tend to think of events as phenomena that 'happen'); it was the *actions* of different players, how they were given meaning and how these meanings changed. The goal was to examine shifts in the parameters of our collective definitions of truth and possibility and the embeddedness of truth claims in distinct language games, which constituted the identities and interests of the different actors.

Consider another example drawn from the hunger strike in the British Maze Prison in the early 1980s, an example which illustrates language as a site of power.[3] A number of IRA activists were sent to prison and the authorities were explicit in naming them as 'criminals'. The prisoners protested this label by refusing to wear the prison uniform, arguing that they were in fact 'prisoners of war'. For a lengthy period of time, a number of inmates would not put on the uniform, choosing instead to wrap their naked bodies in blankets. The symbol of recognition as 'prisoners of war' would be a concession allowing them to wear their own civilian clothing. In this case, it would be difficult to identify objective criteria by which the strikers were either criminals or prisoners of war. Each category belonged to a distinct and contesting language game, which constituted practices of wearing a prison uniform versus wearing civilian clothing. The two meanings were at the core of the conflict. It is the contest itself that is interesting in this case, rather than the 'truth' of one claim or the other. In the end, the 'criminal' label proved hard to maintain in the face of prisoners who were dying from hunger in the face of government refusal to allow them to wear their own clothing; the moral high ground shifted towards the prisoners because of the determination expressed in their own suffering.

In the contest between NATO and the peace movements, it is difficult to ultimately determine whether nuclear deterrence had in fact prevented any

3 The presentation of this context is based on the depiction of the conflict in the film *Some Mother's Son.*

war in Europe or whether it was, at least by the early 1980s, contributing to the possibility of war.[4] The former was accepted as conventional wisdom prior to the conflict over the deployments. By the late 1980s, as disarmament processes were underway and the superpower relationship was changing, arguments about the need for a continuing arms build-up became increasingly tenuous. Throughout the Cold War, it was argued that disarmament was impossible because nuclear weapons could not be disinvented; yet once the political context began to change, once some form of trust began to be established between the two sides, the importance of the weapons began to fade into the background. The point is to examine how new possibilities are constituted as conflicting language games collide in a political space.

The most common explanation of the end of the Cold War posits a zero-sum outcome: NATO or the West was the winner; the Soviet Union was the loser. This represents a packaging of the change which identifies a single cause and a specific end point with the collapse of the Soviet Union. By contrast, I have provided a more multidimensional map of the changes, from Helsinki to Reagan's SDI to Gorbachev's policy changes to NATO enlargement to the Russian response. I have argued that these developments cannot be seen in isolation from one another. Primakov's acts cannot be understood without Gorbachev; Gorbachev or Reagan's acts cannot be understood without the independent citizens' initiatives in East and West; these movements cannot be understood without Helsinki.

The process of change was generated by a conflict between two different notions of security. In one, security is a zero-sum game defined in contrast to an enemy other. In the other, security is a process of dialogue and cooperation with others. The dialectic tension between the two was the motor of change.[5] During the détente process, states in East and West agreed to certain principles that would govern their relationship. Dialogue and cooperation would be sought against the background of a continuing Cold War division

---

4 Lebow and Stein (1994) argue that NATO's deterrence policy prolonged the Cold War.
5 It would be interesting to extend the analysis back further to raise questions about how Helsinki became possible. One reviewer of the text asked whether the earlier Cold War was similarly constituted in language games. Hinds and Windt (1991) have explored the role of US language in constructing the early Cold War. In Chapter Three, I pointed to the role of a grammar of 'structure' at an early stage, as the Cold War was being 'built'. My argument is that actors are always attributing meaning to their practices and the actions of others. Helsinki represented the articulation of a set of *shared* principles to govern relations between East and West. But in choosing this beginning point I do not mean to suggest that questions of meaning only became significant after this time, while power politics dominated the first half of the Cold War. The issue is not one of either ideas *or* materiality, but the role of language in constituting reality. Helsinki, and détente in general, represented a new framework for lending meaning to the relationship between East and West. But power politics has also historically been undergirded by 'rules of the game'.

and an East–West military stalemate. But the balance between the zero- and the positive-sum game proved difficult to maintain. The West had a hard time convincing populations to continue to pay for defence at a time of economic stagnation and relaxed tensions between East and West. Détente began to collapse as groups in the West, such as the CPD, began to argue that arms control agreements with the East had left the West at a disadvantage. Acts by the Soviet Union, such as the invasion of Afghanistan, added fuel to arguments that a new danger was immanent. President Reagan was elected on the coat-tails of the Committee, promising to restore the nuclear deterrent and America's strategic position.

The 1979 double track deployment decision, along with Reagan's loose rhetoric about nuclear war, generated widespread public concern and gave rise to peace movements, which argued that the zero-sum logic of deterrence and the arms race were leading in the direction of fighting a nuclear war and should be replaced by a more political positive-sum game. In the East, Charter 77 and KOR exposed the distinction between Eastern bloc promises to respect human rights, based on the signing of the Helsinki Final Act, and the persecution of those who were pointing out the distinction. Solidarity organised workers' strikes nation-wide to convince the government to enter into a dialogue with Polish society. Citizens' initiatives in East and West held the discrepancy of the promise of Helsinki up against the practices of a renewed Cold War and began a dialogue across the division of Europe for the purpose of restoring Helsinki in a Europe whole and free.

Initially, the persecution of 'dissidents' in the East provided fuel for Reagan's campaign against the 'Evil Empire'. However, against the background of a widespread public fear of nuclear war, he introduced SDI, which was couched in arguments about the desirability of escaping nuclear deterrence and the possibility of a more cooperative relationship with the Soviet Union. Shifts in Soviet policy became evident as Gorbachev came to power. He introduced democratic reforms at home and, at the international level, called for an end to balance of power and deterrence thinking, and for their replacement with a positive-sum game of disarmament and dialogue. NATO initially resisted the move towards disarmament but then, once the INF agreement had been signed, claimed it as a victory. In the late 1980s, NATO began to redefine its mission – articulated in the 1967 Harmel Report as deterrence and détente – as defence and dialogue. As the Berlin Wall and the institutions of the Eastern bloc collapsed, NATO stepped in to make dialogue and healing the division of Europe centrepieces of its policy.

With the collapse of the Soviet Union, NATO declared victory in the Cold War. The zero-sum victory became an argument for NATO survival, as the only remaining Cold War institution fit to provide security in Europe. The need to justify its continuing relevance gave rise, against the background of the West's initial failure in Bosnia, to a decision to expand east-ward. While some feared that expansion would re-create the division of Europe, Russia capitalised on NATO's promise of dialogue to argue the need for a 'true partnership'. The tension between the zero-sum and the positive-sum games continues to shape the possibilities for security in post-Cold War Europe.

Power and strategy

In addition to mapping conflicting language games, this description has been a rudimentary exploration of the relationship between two different types of power as they relate to strategy. Power at the international level is usually conceptualised in coercive terms, as the ability to make others do what they otherwise would not do. Strategy is about altering the frame-work through which others define their options, by means of a threat or the use of violence and the potential to hurt (Schelling, 1966). Power has little to do with language, it is assumed. Power is employed through economic and material means.

Yet there is another form of power and strategy which has historically been employed by the weak or by those playing with a losing hand. In this tradition, strategy is also about altering the perceptions of others (Rubin, 1997: 38). Nonviolent strategy, like coercive strategy, is about the manipu-lation of tensions, but the dynamics of the struggle are different. The goal is to expose the hidden violence in a situation or to place the powerful in a position where the discrepancy between their public claims and more devious intentions is exposed, and thereby to transform the dominant game. This type of power has been expressed in many different forms and with differing degrees of success.[6] Historically, this form of power is associated with nonviolent campaigns such as Gandhi's decolonisation effort in India or the American civil rights movement. The attempts of Charter 77 and Solidarity in Poland to expose the distinction between the signing, by East European governments, of the human rights provisions of the Helsinki Final Act similarly represent, in Vaclav Havel's (1985) terms, 'the power of the powerless'. While the stakes were less great for Western peace activists, the dynamics were similar; they were attempting to expose the discrepancy between a claim that nuclear deterrence would prevent any kind of war and apparent movement towards a strategy for fighting a limited nuclear war. Likewise, the attempt to construct a Europe whole and free through a process of dialogue transcending the blocs dramatised the violence under-lying the division, as peace activists were expelled from Eastern Europe for

6 For a partial listing of literature in the nonviolent tradition see note 2, Chapter Six, p. 95.

attempting to 'talk' to their dissident counterparts.

The two types of power are generally characteristic of different positions. Coercive power is, in Weber's terms (Gerth and Mills, 1946), the power of the politician. Power is utilised to maintain or establish the rules of the game. This power depends on widespread compliance with the rules, even if only in appearance. The power to withhold one's consent is the power of the dissident whose acts cannot be purely dictated by personal gain, given the potential costs.

The point was made nicely in Milan Kundera's (1995) book, *The Unbearable Lightness of Being*. Following the invasion of Soviet troops into Prague in 1968, the main character, a brilliant young surgeon, was called before the authorities and asked to sign a loyalty statement. He refused to do so and, despite his professional prestige, lost his job and was assigned to work as a window cleaner. The tanks which had stormed into Prague were an important element of power, but clearly not the only one. In order to restabilise the situation and the new government's authority, it was essential that the population own the decision. Loyalty statements were obtained under coercion and the consequences for not signing were great. If individuals across the board had refused to sign up to the decision, the Soviets may have continued to rule by force, but over the long term any notion of authority or rule would have been hollow.[7] In the Polish context, over a decade later, the refusal was more widespread and the government could only continue to rule under conditions of martial law, which they could not do indefinitely. In the Czech context, a decade later, individuals who refused to comply attained a greater visibility, particularly in the West. Nonviolent strategy appeals to a more public dimension of power.

Refusing to comply with the dominant rules of the game is often combined with another tactic, which has played a central role in the strategies of the weak: 'acting as if'. 'Acting as if' is not an effective tactic in all contexts. We cannot all simply begin to act as if our interests have been realised and thereby realise them. A graduate student cannot effectively act as if she is a department Chair. It is difficult at best to act as if nuclear weapons do not exist. In the first case the graduate student has no

---

7 Arendt (in Lukes, 1986: 64–5, 71) argues against the tendency to conflate violence and power; instead, she claims the two are opposites. Power refers to the human ability to act in concert and is therefore a property of groups rather than individuals. Violence is distinguished by its instrumental character and the use of implements to multiply natural strength. While opposites, the two usually appear together. However, where one rules absolutely the other is absent. 'Violence appears where power is in jeopardy, but left to its own course it ends in power's disappearance. This implies that it is not correct to think of the opposite of violence as nonviolence; to speak of nonviolent power is actually redundant. Violence can destroy power; it is utterly incapable of creating it.'

legitimate claim to a position of authority in the department; she has no alternative language game within which her act might be meaningfully situated. In the second case, one can only act as if nuclear weapons do not exist by ignoring them, which is easy enough to do; it is far more difficult to find a context where ignoring nuclear weapons becomes a political statement with transformative power.[8]

The power of 'acting as if' resides in a double move, that is, in politicising the rules of the dominant game, by flaunting them and, at the same time, acting within the framework of a more marginal game that already has meaning in a political context. When, during the US civil rights movement, African-Americans acted as if they could vote, sit in the front of the bus or sit at a lunch counter for whites only, they exposed the 'centre of gravity' in the conflict over civil rights.

'Centre of gravity' is a term used by Clauswitz (1976) to refer to the targeting of one's power on the enemy's weak spot. It is a concept that can be appropriated for the discussion of nonviolent strategy as well, although with a somewhat different meaning. The centre of gravity in the latter is located at the intersection of two language games. In the context of the American civil rights movement, acting as if one could sit at a 'white' lunch counter flaunted the rules of the dominant order in the South, which denied this everyday act to Blacks; at the same time, the act was legitimised within an alternative game within which all American citizens should be entitled to freedom of movement in public spaces. The weak spot of Southern segregation was the explicit hierarchy between black and white within a society based on the maxim that 'all men are created equal'. By acting as if, at the centre of gravity, an injustice was dramatised as the keepers of the dominant rules reacted violently in response. The violence underlying the zero-sum game was exposed. The goal of the nonviolent strategy was to heighten the tensions in this context in order to create the conditions for dialogue. As Martin Luther King, Jr (see Washington, 1986: 291–2) said in his letter from the Birmingham City Jail:

> Nonviolent direct action seeks to create such a crisis and establish such creative tension that a community that has constantly refused to negotiate is forced to confront the issue. It seeks to so dramatise the issue so that it can no longer be ignored. I just referred to the creation of tension as a part of the work of the nonviolent resister. This may sound rather shocking. But I must confess that I am not afraid of the word tension. I have earnestly worked and

---

8 The efforts of groups such as the Greenham Common Women to set up a peace camp at the site of a military base might be seen as an expression of acting as if nuclear weapons do not exist. In light of recent celebrations of the transformation of the Greenham base, one might argue that they did in fact transform the political potential of nuclear weapons.

preached against violent tension, but there is a type of constructive nonviolent tension that is necessary for growth ... So the purpose of the direct action is to create a situation so crisis-packed that it will inevitably open the door to negotiation. We, therefore, concur with you in your call for negotiation. Too long has our beloved Southland been bogged down in the tragic attempt to live in monologue rather than dialogue.

In Poland, members of Solidarity 'acted as if' they lived in a free civil society, even against the background of martial law (Weschler, 1982: 56). Their goal was to engage the government in dialogue. In the context of the Cold War, citizens' initiatives in East and West began to 'act as if' the Cold War was over, given the failure of the superpowers to make progress in the negotiations. By engaging in dialogue across the division of Europe, they flaunted the rule by which the 'other' was defined as an enemy; they simultaneously played by the rules of a new positive-sum game which constituted a dialogue of citizens in a Europe whole and free.

Refusal to accept the rules of the dominant game and tenacity in playing an alternative game have a transformative effect over time, which may be almost invisible. Vaclav Havel (1991: 320–1) explored the distinction between the power of the politician and the dissident, and used the metaphor of 'radiation' to refer to the silent power of the latter's acts:

As I have written more than once, I believe the phenomenon of dissent grows out of an essentially different conception of the meaning of politics than that prevailing in the world today. That is, the dissident does not operate in the realm of genuine power at all. He does not seek power. He has no desire for office and does not woo voters ... He can offer, if anything, only his own skin – and he offers it solely because he has no other way of affirming the truth he stands for. His actions simply articulate his dignity as a citizen, regardless of the cost. The innermost foundation of his 'political' undertaking is moral and existential. Everything he does, he does initially for himself: something within has simply revolted and left him incapable of continuing to 'live a lie'. Only then does there follow (and can there possibly follow) a 'political' motive: the hope – vague, indefinite, and difficult to justify – that this course of action is also good for something in general. It is the hope that 'politics beyond politics', that 'politics outside the sphere of power', does make some sense, that by whatever hidden and complex ways it leads to something, evokes something, produces some effect. That even something as apparently ephemeral as the truth spoken aloud, as an openly expressed concern for the humanity of man, carries a power within itself and that even a word is capable of a certain radiation, of leaving a mark on the 'hidden consciousness' of a community.[9]

9 See also Konrad (1984).

Havel has since occupied the seat of the politician. The categories he explores in his earlier text are not intrinsic to individuals; they are relative to a position within a political space, a position of weakness in relation to a dominant game. Subsequently, it is not inconceivable that states which play with a losing hand in the international realm would also employ a strategy of the weak. In the 1980s, the group of non-aligned states made one of the strongest appeals to the superpowers to end the arms race.[10] Gorbachev's strategy of 'winning over' the West relied on tactics similar to those of the social movements. In the previous chapter, I argued that a former superpower, now weak, also employed elements of a strategy of the weak in response to NATO enlargement.

The current relationship between NATO and Russia is not primarily one of coercion but rather of reassurance. Both, as well as the Central and Eastern Europeans, present themselves as engaged in a positive-sum game in which there will be no winners and losers. Nonetheless, in the context of NATO expansion, Russia has been playing with a losing hand, because of her weakness. The question is whether we understand the Russian response as one of concession and defeat or whether a strategy can be recognised behind it. I have argued that Primakov's acts, like Gorbachev's acts earlier, fit more within a tradition of nonviolent strategy. By remaining firm in her opposition to expansion, while calling for a special relationship to NATO, Russia was attempting to 'best' the West, or to put NATO in a position where it would have to live up to its stated intent of dialogue in 'true partnership' or be exposed as the agent in creating a new division of Europe. The defence elite in Russia recognised that expansion would weaken NATO's Article Five guarantee. In this respect the Russian response can be understood as part of a longer-term strategy by which her interest in the transformation of NATO into a more political pan-European organisation might be realised.

By contrast, the continuing importance of the military dimension of international relations and of coercive strategies is evident in NATO's new missions of peacekeeping and crisis management. The use of force continues to play an important role in altering the framework in which conflicting parties define their options, as eventually became clear in Bosnia (Fierke, 1996). But coercion in post-Cold War Europe is being used under very different conditions than during the Cold War. The reluctance of governments to use force has also become an important issue. From Bosnia to Rwanda, states have been hesitant to engage in the use of force, questioning whether these conflicts were in their national interest and anticipating the

---

10 The 'Five Continent Peace Initiative' was signed by heads of government of Argentina, Greece, India, Mexico, Sweden and Tanzania on 22 May 1984.

public response to body bags returning from a far-off war.

Relationships appear to have been turned upside down since the end of the Cold War. States, in the East–West context, all claim to be engaged in a positive-sum game. The coercive strategies of the West are directed more at ethnic groups than other major powers. The interest is less self-defence than stability, that is, in compelling conflicting parties to engage in more peaceful means of dialogue and dispute resolution. Both Russia and NATO claim to be agents of change, rather than protectors of the status quo.

The strategies have changed; the interest is now in a positive-sum game where conflict is transformed. The hope is to replace violent conflict with dialogue. The relationship between the power and the strategies of different types of actor, between states in different positions of relative power, and between state and non-state actors, employing violent or nonviolent strategies, is a central issue in the post-Cold War world. These relationships have not been adequately explored, given assumptions about the primacy of coercive strategies employed by powerful states.

Critical theory and practice

The tension between these two games, and two forms of strategy, continues to be constitutive of the possibilities of post-Cold War Europe. As a result, this analysis has policy implications. Both Russia and NATO, as well as the Central and Eastern Europeans, express concern that others are acting as if the Cold War is still going on, that is, actions are given meaning within a game involving an 'other' who remains a potential enemy. Many fear the game will once again become zero sum. Both sides are also, in different ways, attempting to act as if cooperation is possible, as if a new definition of security in Europe will prevail. In the context of NATO expansion, there are questions about the sincerity of the dialogue and whether the language of dialogue is a cover for a military expansion which will move closer to Russia's borders.[11] But the West's promise of dialogue has given Russia a lever to hold NATO accountable and to take her concerns into account. The next turning point is likely to follow the first wave of expansion, as NATO is called to account for two conflicting promises: the promise to include the Baltic states in NATO's sphere of stability and the promise to deepen cooperation with Russia. The logic of this contradiction is such that it is likely to propel NATO into a choice between the construction of a new conflict with Russia or a redefinition of its own identity in order more firmly to embed the former superpower in cooperative efforts, such that any inclusion of the

---

11 This is consistent with an argument that the expansion is part of an American strategy to re-establish its primacy in world politics. See Posen and Ross (1996–97: 32–42).

Baltic states will not be experienced as a threat. There is every reason to privilege the positive-sum game over the zero-sum outcome of a new conflict in Europe. The post-Cold War identities of NATO and Russia are being constituted through a process of interaction. Russia has made a conciliatory move in agreeing to a Founding Act with NATO against the background of enlargement. NATO's response will play an important role in determining whether Russia continues along this course or makes a hostile turn.

When situated in a context that continues to unfold, the claim of Western governments to a victory must be understood as one move rather than an ending point of the Cold War. The claim to a zero-sum outcome of victory is at odds with the stated intent of all players to engage in a new positive-sum game. A new Cold War is still possible. Avoiding this outcome will depend on a continuing effort by both sides to act as if a different form of security in Europe is possible. Critical actors have an important role to play in exposing the contradictions of this new context and holding states accountable for their words. Critical theorists have pointed to the potential for a new Cold War because of NATO's enlargement. The next move, at this juncture, is to give voice to the potential for a different outcome, given the logic underlying expansion.

Critical theory has emphasised the inseparability of theory and practice. In this light, the continuing viability of realist theory rests on sustaining an argument that the end of the Cold War represents a zero-sum victory. If the end of the Cold War was not zero sum, but rather represents the possibility of a new positive-sum game of security, then realist premises about the inescapability of conflict are on shaky ground.[12] If, contrary to realist predictions, it was possible to transform the Cold War from a zero-sum into a positive-sum game, then other conflicts can perhaps similarly be transformed.[13]

A greater awareness that theory is a form of practice which influences the political world, and greater attention to the practice of political actors as a form of theorising, is required. The conflict between the strategies of the powerful and the powerless is expressed at the level of theory in the conflict between realist and critical theory. Realist strategy and theory are part of a game within which military objects are brought to bear for purposes of coercion. Both validate the role of instrumental reason in international politics. The use of force is the only game in town. The necessity of choices is publicly presented in terms of no choice. Any right thinking individual, it is argued, will recognise that power needs to be countered with power in kind.

---

12 I am indebted to Nicholas Wheeler, University of Wales, Aberystwyth, for articulating this obvious consequence of the analysis, which I had not so clearly recognised myself.
13 For an analysis of the relationship between theory and practice as it relates to the transformation of conflict, see Rothman (1992).

Critical theory, by contrast, began as a critique of the dominant role of instrumental rationality in society. In so far as it situates power in a social and political context, as opposed to an objective order, theory cannot be detached from practice. The second part of this book explored the relationship between the critical concepts of denaturalisation, immanent critique and dialogue, and the practices of actors in the world who were engaged in a critique of the structures of the Cold War. The alternative positive-sum game of dialogue has come to occupy a central place in state-level discourse since the end of the Cold War. The social movements are no longer visible, but the contestation continues over the meaning of this positive-sum game in East and West. For the Eastern Europeans and NATO, enlargement is equal to the positive-sum game of eliminating the division of Europe. For critics in the West and for Russia, enlargement is part of a zero-sum game, harking back to the Cold War; cooperation in dialogue is the only route to a positive-sum game of European security. The positive-sum game is now at the centre of the conflict over meaning. The contest has generated new contradictions, which were explored in the final section.

The end of the Cold War was less a question of winning and losing than the choice between two different games of security. The goal of dialogue, like that of critical theory, is to recover the capacity to be human, to find ways of resolving conflict in such a way that tears in the fabric of human relationships might be healed.

BIBLIOGRAPHY

Adler, E. (1992), 'The Emergence of Cooperation: National Epistemic Communities and the International Evolution of the Idea of Arms Control', *International Organization*, 46: 1, pp. 101–46.

Adler, E. (1997), 'Seizing the Middle Ground: Constructivism in World Politics', *European Journal of International Relations*, 3: 3, pp. 319–63.

Alker, H., Jr (1996), *Rediscoveries and Reformulations: Humanistic Methodologies for International Studies*. Cambridge: Cambridge University Press.

Allan, P. and Goldman K. (eds) (1992), *The End of the Cold War: Evaluating Theories of International Relations*. Dordrecht: Martinus Nijhoff.

Allin, D. (1995), 'Can Containment Work Again?', *Survival*, 37: 1, pp. 53–65.

Anderson, B. (1991), *Imagined Communities: Reflections on the Origin and Spread of Nationalism*. London: Verso.

Anderson, H. C. (1993), *The Emperor's New Clothes*. Loughborough: Ladybird Books Ltd.

Arendt, H. (1958), *The Human Condition*. Chicago: University of Chicago Press.

Ash, T. G. (1983), *The Polish Revolution: Solidarity, 1980–82*. London: Jonathan Cape.

Asmus, R., Kugler, R. and Larrabee, F. S. (1995), 'NATO Expansion: The Next Steps', *Survival*, 37: 1, pp. 7–33.

Barnett, M. (1998), *Dialogues in Arab Politics: Negotiations in Regional Order*. New York: Columbia University Press.

Bell, N. and Kurtz, L. (1992), *Social Theory and Nonviolent Revolutions: Re-thinking Domination and Rebellion*. Austin, TX: University of Texas at Austin Press.

Bennett, P. G. (1995), 'Modelling Decisions in International Relations: Game Theory and Beyond', *Mershon International Studies Review*, 39, pp. 19–52.

Berger, T. and Luckmann, T. (1966), *The Social Construction of Reality*. New York: Anchor Books.

Bernstein, R. J. (1979), *The Restructuring of Social and Political Theory*. London: Methuen & Co. Ltd.

Bhaskar, R. (1979), *The Possibility of Naturalism*. Atlantic Highlands, NJ: Humanities Press.

Blacker, C. (1993), *Hostage to Revolution: Gorbachev and Soviet Security Policy, 1985–1991*. New York: Council of Foreign Relations Press.

Bloed, A. (ed.) (1990), *From Helsinki to Vienna: Basic Documents of the Helsinki Process*. Dordrecht: Martinus Nijhoff.

Blum, D. (1993), 'The Soviet Foreign Policy Belief System: Beliefs, Politics and Foreign Policy Outcomes', *International Studies Quarterly*, 37, pp. 373–94.

Blumer, H. (1969) *Symbolic Interactionism: Perspective and Method*. Englewood Cliffs, NJ: Prentice-Hall.

Bondurant, J. (1988), *Conquest of Violence: The Gandhian Philosophy of Conflict*. Princeton, NJ: Princeton University Press.

Boulding, K. (1989), *Three Faces of Power*. Newbury Park, CA: Sage Publications.

Bowker, M. and Brown, R. (eds) (1993), *From Cold War to Collapse: Theory and World Politics in the 1980s*. Cambridge: Cambridge University Press.

Brown, M. E. (1995), 'The Flawed Logic of NATO Expansion', *Survival*, 37: 1, pp. 34–52.

Bunce, V. (1985), 'The Empire Strikes Back: The Transformation of the Eastern Bloc from a Soviet Asset to a Soviet Liability', *International Organization*, 39: 1, pp. 1–46.

Calhoun, C. (1995), *Critical Social Theory*. Oxford: Blackwell.

Campbell, D. (1992), *Writing Security: United States Foreign Policy and the Politics of Identity*. Minneapolis: University of Minnesota Press.

Campbell, D. (1993), *Politics Without Principle: Sovereignty, Ethics and the Narratives of the Gulf War*. Boulder, CO: Lynne Rienner.

Campbell, D. (1998), 'Epilogue: The Disciplinary Politics of Theorizing Identity', *Writing Security: United States Foreign Policy and the Politics of Identity*, revised edition. Minneapolis: University of Minnesota Press.

Carr, E. H. (1964), *The Twenty Years' Crisis, 1919–1939: An Introduction to the Study of International Relations*. New York: Harper & Row.

Checkel, J. (1993), 'Ideas, Institutions and the Gorbachev Foreign Policy Revolution', *World Politics*, 45, pp. 271–300.

Chilton, P. (1996), *Security Metaphors: Cold War Discourse from Containment to Common European House*. New York: Peter Lang.

Chilton, P. and Ilyin, M. (1993), 'Metaphor in Political Discourse: The Case of the "Common European House"', *Discourse and Society*, 4: 1, pp. 7–32.

Chomsky, N. (1986), *Pirates and Emperors: International Terrorism in the Real World*. New York: Claremont Research.

Clauswitz, K. von (1976), *On War*, edited and translated by Michael Howard and Peter Paret. Princeton, NJ: Princeton University Press.

Cortright, D. (1993), *Peace Works: The Citizens' Role in Ending the Cold War*. Boulder, CO: Westview Press.

Dalby, S. (1990), 'Dealignment Discourse: Thinking Beyond the Blocs', *Current Research on Peace and Violence*, 8: 3, 140–54.

Dallmayr, F. R. and McCarthy, T. A. (eds) (1977), *Understanding and Social Inquiry*. Notre Dame, IN: University of Notre Dame Press.

Deporte, A. W. (1986), *Europe Between the Superpowers: The Enduring Balance*. New Haven: Yale University Press.

DerDerian, J. (1987), *On Diplomacy*. Oxford: Blackwell.

DerDerian, J. (ed.) (1995), *International Theory: Critical Investigations*. London: Macmillan.

DerDerian, J. and Shapiro, M. J. (eds) (1989), *International/Intertextual Relations: Postmodern Readings of World Politics*. Lexington: Lexington Books.

Dolan, A. R. (1990), *Undoing the Evil Empire: How Reagan Won the Cold War*. Washington: AEI Press.

Doty, R. L. (1993), 'Foreign Policy as Social Construction: A Post-Positivist Analysis of U.S. Counterinsurgency Policy in the Philippines', *International Studies Quarterly*, 37: 3, pp. 297–320.

Dunne, T. (1995), 'The Social Construction of International Society', *European Journal of International Relations*, 1: 3, pp. 367–89.

Etzold, T. H. and Gaddis, J. L. (eds) (1978), *Containment: Documents on American Policy and Strategy, 1945–1950*. New York: Columbia University Press.

Fay, B. (1975), *Social Theory and Political Practice*. London: Allen and Unwin.

Fierke, K. M. (1995), *Excavating the Ruins of the Cold War: Recovering the Contours of a Changing Security Culture*. Dissertation Manuscript: University of Minnesota.

Fierke, K. M. (1996), 'Multiple Identities, Interfacing Games: The Social Construction of Western Action in Bosnia', *European Journal for International Relations*, 2: 4, pp. 467–97.

Finch, H. L. (1995), *Wittgenstein*. Rockport, MA: Element.

Flynn, G. and Rattinger, H. (eds) (1985), *The Public and Atlantic Defense*. London: Croom Helm.

Flynn, G., Moreton, E. and Treverton, G. (1985), *Public Images of Western Security*. Paris: The Atlantic Institute for International Affairs. The Atlantic Papers, no. 54–5.

Fukuyama, F. (1992), *The End of History and the Last Man*. London: Penguin Books.

Gaddis, J. L. (1985–86), 'The Long Peace: Elements of Stability in the Postwar International System', *International Security*, 10: 3, pp. 99–142.

Gaddis, J. L. (1992–93), 'International Relations Theory and the End of the Cold War', *International Security*, 17: 3, pp. 5–58.

Garfinkel, A. (1981), *Forms of Explanation: Rethinking the Questions in Social Theory*. New Haven: Yale University Press.

Geertz, C. (1973), *The Interpretation of Cultures: Selected Essays*. New York: Basic Books.

George, J. (1994), *Discourses of Global Politics: A Critical (Re)Introduction to International Relations*. Boulder, CO: Lynne Rienner.

George, J. and Campbell, D. (1990), 'Patterns of Dissent and the Celebration of Difference: Critical Social Theory and International Relations', *International Studies Quarterly*, 34: 2, pp. 269–93.

Giddens, A. (1979), *Central Problems in Social Theory*. Berkeley, CA: University of California Press.

Gier, N. F. (1981), *Wittgenstein and Phenomenology: A Comparative Study of the Later Wittgenstein, Husserl, Heidegger and Merleau-Ponty*. Albany: State University of New York Press.

Gilpin, R. (1981), *War and Change in World Politics*. Cambridge: Cambridge University Press.

Gerth, H. H. and Mills, C. W. (eds) (1946), *From Max Weber: Essays in Sociology*. New York: Oxford University Press.

Glaser, C. L. (1993), 'Why NATO is Still Best: Future Security Arrangements for Europe', *International Security*, 18: 1, pp. 5–50.

Glynn, P. (1992), *Closing Pandora's Box: Arms Races, Arms Control and the History of the Cold War*. New York: Basic Books.

Goldstein, J. and Keohane, R. O. (1993), *Ideas and Foreign Policy: Beliefs, Institutions and Political Change*. Ithaca, NY: Cornell University Press.

Golubnichy, M. (1978), *Détente, the Only Way: The Soviet Viewpoint*. Moscow: Novosti Press Agency Publishing House.

Gorbachev, M. (1987), *Perestroika: New Thinking for our Country and the World*. London: Collins.

Gregg, R. (1966), *The Power of Nonviolence*. New York: Schocken Books.

Habermas, J. (1972), *Knowledge and Human Interest*, translated by J. Shapiro. London: Heinemann.

Habermas, J. (1987), *Theory of Communicative Action*, translated by T. McCarthy. Cambridge: Polity Press.

Habermas, J. (1990), *Moral Consciousness and Communicative Action*. Cambridge: Polity Press.

Havel, V. (1991), *Open Letters: Selected Prose 1965–1990*, edited by P. Wilson. London: Faber and Faber.

Havel, V., *et al.* (1985), *The Power of the Powerless: Citizens Against the State in Central-Eastern Europe*, edited by J. Keane. New York: M.E. Sharpe.

Hinds, L. B. and Windt, Jr, T. O. (1991), *The Cold War as Rhetoric: The Beginnings, 1945–1950*. New York: Praeger.

Hogan, M. J. (ed.) (1992), *The End of the Cold War: Its Meaning and Implications*. Cambridge: Cambridge University Press.

Hollis, M. (1994), *The Philosophy of the Social Sciences: An Introduction*. Cambridge: Cambridge University Press.

Hollis, M. and Smith, S. (1991), *Explaining and Understanding International Relations*. Oxford: Clarendon Press.

Holmes, R. (ed.) (1990), *Nonviolence in Theory and Practice*. Belmont, CA: Wadsworth Publishing Co.

Holt, R. (1997), *Wittgenstein, Politics and Human Rights*. London: Routledge.

Honneth, A. (1995), *The Fragmented World of the Social: Essays in Social and Political Philosophy*. Albany, NY: State University of New York Press.

Hoy, D. C. and McCarthy, T. (1994), *Critical Theory*. Oxford: Basil Blackwell.

Jabri, V. (1996), *Discourses of Violence: Conflict Analysis Reconsidered*. Manchester: Manchester University Press.

Jervis, R. (1976), *Perception and Misperception in International Politics*. Princeton, NJ: Princeton University Press.

Johnston, P. (1991), *Wittgenstein and Moral Philosophy*. London: Routledge.

Kaldor, M. (ed.) (1991), *Europe from Below: An East–West Dialogue*. New York: Verso.

Kaldor, M., Holden, G. and Falk, R. (eds) (1989), *The New Detente: Rethinking East–West Relations*. New York: Verso.

Katzenstein, P. J. (ed.) (1996), *The Culture of National Security: Norms and Identity in World Politics*. New York: Columbia University Press.

Kegley, C. W., Jr (1994), 'How Did the Cold War Die? Principles for an Autopsy', *Mershon International Studies Review*, 38: 1, pp. 11–42.

Kegley, C. W., Jr and Schwab, K. L. (eds) (1991), *After the Cold War: Questioning the Morality of Nuclear Deterrence*. Boulder, CO: Westview Press.

Khong, Y. F. (1992), *Analogies at War: Korea, Munich, Dien Bien Phu and the Vietnam Decisions of 1965*. Princeton, NJ: Princeton University Press.

Kissinger, H. (1977), *American Foreign Policy*, 2nd edition, New York: W. W. Norton.

Kissinger, H. (1994), *Diplomacy*. New York: Simon and Schuster.

Konrad, G. (1984), *Antipolitics: An Essay*. New York: Harcourt Brace Jovanovich.

Krasner, S. (1985), *Structural Conflict: The Third World Against Global Liberalism*. Berkeley, CA: University of California Press.

Kratochwil, F. V. (1989), *Rules, Norms and Decisions: On the Conditions of Practical and Legal Reasoning in International Relations and Domestic Affairs*. Cambridge: Cambridge University Press.

Krause, K. and Williams, M. C. (1996), 'Broadening the Agenda of Security Studies: Politics and Methods', *Mershon International Studies Review*, 40: 2, pp. 229–54.

Kuhn, T. (1970), *The Structure of Scientific Revolutions*, 2nd edition. Chicago: University of Chicago Press.

Kundera, M. (1995), *The Unbearable Lightness of Being*. London: Faber.

Laclau, E. and Mouffe, C. (1985), *Hegemony and Socialist Strategy: Towards a Radical Democratic Politics*, translated by W. Moore and P. Cammack. London: Verso.

Lakoff, G. and Johnson, M. (1980), *Metaphors We Live By*. Chicago: University of Chicago Press.

Lebow, R. N. and Risse-Kappen, T. (eds) (1995), *International Relations Theory and the End of the Cold War*. New York: Columbia University Press.

Lebow, R. N. and Stein, J. G. (1994), *We All Lost the Cold War*. Princeton, NJ: Princeton University Press.

Little, D. (1991), *Varieties of Social Explanation: An Introduction to the Philosophy of Social Science*. Boulder, CO: Westview Press.

Lukes, S. (ed.) (1986), *Power*. New York: New York University Press.

Machiavelli, N. ([Eng. trans. 1640] 1975), *The Prince*, translated by George Bull. New York: Penguin.

Mandelbaum, M. (1996), *The Dawn of Peace in Europe*. New York: The Twentieth Century Fund.

McCalla, R. B. (1996), 'NATO's Persistence after the Cold War', *International Organization*, 50: 3, pp. 445–75.

MccGwire, M. (1991), *Perestroika and Soviet National Security Policy.* Washington, DC: Brookings Institute.

MccGwire, M. (1998), 'NATO Expansion: "A Policy Error of Historical Importance"', *Review of International Studies,* 24: 1.

Mead, G. H. (1934), *Mind, Self and Society.* Chicago: University of Chicago Press.

Mearsheimer, J. (1990), 'Back to the Future: Instability in Europe After the Cold War', *International Security,* 15: 1, pp. 5–56.

Meyer, S. (1988), 'Sources and Prospects of Gorbachev's New Political Thinking on Security', *International Security,* 13: 2, pp. 124–63.

Michnik, A. (1985), *Letters from Prison and Other Essays.* Berkeley, CA: University of California Press.

Milliken, J. (1994), *A Grammar of State Action.* Dissertation Manuscript: University of Minnesota.

Milliken, J. and Sylvan, D. (1996), 'Soft Bodies, Hard Targets and Chic Theories: US Bombing Policy in Indochina', *Millennium,* 25: 2, pp. 321–59.

Nardin, T. and Mapel, D. R. (eds) (1994), *Traditions of International Ethics.* Cambridge: Cambridge University Press.

Naughton, J. (1997), 'Game, Set and Match', *The Observer Review,* 11 May.

Nicholson, M. (1996), *Causes and Consequences in International Relations: A Conceptual Study.* London: Pinter.

Oberdorfer, D. ([1991] 1992), *The Turn, How the Cold War Came to an End: The United States and the Soviet Union, 1983–1990.* London: Jonathan Cape.

Onuf, N. (1989), *World of Our Making: Rules and Rule in Social Theory and International Relations.* Columbia, SC: University of South Carolina Press.

Phillips, D. L. (1977), *Wittgenstein and Scientific Knowledge: A Sociological Perspective.* London: Macmillan.

Pin-Fat, V. (1997a), *Language in International Relations Theory: A Grammatical Investigation.* Ph.D. Manuscript: University of Wales, Aberystwyth.

Pin-Fat, V. (1997b), 'Why Aren't We Laughing?: Grammatical Investigations in World Politics', *Politics,* 17: 2, pp. 79–86.

Pitkin, H. F. (1972), *Wittgenstein and Justice: On the Significance of Ludwig Wittgenstein for Social and Political Thought.* Berkeley, CA: University of California Press.

Polanyi, L., Alker, Jr, H., Lebedeva, M. and O'Donnell, S. (1993), 'Retelling Cold War Stories: Uncovering Cultural Meanings with Linguistic Discourse Analysis', *Working Papers on Security Discourse in the Cold War Era.* New York: Center for Studies of Social Change, New School for Social Research.

Posen, B. and Ross, A. (1996–97), 'Competing Visions for U.S. Grand Strategy', *International Security,* 21: 3, pp. 5–53.

Program on Nonviolent Sanctions (1992), *Transforming Struggle: Strategy and the Global Experience of Nonviolent Sanctions.* Cambridge, MA: Harvard University Press.

Reagan, R. (1989), *Speaking My Mind.* New York: Simon and Schuster.

Reus-Smit, C. (1992), 'Realist and Resistance Utopias: Community, Security and Political Action in the New Europe', *Millennium,* 21: 1, pp. 1–28.

Risse-Kappen, T. (1991), 'Did "Peace through Strength" End the Cold War? Lessons from INF', *International Security,* 16: 1, pp. 162–88.

Rothman, J. (1992), *From Confrontation to Cooperation: Resolving Ethnic and Regional Conflict.* London: Sage.

Rubin, H. (1997), *The Princessa: Machiavelli for Women.* London: Bloomsbury.

Schelling, T. C. (1966), *Arms and Influence.* New Haven: Yale University Press.

Schelling, T. C. (1980), *The Strategy of Conflict.* Cambridge, MA: Harvard University Press.

Bibliography

Schweizer, P. (1994), *Victory: The Reagan Administration's Secret Strategy that Hastened the Collapse of the Soviet Union*. New York: The Atlantic Monthly Press.

Searle, J. (1995), *The Social Construction of Reality*. London: Allen Lane.

Sharp, G. (1973), *The Politics of Nonviolent Action*. Boston, MA: Extending Horizon Books, Porter Sargent Publishers.

Sloan, S. (1995), 'U.S. Perspectives on NATO's Future', *International Affairs*, 71: 2, pp. 217–46.

Smith, N. (1997), *Strong Hermeneutics: Contingency and Moral Identity*. London: Routledge.

Smith, S., Booth, K. and Zalewski, M. (eds) (1996), *International Theory: Positivism and Beyond*. Cambridge: Cambridge University Press.

Stoltzfus, N. (1997), *Resistance of the Heart: Intermarriage and the Rosenstrasse Protests in Nazi Germany*. New York: W. W. Norton.

Sylvester, C. (1994), 'Empathetic Cooperation: A Feminist Method of IR', *Millennium*, 23: 2, pp. 315–34.

Thompson, E. P. (1980), *Protest and Survive*. Nottingham: END and Bertrand Russell Peace Foundation.

Thompson, J. (1981), *Critical Hermeneutics: A Study in the Thought of Paul Ricoeur and Jürgen Habermas*. Cambridge: Cambridge University Press.

Tyroler, C., II (ed.) (1984), *Alerting America: The Papers of the Committee on the Present Danger*. New York: Pergamon-Brassey's.

Vincent, J. (1991), *Human Rights and International Relations*. Cambridge: Cambridge University Press.

Waller, M. (1993), *The End of the Communist Power Monopoly*. Manchester: Manchester University Press.

Wallerstein, I. (1979), *The Capitalist World Economy*. Cambridge: Cambridge University Press.

Waltz, K. (1979), *Theory of International Politics*. Reading, MA: Addison-Wesley.

Washington, J. M. (ed.) (1986), *A Testament of Hope: The Essential Writings and Speeches of Martin Luther King, Jr*. New York: HarperCollins Publishers.

Wehr, P., Burgess, H. and Burgess, G. (eds) (1994), *Justice Without Violence*. Boulder, CO: Lynne Rienner.

Weldes, J. (1998), *Constructing National Interests: The US and the Cuban Missile Crisis*. Minneapolis: University of Minnesota Press.

Weldes, J. and Saco, D. (1996), 'Making State Action Possible: The United States and the Discursive Construction of "The Cuban Problem", 1960–1994', *Millennium*, 25: 2, pp. 361–5.

Wendt, A. (1987), 'The Agent-Structure Problem in International Relations Theory', *International Organization*, 14: 3, pp. 335–70.

Wendt, A. (1992), 'Anarchy is What States Make of It: The Social Construction of Power Politics', *International Organization*, 46: 2, pp. 393–425.

Weschler, L. (1982), *Solidarity: Poland in the Season of Its Passion*. New York: Simon and Schuster.

Wight, C. (1996), 'Incommensurability and Cross-Paradigm Communication in International Relations Theory: "What's the Frequency Kenneth?"', *Millennium*, 25: 2, pp. 291–319.

Wittgenstein, L. (1958), *Philosophical Investigations*. Oxford: Basil Blackwell.

Wittgenstein, L. (1969), *The Blue and Brown Books: Preliminary Studies for the Philosophical Investigations*. Oxford: Basil Blackwell.

Wittgenstein, L. (1979), *On Certainty*. Oxford: Basil Blackwell.

Woehrle, L. (1992), *Social Constructions of Power and Empowerment: Thoughts from Feminist Approaches to Peace Research and Peace-Making*. Syracuse: Syracuse University Press.

Wohlforth, W. (1994–95), 'Realism and the End of the Cold War', *International Security*, 19: 3, pp. 91–129.

Wohlforth, W. (ed.) (1996), *Witnesses to the End of the Cold War*. Baltimore: Johns Hopkins University Press.

Zielonka, J. (1986), 'Strengths and Weaknesses of Nonviolent Action: The Polish Case', *Orbis*, (Spring), pp. 91–110.

Zielonka, J. (1989), *Political Ideas in Contemporary Poland*. Aldershot: Avebury.

INDEX

Note: 'n.' after a page reference indicates a note on that page. Entries in **bold** type refer to main entries